THE LIE ABOUT THE TRUCK

ALSO BY SALLIE TISDALE

The Sorcerer's Apprentice: Medical Miracles and Other Disasters

Harvest Moon: Portrait of a Nursing Home

Lot's Wife: Salt and the Human Condition

Stepping Westward: The Long Search for Home in the Pacific Northwest

Talk Dirty to Me: An Intimate Philosophy of Sex

The Best Thing I Ever Tasted: The Secret of Food

Women of the Way: Discovering 2,500 Years of Buddhist Wisdom

Violation: Collected Essays

Advice for Future Corpses (And Those Who Love Them): A Practical Perspective on Death and Dying

THE LIE ABOUT THE TRUCK

SURV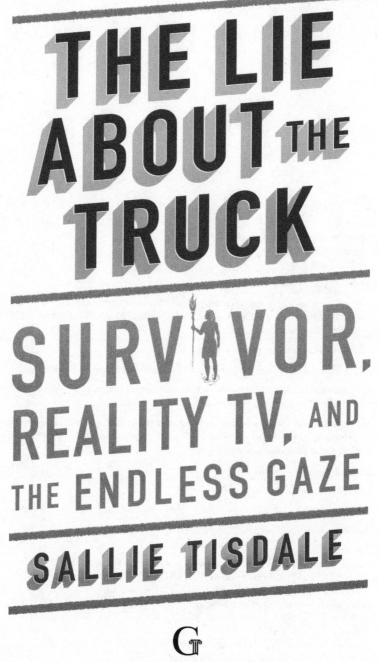VOR, REALITY TV, AND THE ENDLESS GAZE

SALLIE TISDALE

G

GALLERY BOOKS

New York   London   Toronto   Sydney   New Delhi

G

Gallery Books
An Imprint of Simon & Schuster, Inc.
1230 Avenue of the Americas
New York, NY 10020

First Gallery Books hardcover edition October 2021

GALLERY BOOKS and colophon are registered trademarks of Simon & Schuster, Inc.

For information about special discounts for bulk purchases, please contact Simon & Schuster Special Sales at 1-866-506-1949 or business@simonandschuster.com.

The Simon & Schuster Speakers Bureau can bring authors to your live event. For more information or to book an event, contact the Simon & Schuster Speakers Bureau at 1-866-248-3049 or visit our website at www.simonspeakers.com.

Interior design by Jaime Putorti

Manufactured in the United States of America

10 9 8 7 6 5 4 3 2 1

Library of Congress Cataloging-in-Publication Data

Names: Tisdale, Sallie, author.
Title: The lie about the truck : Survivor, reality TV, and the endless gaze / Sallie Tisdale.
Identifiers: LCCN 2021019944 (print) | LCCN 2021019945 (ebook) | ISBN 9781982175894 (hardcover) | ISBN 9781982175917 (ebook)
Subjects: LCSH: Survivor (Television program) | Reality television programs. | Truth.
Classification: LCC PN1992.77.S865 T57 2021 (print) | LCC PN1992.77.S865 (ebook) | DDC 791.45/72—dc23
LC record available at https://lccn.loc.gov/2021019944
LC ebook record available at https://lccn.loc.gov/2021019945

ISBN 978-1-9821-7589-4
ISBN 978-1-9821-7591-7 (ebook)

FOR AUSTIN, TAYLOR, KAYLEE, AND SPENCER:

May you always remember to look up from the screen

CONTENTS

THIS ISN'T WELFARE

On the first day of *Survivor: China,* the 15th season of the show, Courtney turns to the camera and declares, "I am in my own private hell." Courtney, 26 years old, is thin and ghostly pale. She works as a waitress in Manhattan. "People in New York don't act like this," she says. "I'm marooned with, like, flight attendants and Sunday school teachers."

Several weeks later, Courtney is one of six remaining contestants. One of the others is the flight attendant, Todd, a 22-year-old gay Mormon from Salt Lake City. Todd has been in an alliance with Amanda, an unemployed hiking guide from Montana, since early in the game. Amanda says they are playing the same way: burrowing in, lying low. "Doing what we're told. We're doing a lot of work."

At the reward challenge, each player is briefly reunited with a family member ("loved one," in *Survivor* talk) and the pairs compete to finish a maze while blindfolded. Denise, a school cafeteria worker from Massachusetts who calls herself "the old lady"—she's 40—wins the reward. She chooses Amanda and Todd to share it, and their relatives get to spend the night in camp. Denise wanders away with her husband, while Amanda and Todd sit in shallow water with their sisters and talk strategy.

Amanda says, "Honestly, it's not a good idea for us to backstab anyone anymore. But I think as long as we take Denise to the final four, she'll understand." Will she? Every player is given some amount of money, but the top three contestants win big money—$85,000, $100,000, and $1 million—and so everyone longs to be one of the final three. Only a fool is nice about being number four.

"Would you vote Denise before Courtney, or no?" Todd's sister asks.

"Yeah."

"I freakin' love Denise, I really do," says Todd, "but—"

But Denise is a working-class mother who hasn't backstabbed anyone.

"In the final three, she can play her sob story," says Amanda.

"That's right," says Todd. "We, Amanda and I and Courtney, are all pretty much on the same level, because we have pissed a lot of people on the jury off, so it's a pretty even chance between all of us, so—"

"It's like a dream," Amanda adds. "Perfect."

Later, Todd says to the camera: "You can't stop the game. The game keeps going. So, you know what? You want to feel comfortable and you want to feel you can trust people. And you just can't, though. You got to keep on your toes. You got to keep yourself nervous, or else you're gonna get screwed."

For the rest of the day, the remaining players meet in pairs and trios, shifting from ally to declared enemy and back. They tell the same story to different people in different ways, then they tell different stories, and parts of stories; they tell each other the truth and versions of the truth and bits of truth and complete untruths, until no one is sure of anything.

"I'm definitely the swing vote tonight," Denise says, in her broad Massachusetts accent. "For me, personally, I mean, this is do or die. When I get up there—I mean, I don't know right now who I'm gonna pick. What happens when I come back to camp after I make this decision? Who's gonna be flipping out? This is a game for a million dollars, and right now writing someone's name down is a million-dollar signature. I'm a little nervous, I'm a little scared, I'm a little in turmoil, I'm a little flipping out."

Erik is voted out that night. A few days later, Peih-Gee is gone. The remaining players walk back to camp in the odd blue-gray glow of the night cameras.

"Final four, bitches!" says Todd, slapping hands.

The next day, Todd, Courtney, and Amanda talk about voting off Denise. Todd is trying to avoid "them going all girl power on me and voting *me* out." Then Todd and Denise talk about voting off Courtney, while Courtney and Amanda talk about voting off Todd. "Everyone likes him," Amanda, his ally, his closest friend in the game, points out. At last she sees that Todd is her biggest threat. She's afraid he will play the "I'm-the-smartest-guy-here, I'm-the-only-guy-left card."

Courtney, her collarbones jutting out like coat hangers, says, "I know, but Denise is gonna cry." Courtney thinks she's in a great position. In her pregame interview, she said her main hobbies were "reading and learning new things," and her main "inspiration in life" was "the laughter of children." On the show she is brutal, unrelenting, her affect a narrow range between complaint and cruelty. She calls herself "the biggest bitch on the planet." At one point in the game, she says, "I have never been anything except my own winsome personality," tilting her head and smiling with contempt.

Amanda wins final immunity by balancing the tallest tower of porcelain cups and bowls. Now Amanda is the swing vote, because no one can vote for her. Courtney tells Todd that the smart thing is to vote off Denise, as they have secretly planned to do from the beginning of the alliance. Denise was always supposed to be number four.

"You're, like, the schemer, and I'm the tagalong, and she won two immunities," says Courtney.

Todd says, "Obviously, I want to win, but if I have to lose, I don't want to lose to Denise."

"Are you kidding me?" says Courtney. "This isn't, like, welfare. You know? Like, she doesn't deserve it just 'cause, you know, she sucks at life."

PERCEPTION IS REALITY

What the host, executive producer, and kazillionaire Jeff Probst likes to call "the greatest social experiment on television" has been running for 40 seasons over 20 years. After 597 episodes, ratings are stable ("numbingly consistent," said one critic). Viewer demographics are broad. The show usually leads its evening in primetime, as it has season after season, year after year. A critic for *Time* wrote, "This is the real miracle of *Survivor*: It just keeps going—and, so far at least, where it goes an entire genre follows." *Survivor* has been nominated for Emmys 64 times, and won several, including "Outstanding Picture Editing for a Structured Reality or Competition Program." The show has won ASCAP, Gold Derby, OFTA, and BMI Awards. People's Choice Awards. A GLAAD Award for Outstanding Reality Program in 2018. *Survivor* spawned itself in multiple countries, and in turn spawned imitations of many kinds: elimination challenges, castaway shows,

shows about strangers marooned together, and shows about actual survival.

Profits are closely guarded and tricky to define. The first season grossed $52 million. *Forbes* reported that *Survivor: Pearl Islands* a few years later made about $73 million. After 40 seasons, CBS has a loose hand on the reins; as long as the show is a golden goose, they seem willing to leave it alone. *Survivor* is wildly popular around the world. Over the years, it's been played in Belgium, Sweden, France, Denmark, Israel, Norway, and the Philippines; there have been versions in South Africa, India, Slovakia, Turkey, Argentina, Pakistan, Georgia, and the Czech Republic; in Brazil, Finland, and Bulgaria. All these shows are licensed by Castaway Television Productions, based in London, which controls the show's look and is supposed to police the behavior of the production crews. You don't have to speak the language to follow the show elsewhere; there are only a few variations from place to place (usually, the music is better in other countries). Players will be voted off until only one remains. Almost everything else is the same, everywhere on Earth: not just the idol, not just the buffs, but the arguments, the flirting, the mistakes, the acres of bare skin marred by insect bites and bruises, the pseudo-primitive aesthetic and faux-religious rituals. The extinguishing of the torch. *The tribe has spoken.*

The seeds of *Survivor* were planted in Britain, when a producer named Charlie Parsons created a show called *Expedition: Robinson* with Bob Geldof. (Parsons is now an executive producer of *Survivor*.) The BBC rejected it, and the show ended up in Sweden, where it ran as *Expeditie Robinson* until mid-2020. At the suggestion of Lauren Corrao, a Fox executive, the freelance producer Mark Burnett bought the idea after Parsons's production company was sold. The idea was rejected several times, including twice by CBS, before Burnett finally got a deal. (From the point of view of Swedish viewers, *Survivor* is the stepchild.)

The concept is brilliant and simple: a small group of strangers are stranded in a wild place with few resources; they must band together to survive but also vote one another off. Most of their time is spent on the fundamentals: shelter, fire, food, and getting along with one another somehow. (Or not.) They also compete: at first, tribe against tribe, the winning group sharing the spoils. Eventually, the tribes merge and players compete against one another as individuals. The game typically follows a three-day cycle: reward, immunity, elimination. One day they take on physical and mental challenges for rewards like fishing gear or peanut butter sandwiches. The next day, they do the immunity challenge: the winning tribe or the winning person is safe from elimination. (Read: execution.) That night or the next, the losing tribe—or everyone, after they merge—meet for Tribal Council, where a person is voted out. By then, deals have been made and players have formed alliances; such agreements may be secret and sometimes transparent, and they are almost always temporary. After the vote, Jeff snuffs the loser's tiki torch—"Because fire is life"—and says, "The tribe has spoken."

Players who are voted out after the tribes merge become members of the jury. They are taken to a kind of resort nearby called Ponderosa, where they eat, drink, sleep, and bicker. The jury members attend each Tribal Council but aren't allowed to speak. (Oh, but if looks could kill . . .) The game ends when there are only two or three players remaining, and then, as Jeff puts it, *the power shifts*. At that Council, the jury asks questions of the finalists, supposedly about the *Outwit, Outplay, Outlast* aspects of the game, but often they are simply airing grievances. Then the jury votes for a winner.

Producers weren't sure what to expect from the first season of the American version, in 2000. Would anyone want to play? More than 6,000 people applied for the first season. The producers conducted hundreds of interviews, dozens of physical exams, background checks, and psychological evaluations, until 16 contestants were chosen. They ranged in age from a 22-year-old rafting guide to a 72-year-old ex–Navy SEAL.

The first season took place on a small island in Borneo called Pulau Tiga, a place about a mile wide and three miles long with snakes, sharks, and plenty of insects. Burnett, who once said in an interview that because he was British, "I don't know from racism," said he chose Pulau Tiga because he wanted a setting that "looked like something straight out of *Apocalypse Now*."

In those first episodes, the visibly nervous host strolled along the beach and talked into the camera. Prior to *Survivor*, Jeff Probst had been host of VH1's *Rock & Roll Jeopardy!* On *Survivor*, he started out as a proxy for the audience and a friend to the players; his job seemed to consist of explaining the rules in the manner of a wide-eyed rookie. The contestants were equipped with good shoes, yellow rain slickers, pencils and paper, needle and thread, sunglasses, sunblock, a first aid kit, flashlights, even sparklers. The women wore jewelry. As the show opened, they were given two minutes to grab whatever else they could get off the boat, and they grabbed a lot—a frying pan, fishing traps, rope, life jackets, buckets, a machete, a mallet, a raft, canned food, kerosene, mosquito nets, blankets. Each contestant also had a backpack with ziplock bags for their personal gear, and each was allowed one "luxury item." One man brought a Bible; one of the women brought a ukulele. In the middle of the season, the players received care packages; Sean got a razor, which he used to shave the hair around his nipple ring. The women borrowed it to shave their armpits. (Razors are no longer allowed. But many women wear bikinis and never show a hair, so perhaps a wax is mandatory. Inquiring minds want to know.)

The first Tribal Council set was little more than a log bench and a fire, and players stopped to ring a gong as they entered. The meetings were like gentle deprogramming sessions; in one episode Jeff even handed around a conch shell to use as a talking stick. (Jeff nixed this for the future; it left him with too little to do.) "What happens here is sacred," he said soberly. "It needs to be respected." He wanted "to see if we can get a little more truth," because "you ought to be able to feel safe to say things here that maybe you can't say back at camp." Everyone pretended this nonsense was true. There was no discussion of voting strategy. In the first episode, Sonja and her ukulele were voted off, to no one's surprise. Almost a fifth of the American population—51.7 million people—tuned in to the finale.

Recliner, sofa, and recliner in a semicircle, backed against the windows with the curtains closed so we could watch the TV set without glare. *The Merv Griffin Show* on weekday afternoons and *The Wonderful World of Disney* on Sunday evenings. Any movie starring John Wayne. The sad-sack longing of *Queen for a Day*. *Voyage to the Bottom of the Sea*. *Captain Kangaroo* and *Bonanza*. *The Beverly Hillbillies* and *Hogan's Heroes*. *Colombo* and *The Mod Squad*. We were readers, all of us, but we read with the television on. We played Monopoly with the television on. We ate dinner with the television on. I think we might have opened our Christmas presents with the television on. Even during my delinquent years the television was on, but instead of sitting between my parents, I went over to Terry's house and sat between his parents, in a semicircle with the curtains closed against the glare to watch professional wrestling.

I grew up with the television on all the time and then left home and didn't watch much television for years. There was one set in our college dorm, but I don't recall seeing anything other than the Watergate hearings and the occasional episode of *Star Trek*, with the sound turned down so we could make up our own dialogue. I took pride in my newly elevated tastes. When I visited my parents, I joined the circle in front of the TV, but I was pointedly reading Alan Watts at the same time. When I found myself living with a television again a few years later, it wasn't my fault; it wasn't my TV, but it's a slippery slope and down I slid.

Stories. That is my drug. I am addicted to stories and I take stories in every form. I make up stories and I love to hear stories. I read a great deal, I watch a lot of movies, and I watch television. I like action films and comic books. In Thomas Hardy's words, "I like a story with a bad moral." My taste is more broad than low (and I can find any number of people willing to defend the artistic merits of action films and comic books). But for a long time, television was background companionship, less of a story than the Top 40 countdown. I went to the movies almost every week of my childhood; we watched previews, a cartoon, and the double feature. I was born just a bit too late for the serial, sometimes called a chapter play. What a great idea: a story progressing from week to week. But all the television shows I watched were self-contained. Colombo always had just one more question. Granny sent the neighbors a bottle of tonic on *The Beverly Hillbillies*; by the next week, the tonic was forgotten. Even *Star Trek* wrapped everything up by the end of an hour. But television got better. Characters began to move through time. They changed and grew and suffered the consequences of mistakes. We watched *Hill Street Blues* and *Dallas. St. Elsewhere* and *L.A. Law* and *Twin Peaks.* Television began to require attention. *The Sopranos. Breaking Bad. Six Feet Under.* And now? *The Expanse. Schitt's Creek. Trapped.*

I'm not here to defend anything, but I'd rather surf the channels than the web. The artist Daniel Rozin made the "Self-Centered Mirror," a sculpture of 34 vertical mirrored panes. The panes are arranged in such a way that standing in front of the mirror, you will see yourself and only yourself reflected in every pane. The web feels this way to me sometimes; it's a useful tool, because it does what I tell it to do and goes where I tell it to go. (The internet also watches me in a disturbingly precise way; as far as surveillance goes, I prefer television's blunt reflexes to the fine algorithms of data miners.) Grab the remote to surf the channels and it's like riding the subway; it's where everyone is. Everything is on television and almost everyone in the world is watching. People sometimes tell me they don't watch TV, with a hint of pride. Instead they send me YouTube links and stream Netflix.

As a child, I watched *Candid Camera*, because didn't everyone. But I was in my anti-television years before the Loud family decompensated in public view, and I was well into plot-driven dramas by the time *The Real World* appeared, well off my radar. Except for the comedic stylings of Pat Patterson on WWE, I didn't know what reality TV was, exactly; I had a vague and critical idea of some amalgam of *Jerry Springer* and *Cops.* (Which isn't entirely off base. The list of failed reality shows is long, with a throw-it-at-the-wall-and-see-if-it-sticks quality. There's *Shattered*, where players have to try and stay awake for a week. *Who's Your Daddy?*—a Fox show from 2005 in which a woman tries to guess which of 25 men is her biological father. *Splash*, a competition where celebrities perform high dives; many people were injured before the show was cancelled. *Space Cadets*, a Channel 4 show from the UK in which people were told they'd been picked to be astronauts and were sent into "space." Few people were fooled. A few years ago, a reality show called *Eden* was filmed on a fenced 600-acre estate in a remote area of western Scotland. Twenty-three men and women were left there for a year to start "building a new life and creating a society from scratch." They had personal cameras, a skeleton crew, and remote cameras around the property. Over the course of the year, many cheated and more than half quit. The show aired four episodes before being cancelled. But no one bothered to tell the remaining players that it was over. They just kept trying to create a society from scratch for seven more months.)

Reality television is not one thing. Are quiz shows and game shows reality TV? Maybe. A case can be made. Talent competitions are a kind of reality show. But the core, that which feeds the wildly popular and surprisingly diverse human preoccupation with each other, is where we find makeover shows and slice-of-life shows and so-called adventure shows. Such shows feel like a kind of espionage. At the center of it all is *Survivor*, one of the most influential shows ever broadcast. *Survivor* forces people to rely on one another and eliminate each other at the same time. It swings between the tedium of real housewives and the adrenaline rush of a footrace; *Survivor* puts people in faux danger and real discomfort and watches as they half-bore one another to death. It's a little bit of everything and became the blueprint for countless other shows.

One day some years ago, and I cannot tell you why, I watched *Project Runway*, a fashion design competition. Fashion design does not interest me. But I was mesmerized by smart, creative people doing ridiculously difficult challenges under crazy time limits. My own work involves language and interior life as much as anything that happens; the problems I have to solve are often hard to frame. I do solve most of them, sometimes with a jolt. Watching people design and tailor a red-carpet look based on New York City architecture in 24 hours felt oddly familiar. I could see—I recognized—the small *aha* slide across a person's face like a brief spark. I fell in love with *Project Runway.* I was struck by the weirdness of it all—not the thrill of solving a tricky problem, but the very idea of doing it on camera, in view. I'm a little introverted and private. (This surprises many people. I'm not shy; I'm comfortable with public speaking; I'm opinionated. And I've written at length about private matters. But if a writer does their work well, the work of it disappears and the words seem artless, natural. This can fool a reader into thinking they've seen behind the curtain. But writers reveal only what they wish to reveal, and take great care about it. You have no idea what I've left out.) I am perhaps more private than is good for me and certainly more private than is considered normal in current times. I was curious about the idea of so-called *reality* as a so-called show, with elements of games and documentary and improvisation and manipulation and rules all blended together. And the very idea.

The fact is, I watched *Project Runway* because a smart musician I know told me, with some embarrassment, that *she* liked it. And I was embarrassed, too, for a while; then I found out that another friend—and another—were watching secretly, too. So I'm not here to defend anything, especially myself, but I'm still a snob. It's just that being a snob about reality television is a little different from being a snob in the world of, say, quantum physics. I knew I was getting sick when I watched *America's Next Top Model*—once. (Okay, I watched it more than once.) I watched *American Idol* a few times. So did a lot of other people. (When *American Idol* first aired, only 27 of 140 million cell phones were used for texting. A third of the phones used for voting in *American Idol* had never been used for texting before. An ATT spokesman said that the show had done more to "educate the public and get people texting" than their marketing.) I watched *Survivor*. I watched *The Amazing Race* because I like to travel, but wouldn't want to travel like that. I watched *Top Chef* because I like to cook, but I can't cook like that. I watched *Dirty Jobs* because I don't have one. A pattern, perhaps. Being private and avoiding social media means not always seeing other people's lives as intimately as my native curiosity would like. A little reality television fills the same appetite that I think drives a lot of social media. These shows were about life, but they were not about my life. Maybe that is what I want from stories most of all.

More than 700 reality shows are being produced now around the world. I've never watched *Big Brother*, a show in which strangers are isolated together and kept under 24-hour surveillance. *Big Brother* may be the biggest reality show in the world, with hundreds of seasons in more than 50 countries. I had always assumed reality shows were a peculiarly American invention. Not so: *Big Brother* began in the Netherlands. The company that started *Big Brother*, Endemol, got very rich. There have been many imitations, like *Star Academy*, which aired in Lebanon, among other countries. A pan-Balkan show called *That's Me* brought contestants from several former Yugoslav republics to live together in a *Big Brother*–style house. (Do we believe the producers' high-minded emphasis on peace and harmony among former enemies? Perhaps you can imagine how it worked out.)

You've read this far. So maybe you're not one of the people I've talked to lately who are dismayed at my choice of subject, who trash all of reality television and then admit they've never watched it, who are otherwise discerning and curious but willing to dismiss one of the most influential entertainments in the world. Reality shows have changed television, changed culture, affecting everything from the beauty business to the travel industry, yet a lot of people ignore them. Theodore Sturgeon famously responded to the complaint that 90 percent of science fiction is crap by saying, "90 percent of everything is crap." When I tell people what I'm writing about these days, the blinds come down. I'd be curious about this if people had actually checked it out—I didn't decide that soccer bored me until I suffered through an entire season of it. When I ask people how they came to the conclusion that, as a good friend said with a sneer recently, "Reality television is awful," I get a whiff of internet conspiracy. Maybe they watched one episode of *Real Housewives* or *The Bachelor* several years ago, hated it, and thus proved that the entire ill-defined genre is terrible. Maybe they just assumed, and didn't bother to watch at all.

Besides, the fact that we produce so much crap is interesting, too; so is the fact that we don't agree on what crap is. I may think *Real Housewives* and *The Bachelor* are terrible shows, but an awful lot of people like them.

Talent competitions are popular everywhere. There's a lot of singing and dancing but also pottery, tattooing, glassblowing, dog grooming, acrobatics, and drag. Poetry competitions are popular in the Arab world. *The Holy Qur'an Caravan* is a Koran-reciting competition in which the winners are voted on by the audience. A show called *Green Light* that aired in several Muslim-majority countries required people to compete on doing good deeds. *Rough Science*, a BBC show, landed teams of scientists in a strange place and challenged them to solve puzzles, like determining the latitude and longitude or making soap.

I followed *Queer Eye for the Straight Guy* with something close to delight, but I can't get interested in any other makeover shows. The rest of the world can, though; makeover has a big audience, whether it's about dieting, plastic surgery, interior decorating, fashion, cars, makeup, preparation for marriage, or life in general. I want stories, which means pitting strength against weakness, sending a character on a journey and into conflict. It means an end that is unexpected or an end that is expected but complicated or an end that never quite arrives. I've never been able to tolerate the slice-of-life shows like *Jersey Shore* or the many *Real Housewives* shows, because like *The Real World*, the only things that happen just happen. They're like experimental films in which all the dialogue is the stream of consciousness in an unnamed narrator's dreams. I don't care what happens next.

The Amazing Race, in which pairs of people travel around the world as fast as they can, should be one of my favorite shows. Players go from Burkina Faso to Vilnius and then hand-deliver several packages without speaking any Lithuanian. They go from Singapore to Manila, where teams have to plow a muddy field with an ox. They fly from Auckland to Siam Reap, where they retrieve baskets of fish out of the harbor. From San Diego to a small town in Argentina, where they have to make 120 empanadas. There are petty pleasures to be had. In season 20, Rachel and her partner can skip to first place if they will shave their heads. She looks stricken, then begins to cry. "I don't wanna shave my head! I paid five hundred dollars for extensions!" I like to travel, especially to places I've never been and where

I don't speak the language, but I wouldn't want to travel with Rachel. And the show makes me nervous. There's a lot of pressure and plenty of luck involved; taxis get lost and bicycle tires go flat and dancing with a bottle on your head is about as hard as it sounds. *The Amazing Race* can be like a bad dream where you run without getting anywhere and then stop to plow a field with an ox or make empanadas.

Last year, late at night in a hotel in a foreign city where I knew no one and couldn't sleep, I discovered *Lego Masters*. It's an improbably hypnotic competition, oddly soothing. Lego building has its own vocabulary, its own stars, its own genius hacks, and the obsessives who spend their hours at this are full of admiration and curiosity about each other's work. Let's face it; the last few years have been a slog for a lot of us. Maybe I need a competition for good deeds. *Lego Masters, The Great British Baking Show*? There's goodwill in these shows. *Floor is Lava* and *Holey Moley*? The stakes are so low. These are the Vanilla Wafers of reality television.

But I can't live on Vanilla Wafers. The stories I like are the ones where problems get solved. Make a garden party dress out of actual flowers, cook breakfast with this weird fungus you've never seen before, get across Saigon at rush hour on a bicycle. Scale this wall and solve this puzzle. Live with these people (yes, *these* people) for 39 days, on a tiny beach. I know I'm not alone; a lot of us have turned to this kind of entertainment in the last few years, as a kind of Novocain. I admit to a bit of numbing, but I'm also prone to the deep dive. I think of the unresolved in life as problems: that which I want to understand, that which slips out of my grasp, becomes the next thing to tackle. My love of other people's stories, my urge to escape my own, the vast audience of strangers doing the same thing: this was worth investigating. The irony, of course, is that I can't dive deeply into why we disappear into television without doing so myself. I started watching *Survivor* again a few years ago: tropical island, physical challenges I could probably never finish, a chance to break out my genetic tendency toward sarcasm. I watched off and on. Then I watched regularly. And then I went nuts.

Mark Burnett became known to some fans of *Survivor* as EP, which can refer to his role but more commonly means Evil Pecker. Mark Burnett is also responsible for *Shark Tank*, *The Voice*, and *The Apprentice*, the latter of which made him literally hundreds of millions of dollars. Burnett and a ghostwriter, Martin Dugard, wrote an unintentionally hilarious book about the first season of *Survivor* and its meaning to the human condition. He claims that they didn't know what would happen in the first season, but they knew what they were after—in the words of a producer, "dramality." That means reality with a story, contestants playing a character based on themselves, playing through a loose plot outline with an unknown end.

Burnett grew up in London, the child of factory workers, and then joined the British Army. He's a self-made man and seems to believe his own press. He has a lot of self-esteem. I've read both his memoirs, thus saving you the work. (My task was made easier by the fact that entire sections of the books are identical.) I can tell you that Mark Burnett is a brave, persistent man with a vision; his style is "quiet micromanagement." (Remind me not to work for him.) He describes a thunderstorm during an early season of *Survivor*. Lightning is flashing overhead, and it had rained so hard that the camera operators were standing in water. Burnett was confident that lightning wouldn't strike, and refused to let people take cover. "There was never a question of stopping due to this storm. *Survivor* was real. Period. Real meant shooting until it was unsafe. . . . From that moment on, *Survivor* would have the stamp of authenticity."

In early seasons, *Survivor*'s narrative floated the idea that the "castaways" might create a new civilization. "This is their story," Jeff told the viewers. "Sixteen strangers forced to band together to carve out a new existence." "Great waves, great beach, beautiful girls!" says Sash, in the first episode of *Nicaragua*. "It doesn't get much better than that, does it?" In *Worlds Apart*, Joaquin is thrilled: "Fast money, loose women, lots of champagne—are you kidding me?" There's no champagne or money yet, and he's just met the women. It's not clear if he's referring to the moment in which he finds himself or the fantasy of what might happen if he won. I'm not sure he knows. Burnett has been known to wax philosophical about the transformative nature of a season on *Survivor*, that the players are "fighting for their existence, their mental health, their self-respect. Their money. If ever a device were invented to help men and women gauge the caliber of their character, *Survivor* is it." The game changes people, he thinks, because they discover Maslow's hierarchy. "The clothes go first," he wrote. "Soon all life is fluid." Burnett, who lives in a $25 million house in Malibu and whose net worth is around a half-billion dollars, added, "I cannot begin to describe the simple wonders of life on a deserted tropical island."

Survivor sells us spontaneity, the fantasy that we are seeing people as they really are. If you like reality shows, it is partly to see people in spontaneous—unscripted—moments. *Survivor* is disconnected from daily life. (And yet so much of the show is built on the mundane chores of daily life.) It exists in unstructured time, ahistorical time, with no calendar, no watches. Sunrise and tides mark the days; lost weight and beard growth mark the weeks. The show is so dislocated in time and space that episodes from 20 years ago can feel as fresh as the most recent one. The producers seem to edit out telling slang or newsy comments, clothes don't look like much after a few days, and everyone's hair is a mess. The only person who changes is Jeff, and just barely.

Reality television sells a hologram of real life—which is (of course) the opposite of real life. But I am not sure it is all that different from the way many of us watch the greatly varied human circus stroll by. We have no idea who most people are, *really*, but that's no obstacle to our opinions about them. We can guess. And we can judge. "Maybe that's the unspoken contract: to be blank spaces for each other, holding the maps of desire that are projected on our skins," wrote the artist Akwaeke Emezi. She was talking about the isolation of the pandemic, but her words are easy to apply to the hours of viewing. "Maybe we are alone together and that is a tender choice."

The many academics who have studied reality television—alternately puzzled and offended by its success—have plenty of theories for why we watch. Perhaps we are reacting to the loss of a sense of reality in daily life, a growing inability to recognize what is true. Are reality shows part of the shared construction of reality that includes everything from Photoshop to QAnon? Or is it a "dialectic between affiliation and self-assertion" mirroring our childhood experience, as one psychologist says, which is altogether more theory than I need. Some of us are voyeurs and many of us are lonesome. Is that so complicated? When a friend recently told me in strong terms that reality television was simply awful, my reaction wasn't just that he was tarring with a very broad brush. I felt he was missing something about our condition. I am eternally curious about people, even when I can't stand them, even when I don't understand anything about people. And if you're curious about people, then you are curious about what drives them, compels and attracts them. There aren't many better places to go for *that* kind of people-watching than a genre of performance in which people pretend to be real, think they are being real, are challenged to be real, and maybe fail to be real—and in the process, uncover something real they would never have shown us otherwise.

Then again, maybe I'm reaching. Maybe I'm feeling a little defensive.

A 2010 survey found that registered Republicans are more likely to watch *Survivor* and reality television in general than registered Democrats. (In the survey, Democrats seemed to prefer "character-driven dramas, like *Dexter*.") The show practices a cheerful, unembarrassed product placement—Sprint and Outback Steakhouse, I'm looking at you. My favorite is the Charmin Café where the reward is a "modern toilet and plenty of Charmin." On CBS All Access (now part of Paramount+), the commercials for *Survivor* are an odd mix: military recruitment, medications for ulcerative colitis, a variety of detergents, the deeply annoying Progressive Insurance campaign, ATT, and the Sleep Number mattress. I see the same ads over and over and over and over until I can recite them with the sound muted.

I've read so many pages trying to explain why people like *Survivor*, and it doesn't seem that hard to understand. The show partakes of base archetypes, rewards bad behavior and sometimes punishes it, punishes good behavior and occasionally rewards it, and indulges a few impulses we like to imagine indulging. There's satisfaction in seeing the strange bedfellows—people who would never meet otherwise are suddenly wrestling in the mud or fighting about whose turn it is to get water. Unlikely friendships develop, such as the one between two of the finalists in *Gabon*: Bob Crowley, a high school physics teacher who looks like Bill Nye the Science Guy—still the oldest player to win—and Sugar Kiper, a swimsuit model who looks like a blond Betty Boop and came in third. One kind of viewer is a technician, checking strategy and examining methods. Another watches in sympathy, to be able to say, *That's just what I would do.* Another waits for the exquisite cringe of failure. And some of us lean forward as though we are in the Colosseum and the lions are strolling in. (The political writer Christopher J. Wright did a painstaking survey of viewers to find that a person's social class and voting history could predict which contestant they preferred.) After the original season of *Expedition: Robinson* aired in Sweden, the chief of the network there said, "You felt embarrassed watching it, but you couldn't stop."

A lot of people want to play this game. Money is just a part of it. The winner, as everyone knows, gets a million dollars. The person in second place gets $100,000, and third place wins $85,000. But every player gets paid. Being on the jury is, according to a few sneaky sources, worth $40,000. Even the first player voted off gets $3,500—unless that person is a returning player, in which case it goes up to $25,000. For the reunion show, everyone who attends is paid again, reportedly $10,000. This, free travel, and a nice vacation after being voted out. But the money is part of a complicated equation: people are playing *for their families, for their children, for their own self-worth, to prove something, to be something, to become something, because they love it.* They've grown up watching the show and imagined themselves on that island many times. In *Worlds Apart*, at her first Tribal Council, Jenn says, "It's *fun* being here—it's Tribal Council! I've been watching this since I was eight! I still feel like I'm watching you on television right now!" She is smiling, self-aware, but it's still true. "I can't believe I'm here! I'm losing my mind! You have no idea!"

There are ways to win *Survivor*, though none are guaranteed. Success is not just about being strong or likable, and sometimes neither counts. Good players tolerate heat, cold, damp, discomfort, hunger, and boredom. They are willing to throw themselves into physical challenges, even if they have no skill. They are willing to eat food they've never considered eating. Good players can stand on a small shelf for hours, be rolled in a barrel down a hill, and answer trivia questions. They do hold-coins-between-your-fingers-while-standing-in-an-uncomfortable-position challenges and carry-raw-fish-in-your-mouth challenges and stack-blocks-on-a-wobbly-table-held-by-a-rope-while-walking-backward challenges and dig-chop-climb-swim-pole-vault challenges. There are many, many puzzles to solve and locks to open and knots to untie. Bridges to build, tightropes to walk, and, often, mud. Fire is key to what little comfort the players have, to clean water, light, warmth, and meals. But few people know how to start a fire. On *Kaôh Rōng*, the 32nd season, the Brains tribe wins a fire-making kit that includes kerosene. One of the men promptly uses most of it on their first fire and the brainy tribe is stymied about what to do next—they have fire, but they don't seem to know how to keep fire. A few people have started fires using their eyeglasses and now and then a great effort results in fire by friction. Often, a great effort does not. When a player who says he's a longtime fan of the game announces that he's been practicing starting a fire by watching YouTube videos, and then actually starts a fire, all I could think was, well, at fucking last.

I watch in wonder, that you would go through the elaborate process of applying to be on *Survivor* and sign life-altering contracts and travel to a foreign country to live on an island, yet make no effort to learn how to build a fire, solve puzzles, catch fish, make shelters, or follow a map. People end up on the game without a base tan, unable to swim, scared of crabs, having never been in a boat. People come to the game so woefully unprepared that it makes me wonder if they are coached. On season 38, a woman from New York says her sole outdoor experience is that she once peed in the bushes in Central Park, and "that was an emergency." On *Fiji*, Cassandra, a middle-aged college administrator, says, "My outdoor experience up to this point consists of being maybe 20, 40 feet off the road. I love coconut, but it's granulated and already shredded in the grocery store." But having good survival skills won't get you to the end. Winning requires a social game—the ability to make friends or the semblance of friends; to convey trust or the semblance of trust; to build an alliance, until an alliance is no longer worth keeping.

I hate the idea of *Survivor*, even as I am seduced, even as I give in. Why do *I* watch? Not because it's real and not even because it's good. As a whole, the show is sort of awful a lot of the time. Watching more than one episode in a row can make me feel a little sick (of television, the contestants, Jeff Probst, psoriasis medication commercials, myself). But I always come back. *Watching* is a verb: I'm *watching* the show and watching myself watch. I am torn between wondering how I would fare on the show and passing judgment on the people who are. I think, *Why in the world would anyone do this?* And immediately add, *If it were me*— Sometimes during the live finale, viewers can see a replay of the audience watching the final episodes. We are watching the audience watch the show we are watching.

I like the rituals of reality television—of television. There are so many tropes built into reality television that websites are devoted to collecting them, capturing all the recurring moments, objects, sayings, and characters, from "limited wardrobe" to the "dumb blonde" to the "oh crap" expression. I like the sing-along nature of the shows. *Please pack your knives and go. That means you're out. The tribe has spoken.* I like that it's kind of boring. Sometimes the tin pot dictators and tiny cold wars of *Survivor* are more manageable than the evening news.

Often the face the players present to me as a viewer is completely different from the face they present to their peers. In almost every season, someone will say, "Perception is reality." These conversations happen within the conventions of performance—that is, players confess as castaways. Often what they are doing is confessing the way they've lied to the others. They are not breaking out of their performance; they speak to the eye of the camera as part of their performance, helping us build the shared reality of marooning. Now and then, a player is able to speak *through* the screen, directly to the viewer—in on the joke. We are reminded of the layers of deception at work: between player and player, player and viewer, camera and player, camera and viewer. Is Courtney really like that, or is she just filmed that way? Is she like that because she is being filmed? Is she *being like* "Courtney on *Survivor*"?

I'm curious about how it feels to become a character, to live behind a veneer in a state of ceaseless deception in this way, because I think this is how most of us live most of the time. Our interactions with each other are a kind of presentation, a performance. And we love to give confessionals. I watch because while I'm watching a swimming-climbing-hauling-weight-across-a-balance-beam-and-solve-a-ball-maze problem, I'm not worried about my own. I watch Ben and Chrissy go head to head guiding small white balls through a maze while standing on a balance beam. Because it might be a million-dollar challenge. Because fire is life. Starting to watch a new season sometimes feels like eating too many cookies. They do all taste the same; there is a sweet predictability in each bite. It's too much, but I still want another one.

The social psychologist Erving Goffman described the conscious and unconscious behaviors of meeting other people as "a potentially infinite cycle of concealment, discovery, false revelation, and rediscovery." We are stuck with first impressions, because we keep having them. (We are stuck with them even if they are filmed and edited.) Goffman used the word "performance" to describe how we try to impress others; he saw all shared and public experiences as fundamentally theatrical. All of us are actors in relationship to others, taking our parts in a complex play; all of us are audience to the relationships of others. By watching the game we are already playing it, and playing in the same way as the contestants. That is, we know some, but not all, of the players; we trust some, but not all, of the process; we are never sure if we've made the right choice about whom to trust. By watching, we connive to keep the game going, and even to keep the conniving going, because we like the game and we like the contrivances. That makes us collaborators, and part of the role of collaborator is to always pretend one is not collaborating. We join in the big and small and tiny lies. *We're not evil,* says one of the first contestants. *That's just who we play on television.*

WORKING BACKWARDS

Television, once the most evanescent of media, never dies anymore. It barely fades. But when *Big Brother* first aired, people were alarmed at the idea of constant surveillance and the caching of filmed lives. *Survivor* is very good at making it appear as though the players—often called "castaways" on the show, but also simply called players or contestants by the viewing world—are isolated. But there are so many cameras, cameras everywhere, GoPros and drones and dozens of cameras and microphones at the edge of every scene, hidden cameras in the trees. The timing of the confessionals is up to the producers, who watch and wait for the story arc to appear. In one behind-the-scenes photo, a player is surrounded by a cameraman, a boom mike operator, a guy holding a reflector, and the producer asking questions—questions that are never heard in the show. The camera lighting at night washes every face into a bluish white and the rest of the world into shades of dark gray. The players, their eyes shaded to a dull black, whisper and shift from the glow of the firelight to the shadow, like wraiths. Boats with camera operators follow when the players go out on a raft. It looks like two people are taking a private stroll along the beach, but they are not. They are strolling inches from several camera operators laden with equipment, one camera per player, and a couple of other people holding microphones or reflectors. Tyson (and one of the results of *Survivor*'s long popularity is that he doesn't need a last name) says you can tell if people are talking strategy because of the way the camera operators behave; if they are clearly focused on a conversation between two people down on the beach, take note.

Whenever players are together but not on camera, such as waiting in a tent for Tribal Council to start, they aren't allowed to speak. They are ferried to Tribal Councils and challenges to prevent that. We see them set off into the sunset, trudging along the beach, but that's it; then they get a ride. Players aren't allowed to wander too far away from crew—off-stage, as it were—and aren't supposed to talk to the camera crews. If they do, the crew isn't supposed to respond. Veteran players say you should still try to make friends with the crew any way you can, so they'll give you a little leeway. If you're really careful and quick, you can get a few whispered exchanges in before they catch up to you.

A group of college students supposedly known as the "dream team" are hired to test and run the challenges. (It's a dream job.) They are filmed on the courses and sometimes function as stand-ins for long shots or reshoots when a crucial moment is missed. In aerial shots of the challenges, the course is surrounded by empty sand and water, but these are setups. Actual challenges may take hours to run instead of the 10 or 15 minutes we see. The players are given individual explanations of what the challenge will require, and they can ask questions. Then the players are tested for fitness before the challenge begins. During the actual race, a crew member may be just out of view, holding parts of the shaky course together. The viewer never sees any of this; we don't want to see this.

Players can be alone sometimes. Rick Devens, who played a nearly flawless game on *Edge of Extinction*, said in an interview, "There are people around all the time, but there is definitely not always someone there to keep you from getting hurt. I remember one time going fishing out on the reef, and going out past the reef where it just drops down. And my whole heart just turned cold. There was no one around." When Mike Skupin fell into the fire in *Australia*, he was alone and the cameras didn't capture it. When the crew heard him screaming, camera operators came running. Later the editors applied "a very Hitchcock technique using just sound and nature B-roll to tell the tale" of what happened before they started to film.

The show is more or less made up. Sort of. It's not exactly real. Julia, who played *Edge of Extinction* and took exception to how she was edited, wrote later, "The 'reality' of it is that you truly only see 1% of what happens." The editors pare about 25 hours of footage down to each 40-minute episode. At times editors have shown scenes out of order or spliced conversations together, messing with the chronology of how relationships develop. There are separate editors for the challenges, the councils, camp life, for teases. They have on-site producers who keep track of the "important beats" for each episode. The producers claim to have a loyal crew that has lasted many seasons. But the filming of the 29th season was interrupted by a strike by the postproduction crew, demanding a union contract with health and retirement benefits, something they still didn't have after 29 seasons of a successful show dependent on skillful editing.

The first season was an experiment. "There was no blueprint," says Sean Foley, director of photography for many years. "We began to emulate traditional drama, crafting scene work from scraps of moments to create a sense of cause and effect." There was a kind of blueprint, though. Game shows in the 1950s were, in the phrase of the time, "controlled." That meant they were fixed. It wasn't uncommon for contestants to be fed questions in advance and sometimes answers, to be scripted to lose or win after a suspenseful race. Players were coached in how to behave, taught to look thoughtful or worried, to make the occasional unimportant mistake. All to "make it real," in the words of the producer Albert Freedman. I don't think *Survivor* editors script the events and the producers don't decide who wins or loses, but the story is a kind of fiction nonetheless. As with everything from Shakespeare to *Twenty-One*, part of the story is that we get to pretend that all of it is real.

Jeff Probst—Jiffy, to fans—has said that his job is about "how to tell a story in a jungle with heroes and villains and archetypes and underdogs and all that stuff." He wants to find "every player's dramatic arc," the "beginning, middle, and an end" to every player's story. The writers' strike in the summer of 2001 helped create the reality genre. What to do when the writers quit? Make a show that doesn't need a script in advance. Probst was giving an interview after signing a new contract to stay on as host. He'd quit and negotiated his way back to a raise and a role as executive producer. "There's a central dramatic question of the episode: Who is going to be voted out tonight? And then we work backwards: Bill is going home tonight, the story starts, and we start laying clues to help you try to figure out what's going to happen." Or, in many cases, keep you from figuring it out. For months, the players keep mum under the threat of painful fines and they don't know the final outcome. But the editors know. They know who wins and who comes close and who never has a chance. They know who is going to make the biggest mistake and when the wrong words will be said. Out of a mountain of raw material emerges a villain, a mentor, a pawn, a surprise, the hero's quest and the fool's comeuppance. The players and their "journey" (often a "transformative journey") are constructed into a narrative familiar to anyone who has read myth or fairy tales. And I fall into the story line, a story that is created to predict the results after the results are in, a story that pulls us along to its inevitable end. Even the outtakes are controlled; we see what we are allowed to see, and often the purpose of outtakes is to add to the impression of artless spontaneity, when it is anything but.

Probst said last year that he wants to stop being "so literal" with interviews in the editing process—that is, linear is so yesterday. "Anything to keep it feeling fresh," says Brian Barefoot, a current editor. Recent seasons involve more cross-cutting and combining of scenes, to the point of creating conversations that never happened. Or didn't happen exactly that way. We pretend there's no rescue, just as we pretend that no one's watching. We pretend that a game this fake is a gateway to self-awareness, that a game played for money in which lying is essential is the equivalent of a spiritual retreat. "Nothing is taken for granted about any version of self, relationship, or reality in general," writes the psychoanalyst Roy Schafer about therapy. The musician and painter John Lurie, talking into a camera, mused that anyone who can do so naturally is "probably a sociopath." You can make a lot of money doing it," he adds, but as he got better at talking to cameras, "I became a worse and worse person." One player on *Survivor* said in an interview, "I think the cameras are there, but I am not acting for them. This is just me. This is *real.*" *This is just how I am when I am in front of a camera.*

I don't much like the "very special episodes" sewn onto a season—the deleted scenes, audition tapes, extra interviews, and revelations of real-life problems. That's not what I want; they violate the frame. What I want is the story, the slowly unfolding revelations of motive. It isn't just that I usually respond the way the editors want me to respond. I *want* to respond the way they want me to, as I want to be scared and then relieved when I read a thriller or moved and then satisfied by a drama. I'm choosing my manipulation. I know the story is built: like all stories, it includes secrets, diversions, buried truths, half-told tales. All the stories that I like are *built*. The skill in storytelling is in letting me forget that for a moment. Artlessness is difficult to achieve.

Am I proud that my dopamine triggers get popped? No. But they do. I am not immune to any of this manipulation. It's a blunt tool much of the time: the flash of a shark's fin or a spider spinning a web during a conversation between two supposed allies. Scenes of young women sunbathing cut with one of an older woman chopping wood. It took me a while to realize how curated the show is, and longer still to let go of my arguments about that fact. I wanted it to be what it appeared to be and what it tried to convince me it was. (And yet people really do say these things.) I don't entirely believe anything I see—not the arguments, the tears or the hugs or the blindsides. But I don't really care anymore; I watch *Survivor* the way I watched *Deadwood* and *Nurse Jackie*. I know it is fiction, but fiction of a particular kind; it *feels* real. It's dramality.

Fredric Jameson thinks that we rewrite history and experience to fit into foundational narratives. I know I'm *susceptible* to foundational narratives. I like foundational narratives. The anxiety. The scheming. The struggle. The old dream of a clean slate, the chance to start over. It's our fantasy marooning.

EVOLUTION

The early seasons of *Survivor* focused more on actual survival—the harrows of deprivation, building shelter, and struggling to find food. In *Survivor: Africa*, the third season, the players are driven into dry, empty land along a dusty road. "We are carving a path along the equator, through the scorching desert of Kenya in East Africa," says Jeff, rocking in the truck. "They are about to be abandoned in the heart of one of the most diverse and dangerous collections of animals anywhere on the continent." Their camps are behind thorn fences, and they are told to repair the enclosure because it is their "only protection" against dangerous animals. They must keep a fire burning and have a night lookout. All this is being filmed by crew, whose own accommodations are not far away.

Even though earlier seasons focused more on physical survival, they were easier in physical terms. The contestants in Africa had more supplies than they could carry, including canned food, water, and a medical kit. Most groups now start with no tools, shelter, food, or fire-making supplies. No more care packages or luxury items. (I used to imagine what I would choose as my luxury—probably a notebook or dental floss. Over the years, people have lugged along an American flag, a Texas flag, war paint, massage oil, fire dancer torches, lipstick, a Magic 8-Ball, a bottle of cologne, a skateboard— to the beach—and a bongo. A *bongo*.)

The focus now is on relationships, alliance-building, deceit, and secrets. Despite the more demanding conditions, the show tends to skim over or even ignore such things as leaking shelters and the search for coconuts in favor of the social game. We all know the contestants are hungry, that they are cold sometimes and hot sometimes and wet a lot of the time and that they all smell pretty bad. This is a given. On *All-Stars*, a big storm floods the camps, leaving everyone miserable. Ethan says some of the tribe thought the producers would come and rescue them. "What are you, nuts? This is *Survivor*." The rules state that a player can't hurt another player, but also, explicitly, that the *show* can hurt anyone. For the most part, they are uncomfortable rather than endangered and suffer as much from boredom and irritation as hunger. The discomforts of *Survivor*, the dampness and dirt and cold and heat and bug bites, the aches and minor injuries, the empty stomachs, are genuinely limited in both time and scope. This is voluntary suffering, part of the treasure hunt, the price paid. This is one of the transformative lessons.

The end of almost every episode is a meeting called Tribal Council, where a player is eliminated. (After people vote but before Jeff reads them aloud, a producer arranges the votes in the order that will produce the most suspense.) The Tribal Council set is elaborate now and most of the time spent there is devoted to dissecting each other's game: who's strong, who's popular, who could win, who screwed up, who is sympathetic, who is irritating, and who has burned too many bridges. (Burnett calls Tribal Council a place of "brutal, unscripted truth.") The set is still mocked-up aboriginal, but the sessions are longer and more chaotic, an odd combination of group therapy and bipartisan negotiation—free-for-all, chest-baring anger management sessions that sow mistrust and disrupt relationships. I am still surprised at how people let it all hang out during the Council. Jenny claims she was lying to Alecia all along so she could "give her a good last day" and Alecia says that being lied to doesn't make for a good day and Jenny replies, with the passion of the unfairly maligned, "I'm not saying it's the best decision or the right decision, but that's who I am as a person! I care about people's feelings!" The plotting is so bald and badly done, and then I remember a few of the ways I've misspoken: impulsive, unthinking words can appear without warning, as though without intent, and change everything. The players are tired and hungry and worried and *on camera*. I can't believe I would make such mistakes; I would probably make such mistakes. The meetings last for hours, but surely there are ways to dodge Jeff's leading questions. (Are there? Probst isn't just host and executive producer; he's God.) There may be ways to dodge questions, but he asks them, and people just start unloading their resentments and fears, their secrets and plans. Now and then you see a flash across someone's face: *Oops.*

Over the years, the babelicious score has gone way up. On fan sites, there is always talk about the game "evolving," as though it were an organism. A writer on *The Ringer* said the show is "a bit like pizza—even when it's bad, it's still good. And when it's good, it's *really* good. Sometimes, though, the producers pulling the strings throw pineapple on the pie just to try to jazz things up." On *Pearl Islands*, season 7, the contestants were tossed overboard with only their clothes instead of a backpack with a few changes and a swimsuit. In season 11, *Guatemala*, a hidden immunity idol was introduced. Several twists have allowed cast-out players a chance to return. And the producers are always trying to undermine the plans of players who think they know how to play the game. Jeff explains a reward challenge: two teams will run through the surf, cross a rope bridge, and toss rungs onto a ladder target. "You do not practice this at home on the weekend," he shouts, because he knows that lots of fans practice all kinds of things like this at home on the weekend. "These are the *Survivor* guinea pigs right here!" Describing a challenge requiring people to squat while balancing a vase, he says, "Another brand-new *Survivor* torture device!" In season 37, players have to swing a pendulum around and through a frame to keep a statue upright while balancing on small wooden blocks. "Something you're not going to be practicing in your backyard." They will be now.

The show appears lodged in Fiji now, and concerned with various themes rather than locations. The show has filmed in 18 locations, and for many years, two seasons were filmed back-to-back every year in the same place to save money. Probst decided that Fiji had everything they needed, and he was more interested in the show having themes than moving from one country to another. Just as television has always been more reflective than anything else, *Survivor* has been forced to up the ante on itself as imitators appear and other shows increase the noise. More drama, celebrity, shocks, complexity. Media grows broader, shallower, forming a kind of estuary of reflection. So teams have been divided into "heroes and villains," "fans versus favorites" and "beauty, brains, and brawn," divided by age, gender, race, and class, and composed of paired relatives playing together. Now there are steal-a-vote advantages and double-vote advantages and the Safety Without Power advantage and an idol split in half and idol nullifiers. Not every twist succeeds, and negative reaction from fans is noted. *Redemption Island*, in which booted players competed for a chance to return later, wasn't popular and seems to have disappeared. The "Outcast Twist" in *Pearl Islands*, when two booted players were allowed to return, was deeply resented (and not just because it brought Lil's scoutmaster uniform back into view). *Cambodia*, the 31st season, introduced the "Second Chance" twist, in which fans had the opportunity to vote for the cast from a pool of players who had only played once.

Probst said a few years ago that he wants the show to reflect the culture, to be "of the moment," and right now, our moment is "a really exciting, risky, all in, winner take all mentality." *Survivor* is a kind of experiment. But I'm more inclined to think of a peculiar tangle of wires in a dusty basement laboratory than any careful investigation. Jeff lays this out explicitly in *Edge of Extinction*, the 38th season, which sent expelled players to a barren camp to wait for a chance to return. "The idea behind *Extinction* was not just a second chance," he told the players later. "It was to further explore the social experiment, with the questions, 'What would happen if you took somebody, and you sent them off to an island, with no idea how long they were going to be there, no idea what to expect? What would happen?'" (The jury is one of the strangest things in the two seasons with the *Edge of Extinction* twist. All the eliminated players form the jury, but remain huddled in barrenness on another island. When they walk into Tribal Council, instead of being freshly showered and fed, they are ragged and thin and look like they've just been rescued from a natural disaster. And they aren't smiling.)

Probst, who claims to have about 20 possible twists in mind for every season, says that the producers ask, *What is the invoice?* What tension or risk is involved? What is the price of a twist? The last six winners have been men, and the game's challenges are more physically punishing than they used to be. That's part of the invoice these days. "It's not enough to think about how a new twist or advantage can create good TV," wrote Riley McAtee in *The Ringer*. "It's also worth thinking about which kinds of players these new wrinkles in the game are rewarding." The game now rewards players like Tony, who spend all their time scheming and plotting and digging spy shacks instead of catching clams and getting to know people. I miss the day-to-day demands. I miss just watching people figure out how to do this, how to be in this strange situation for 39 days. With less time spent on mundane moments, we have a harder time understanding conflicts and alliances. Why do those two get along so well? Why does he hate her so much? Sometimes we haven't got a clue.

The 34th season, filmed in the Mamanuca Islands in Fiji, was called *Game Changers*. All the contestants were returning players who, in the words of CBS, "helped evolve the game even further by launching an accelerated level of competition" and who showed the "willingness to risk it all in order to become the Sole Survivor." (CBS does not explain that in this pursuit some of them played the game *badly*.) To combat the players' supposed prowess, the entire season was filled with new, mildly desperate twists. The producers have to insert surprises without losing sight of that patented *Survivor* world. We want the same old, same old, in new clothes. There are twists, but one familiar part is that there are twists. So the opening changes. Sometimes it's another "jump off the boat" free-for-all and sometimes it's a divide-into-tribes-on-the-beach scene. In season 39, the players are dropped off at their camps with no one greeting them and no instructions. In season 24, *One World*, Jeff says in the voice-over, "They think they've got *Survivor* figured out. They think they know the rules. They think they've seen everything. But they're in for a *huge* surprise." In the first episode of season 14, the players are given a map to supplies. They start to get excited, and then Alex remembers: "Wait a minute, this is *Survivor*. Something cruel is about to happen." Oh, it does. On *Palau*, the tenth season, Jeff narrates in portentous tones as the players arrive. For the first time, there are 20 of them, "set adrift with only the clothes on their backs and one canteen of water each. Everything they've come to expect about the way this game begins will soon be wiped out." As the contestants struggle to row a heavy boat to shore, Jeff skids up beside them in a fishing yacht. He tells them that the first woman and the first man to get to shore can claim immunity necklaces. Of course, the two who jump in the water are immediately left behind by the boat. Then the two who do get the necklaces are made to choose the tribes and must give back the necklaces.

"Jeff's a sumbitch, let me tell you that," says James, a steelworker from Mobile, Alabama. "Hell, I thought we were gonna get, ya know, some breakfast food and water, somethin'. Hay-ell, no!"

Still, the core of the game remains. Enemies win a reward together. People make moves. Someone lies and swears they've never lied. The one most likely to go home wins immunity by a hair. People cry when they see their loved ones. The weakest person loses a challenge for their team. The most forgettable young woman flies through a weird physical challenge. A guy acts nuts and thinks he's the favorite to win. Another guy can't stop talking, and someone gets paranoid and nervous and ruins his chances by driving everyone crazy. Someone cries. Someone pukes. People climb out of the shelter in the middle of the night to dig in the leaves for an idol.

A recent season, *David vs. Goliath*, pitted a tribe of Davids (people who have "spent their life battling adversity" as underdogs) against a tribe of Goliaths (people who have always "capitalized on their assets and are always considered the favorites"). The tribes assemble on a small cargo ship. They don't know their tribe names or how they're divided yet; it just looks unfair. A Goliath says of his team, "We just look stacked. So much strength, so much beauty, some clear brains." Then the Davids arrive. "As I look at the other tribe, I have the biggest smile on my face. The cards are just stacked completely in our favor." Guess what?

Jeff tells them, "*Survivor* is a game of social politics that often revolves around the story of the underdog versus the favorite." He explains the tribe divisions. "But what complicates *Survivor* is the unknown. You have no idea what to expect. You don't know which skill set will come in handy. And you know very little about the other players. So the question every day is the same. It's not, 'Who has the advantage?' It's '*What* is the advantage?'"

Jeff asks the biggest man, "Have you always felt like, 'Yeah, I am a Goliath'?" John, a professional wrestler, laughs. "Well, *obviously!*" The Davids are not amused. Jeff has the Goliaths choose the weakest of the David tribe, and they pick a skinny guy with glasses they call "Big Bang Theory." Then the Davids choose the strongest of the Goliaths. But the Davids get to assign the parts of a challenge requiring balance, crawling, and a puzzle. Big Bang Theory, whose name is Christian, chooses a slide puzzle. After the Davids win handily and get a shelter kit, Christian is shown in a confessional. He explains that he has a PhD in robotics and wrote slide puzzle algorithms as an undergrad. He starts explaining the mathematical nature of slide puzzles in great detail, and the screen fades out while he's still talking. (Christian will later bring on the "charm-pocalypse," and go far in the game, a big fan favorite.)

The audience has no idea how accurate the aired footage is to the actual game, and, except for a few tantalizing details, will never know. As I write this, in the months after Trump left office, complaints about subjective editing seem odd. From controlled game shows to awards for structured reality—this is the story arc of our time. Reality television is partly about reality, after all, about how we perceive reality, just as it is partly about fantasy. Reality television is also about television as the primary mediator of shared reality, a source of dreams for the culture. If you don't believe this, you haven't been reading the news for years. The act of watching creates what is watched and then creates a world in which the watchers participate; we see ourselves mirrored and then enlarged in the act of watching. We do this all the time, of course. This is the work of memory for much of our lives. We look back and remember what happened and ask, *How? Why?* We sift through the raw material of our lives to find the logic in it, to find a line we can follow from *then* until *now.* Life is a tragedy and a comedy, a fool's comeuppance and a hero's quest. The producers edit the game in all kinds of ways to create a narrative; Jeff edits the story in real time by commenting on performance and asking extremely leading questions. I edit as I watch, turning toward one player, paying little attention to another. And I'm editing the way I write about the way I watch the show in an attempt to make you, reader, feel certain things or react to characters in a particular way and (especially) so that you will like me. You will want me on your tribe. You can trust me. I swear.

FANS AND SCHOLARS.
MOSTLY FANS.

People study makeover shows in Asia, the psychological types of players, the class-based concerns in British reality television, the "nonverbal communication of trustworthiness," and how reality television constructs masculinity, usually in the disciplines of media studies or social science—but also psychology, communications, history, philosophy, and political science. A fair amount of such work involves turgid discussion topics like semiotics and intertextuality. An academic subspecialty is devoted to *Survivor*: "This argument is grounded in the idea that regardless of whether or not Campbellian structures are self-consciously drawn upon by the creators of long-term immersive narratives such as reality television, they serve as a powerful analytical tool for making sense of those narratives" and *Emotional and cognitive predictors of the enjoyment of reality-based and fictional television programming: An elaboration of the uses and gratifications perspective.* These authors tend to be sober and discursive. How do you explain the show? One writes, "The *Survivor* experiment proves, with unusual clarity for social science, the paucity of meaningful strategic rationality in human behavior."

The scholars occupy a corner of a field crowded filled with amateur critics, wonky analysts, obsessives on the continuum, and plain old panting fans ("i think Abbi is really good at manipulation and that is what she is doing, playing them big time. She is playing the poor, pitiful me card and Malcolm is falling for it to some extent."). The seriousness of the one body of work is so grandiose at times it approaches absurdity; it is mirrored by the frivolity of the other, in its solemn dedication to minutiae. The quality of writing in both cases varies from mediocre to accomplished, but the level of wit is much higher among fans. Irony is almost nonexistent among academics, but that's not news; among *Survivor* fans, irony is the default voice.

If I were a truly serious fan of *Survivor*, I would have subscribed to CBS All Access as soon as it appeared so I could watch videos of Ponderosa, the resort area where jury members wait between Tribal Councils. (Players voted out earlier than this are sent on a nice, long vacation where they are kept incommunicado.) At Ponderosa, players are still being filmed a great deal of the time, but now it's while they drink, flirt, get makeovers, cry, do revenge confessionals, meet with psychologists, and gang up on each other. (According to the contract, if you end up at Ponderosa you "may be obligated to undertake numerous practical activities and chores as part of my daily schedule and routine.") The CBS website has a lot of videos of very special moments, trivia contests, interviews, and spoilers, but YouTube carries hundreds of fan-created videos about *Survivor*. Maybe thousands. Videos about Ponderosa. Compilations of challenges. Best moments, worst moments, challenge-hacking moments. *Minecraft Survivor*—entire seasons. Episodes from other countries. The best of Sandra, funniest moments, Jeff being sassy, "Jeff being Jeff," *Survivor* secrets, locations of hidden idols, "Survivor moments that cured my depression," 17 minutes of people falling over, "Cringeworthy Survivor moments," Jeff's funniest insults, and, of course, videos asking *Where are they now?* Not to mention the behind-the-scenes videos that show how it is all filmed. If I were a real fan, I'd be listening to the *Survivor Know-It-All* podcast—or the *Outlast* podcast or *The Tribe* podcast or the *Survivor Historians* podcast. I'd join the *Survivor Romania* group on Facebook. I would have followed the Mr. and Miss Survivor contests on *Rob Has a Podcast*; mercifully, these were cancelled in 2015. I'd have followed the defunct live-streaming series called "Beyond the Buff," which sometimes featured "a rotating group of *Survivor* experts, celebrity super-fans, and former players to weigh in on the biggest moments" of each week's episodes. I'd be registered in one of the major *Survivor* chat rooms (there are many) and looking up "buff" on *Survivor Wiki* to find out who first wore the buff as a skirt and who first threw a buff into the fire at *Redemption Island* and what font the show's name has been in.

If I was a real fan, would I get lost? Angelina targets Christian first but then targets Elizabeth while telling Elizabeth that she is trying desperately to save her. Liar, liar. Or am I confused? Is the story that I can't quite follow what's going on? Thirteen people at Tribal Council form a complex Venn diagram; the conversation devolves into cross-talk and whispers, then Jeff interrupts and Gabby breaks down in tears again and Angelina starts to cry, saying she "just couldn't lie" to Elizabeth. But she *lied* to Elizabeth. Didn't she?

I am watching during the pandemic, when new production is shut down because visiting Fiji is forbidden. Fans complain that *Survivor* is a perfect quarantine situation. Why can't they film in the

Outer Banks or the Channel Islands off California? Many inquiring minds want to know. Fans are getting through the drought by watching old seasons and opening old arguments again. I've been thinking about how streaming is changing the show—how having all the parts of a story available all the time changes a story. The continual access to a story seems to disrupt the concept of *story* itself at some level. Academics are used to working on past events, examining the fine details through repetition. *Survivor* fans do this, too, but the timeline is deformed. People who used to have an ongoing relationship with a changing but familiar set of plot points in a series now have a continuous relationship to all of it—not as something once heard and remembered, but ever present through 40 seasons and beyond. Players return to play again, but also as mentors, commentators, critics, and relatives of new players. And the show itself returns, whole seasons and "best episodes" and "beloved moments" and "craziest scenes." There seems to be no end to it, no amount of commentary that is finally enough. As I write this in early 2021, people are engaging in long, passionate, extremely detailed discussions about seasons of *Survivor* that aired 15 years ago. One posted to Facebook recently that "*Survivor* is the glue that helped hold my marriage together."

You can find a set of elaborate spreadsheets covering the number of times people have made on-camera confessionals, with averages figured for every season. You can read posts like this: "What is the 'fly theory'? SM claimed way back on the original ASS that the fly represented 'death/disaster' and getting hit by one was significant enough to eliminate a player from contention. Mariano Man picked up on this theory last season and disproved Panurge's storyline thread by using the 'fly theory' to eliminate Cochran. When Edgic had reduced the prospective winner field down to 2 players

(Sophie/Coach) MM used the fly theory to correctly pick Sophie as the winner, because the fly had hit and thus eliminated Coach (as well as Ozzy, Cochran, Rick and Brandon)." You, dear reader, don't need to know what this means, because a lot of people already do. Post a question or list—"favorite second-runner-up" or "Do you think Rick will ever play again?" or "most delusional players"—and the comments will roll in. (Coach. *Coach.*)

In the chat rooms, an old thread comment—"Jerri Manthey was one of the first four Ogakor out, she was last of the first four of them out, so she kind of statistically sucks. I like Heidi Strobel sometimes when I re-watch, but other times I just think she's kind of dumb, a bimbo, or like, stupid"—doesn't seem any less relevant than one from November of 2020, referring to season 23, *South Pacific*, which aired in 2011: "If Ozzy or Dawn gave Cochran some form of immunity, he wouldn't have to worry about drawing the odd rock because if there was a 6-6 followed by a 5-5 deadlocked tie, he wouldn't have to reach into the bag and would therefore be safe. If this had happened then Cochran would've been safe with let's say hypothetically Dawn's necklace, Whitney would be safe because Ozzy used the idol on her, Ozzy would be safe because he'd have immunity, and Keith would be safe from drawing a rock because he'd be in the tie. That would mean that Jim and Dawn would draw rocks for Savaii and all the Upolus except Rick would have to draw rocks because Rick was in the tie and would therefore be safe if there was a deadlocked tie. This would mean that there'd be a 71% chance that an Upolu would draw the odd rock." The *South Pacific* season aired ten years ago, but this observation drew a number of informed responses.

Former players have become discerning commentators. "When J.T. stood up, it was like showing up to a black-tie wedding wearing speedos and a Viking hat. If Probst were wearing a monocle, it would have popped off," writes Stephen Fishbach on his blog for *People*—a fine source for *Survivor* microscopy. Fishbach has played the game twice and knows of what he speaks. "Of course, what happened next was a catastrophe for J.T." Rob Cesternino's wiggling, temporary loyalties in the sixth season, *The Amazon*, made him popular with viewers. He was particularly well-liked by fan nerds because he was one, too, commenting on the play, trying to manipulate the play the way fans dream of doing. He was snarky but invested, caring about the outcome but not getting lost in the game. Jeff Probst once called Rob Cesternino "the smartest player to never win." One commentator said that, in *Amazon*, he was "playing chess while others were playing duck duck goose." Cesternino was crafty and disloyal; he somehow got away with a long series of obvious lies and came in third. But he didn't win and was out early the second time he played. Cesternino created *Rob Has a Podcast*, and made a career. Self-appointed experts who call themselves *curators* and *historians*, who watch the show obsessively so they can summarize and critique each moment of each episode for other fans, create a kind of superstructure. I am indebted to them, and to many anonymous teams of closed captioners who labor in windowless rooms trying to figure out what people say (and without whom this book would be shorter).

Many *Survivor* fans follow other reality shows and are thus able to speak with confidence about the third season of *Big Brother* and whether Arsenio deserved to be on *The Apprentice* and which housewife is the most wretched. Others are simply *Survivor* super-fans, the kind of people who collect replica buffs and give each other tests: "Name one of the only two seasons to not have a debutant [sic] return in a future season?" and "What was Clarence Black's luxury item in Survivor: Africa?" and "Which female castaway has held the most weight in the 'Shoulder the Load' challenge?" (I know, I know!)

The actual show, what we might as well call the primary reality because there is no way to know what really happened, is enveloped by a secondary reality of "must-watch" moments and "secret scenes" and spoilers and recaps and trivia and highlights and bone-headed mistakes, which in turn is wrapped in the tertiary reality of endlessly reproducing threads of arguments and gossip. There are blogs by fans, blogs by contestants, blogs by fans in praise of contestants, blogs by fans complaining about contestants, blogs about Jeff Probst. Blogs about being a *Survivor* blogger. There is far, far more fan action than I can absorb. The intensity, the detail, is remarkable. There is much shorthand: the Black Widow Brigade, Erik's necklace, the dead grandmother. You can watch hours (literally: many hours) of archeological research into female finalists or blindsides or how alliances are formed. The granularity of it all!

People bond deeply to the contestants in packed and dissonant ways: as the archetypes they fulfill on the show, as the personalities they appear to be, as the "real" people they are revealed to be in interviews and packaging before the show, as the people they seem to become when the show is over. Fans are invested with each other as well: as fellow fans, as competitors, as audience for the show playing in their heads. They are emotional and contentious and focused. The sheer activity of *Survivor* fans impresses me; there's nothing passive about their experience. This whole thing is partly the fault of CBS, because the official *Survivor* site is scanty and cautious. The producers create confusion by planting misleading clues on the website and in the credits. Producers supposedly have planted false images deep in the website programming to fool hackers. Since the first episodes generally air before the editing is finished, the producers can watch public reaction and edit the later episodes in such a way as to misrepresent the outcome. Thus fans ally together against the network;

the network essentially creates the fan world as an opponent in the game. (I feel the need to say that the reader may notice a certain hedging quality to some of my prose. CBS takes the show, and itself, seriously, and has maintained an almost total wall of silence around many of the rumors and stories told about *Survivor.* Jeff has gotten a lot looser about telling stories on himself, but not CBS. The network doesn't comment on things like leaked contracts and cheating rumors, but they don't hesitate to punish those who do. I've been advised to be careful. But rumors repeated endlessly and never denied become a kind of fact. Allegedly. Supposedly. Perhaps.)

The *Survivor Wiki* website on *Fandom* has been in continuous operation for almost 15 years and has 5,061 pages today. (There are a few more pages almost every day.) It has a "random page" option; I click and get sent to a page on episode 23 of the Australian franchise's 2019 season, then a page on Marisa, who played in Samoa in 2009 and was voted out first, and then a page on the 11th season of *Expeditie Robinson.* The *Survivor Fanon Wiki* site, also on *Fandom,* covers fictional seasons of the show and it is almost twice as big as the one covering the real show. The *Fanon* website looks almost exactly the same, but has more annoying ads. I've been briefly fooled a couple of times. *Fanon Wiki* is only one of many sites where fans create fictional seasons, with contestants, challenges, and elaborate conversations covering alliances, betrayals, and conflicts. In the *Fanon* world, there are seasons in Laos, the Galápagos, the Gobi Desert, and of course North Korea. Many fans would like to see a season in the United States, as long as we're stuck here anyway, the world's lepers. I like the idea of *Survivor: Des Moines.* A memorable post on Reddit lists possible themes for future seasons, including *Survivor: Chernobyl, Survivor: IKEA,* and *Survivor: The Moon.* We can dream.

Mario Lanza is a self-appointed historian and compiler of *Survivor*; he's written a memoir of what it's like to be a self-appointed historian and compiler of *Survivor*. Lanza has also written a particular kind of fan fiction by creating imaginary seasons based in Greece, Alaska, and Hawaii, but using real players. Unlike the entirely imaginary seasons on *Fanon*, Lanza makes fictional character arcs and interior lives for the semi-fictional characters already created by CBS from real people, and imagines how these real/not-real people/characters will behave in an imaginary series based on how they were edited to behave on a real series. A Georgetown University student "interviewed some of these players and found that they often felt Lanza's fiction more accurately reflected their real personalities and strategies than the television program itself because it was less reliant on stereotyping."

Because all of *Survivor* is streaming now, *Survivor Wiki* is a "nonspoiler" site. Spoilers emerged after the first season. The final vote is filmed with unmanned cameras, and the monitors are covered to keep the people who know what happened to a bare minimum. Spoiling a show like this requires doing a frame-by-frame analysis of credit sequences, stalking players who have returned home to compare their weight loss, limps, and beard growth, and trying to bribe or coax crew members into giving away secrets. In the early years, two prominent posters spent untold hours trying to pinpoint locations through contacts in the travel industry, looking at climate and latitude, demographic maps and satellite images. One fan wrote a massively detailed exegesis of a lens flare that looked to him like a Star of David, which he took to mean that Jewish Ethan would win the prize in Africa. (He did.) Early on, a group called The Ellipsis Brain Trust found out who designed the CBS *Survivor* website, broke into their email, and found a list of 16 URLs linked to names.

Then they went looking for people with those names around the country, eliminated many through age or health, and were able to confirm all the players of a season ahead of time. Why? Why not?

The anonymous poster ChillOne went to the hotel in the Amazon where the crew was staying during production of the sixth season and spent a long time bribing, drinking with, and interviewing locals to determine the two finalists. His claim (ChillOne eventually revealed himself as a photographer named Bill Marson) ignited long, detailed arguments about accuracy and methods. Is examining the methods of an anonymous blogger who tried to spoil the ending of *Survivor: The Amazon* less obsessive and meaningless than *Survivor: The Amazon*? What about the fact that ChillOne was right? What about the fact that ChillOne then wrote a book about it?

"Spoiling *Survivor* is a game. Spoiling the *Survivor* spoilers is a game. Planting fakes to see how long they go is a game. Spoiling certain elite spoiling groups is a game." So wrote an anonymous fan, who calls the fan world "this big wide open amusement park" in which anyone, absolutely anyone, could be playing with you.

Edgic, a combination of editing and logic, is a blend of sabermetrics and a kind of literary theory intended to break through the show's editing tricks and predict the winner, even before the tribes merge. If you want insider stuff for *Survivor*, here it is. A lot of fans have never heard of it. Edgic began not long after the show itself, and exists in a lot of corners of the *Survivor* universe. There's a subreddit forum for Edgic with thousands of members. *Unspoiled Edgicers Unite* (known as UEU) has a 5,000-word primer and more than 240 pages on the thread for the most recent season alone, as well as transcripts and video compilations. Edgicers get into arguments with each other but also with regular viewers (and "regular viewer" is a bit of an insult in this world). But nothing is official; official doesn't exist here. "Every edgic convert meets their Morpheus and discovers how deep the rabbit hole goes at a different stage of *Survivor* fandom," wrote Ben Lindbergh in an analysis of the analysts in *The Ringer*. The point of Edgic is to see past the narrative manipulation that interests the fan in the first place; suddenly, it's the Wizard behind the curtain and he's just another guy, but let's check out that machinery.

In Edgic players are classed as "invisible," "under the radar," "middle of the road," a "complex personality," and "over the top." This rating is based on everything from how many sentences they speak to whether they answer questions during Tribal Councils. They get more or less SPV—"second-person visibility"—when they are discussed by other players. And finally they are rated by tone, which is based on everything from the music accompanying their scenes to any comments by Jeff to which animals are flashed on the screen when they speak. Edgic is so wonky that I can barely follow it. All this data is plugged into a complex formula to reach a rating, then that rating is posted into forums, and groups of Edgicers will rewatch the show, debate, and ultimately vote on final ratings. (There are open and closed voting sites.) And *then* this is turned into color-coded spreadsheets covering every player's position in every episode, with a winner predicted each week. It's crowdsourced deconstruction.

Over 40 seasons, Edgic has often gotten it right. The show's editors claim to disdain Edgic, saying there is no such thing as a winner's edit. Or rather, "We try and give everyone a 'winner's edit,'" says Matt Van Wagenen, an executive producer. Fat chance. Winners generally have more CP, or complex personality, ratings. They may have a low profile or look MOR for a time, but most winners grow in complexity and have generally positive tones. Season 28 in Cagayan "broke edgic," says one analysis, because the winner, Tony, had a fairly unpleasant character arc. (It broke me, too.) Maybe the editors are trying to "break edgic" in their turn, but many fans are distressed when an unpleasant player wins. It's a bit like having an unreliable narrator; they can be interesting but we don't usually love them. You can apply Edgic to all kinds of stories, but it hasn't caught on. One edgicer claimed that he knew Bran would be crowned king in *Game of Thrones* because "the start is the most important," and Bran had a big role in the very first episode. Since the writers made it clear they didn't know how the series would end until very late in the process, I don't buy it.

If Edgic is one end of the fan's long bench, then *Backyard Survivor* is the other. The show is big in Australia, which has its own franchise. A couple of self-described super-fans there created *Backyard Survivor* for all those people who will never get to go on the show. This is exactly what it sounds like: all the elements of the show, including idols, challenges, alliances, and voting, in a backyard.

An entire generation has grown up watching the show and dreaming of being on it, applying year after year, and players say that getting on the show—or winning the necklace—or going to Tribal Council—or just meeting Jiffy—is the best day of their lives. On season 35, Chrissy, a 47-year-old actuary who had applied to the show for 16 years, wins a wheelbarrow-obstacle-course-puzzle challenge. She says, "I've been waiting for this for 16 years!" Jeff is pleased, of course. He asks, "What is this feeling, when you dream about playing *Survivor* for sixteen years and you pull off one of the most iconic moments, winning individual immunity?" (Well, Jeff. It's *great*.) The finale for that season begins with a "*Survivor* fan's fantasy," a kind of street fair with miniature versions of challenges hosted by popular players. Jeff stands in the rain—"perfect for *Survivor*"—and explains why *Survivor* is such a good family show. Later he interviews Mike, one of the contestants, who calls it "the greatest game ever invented." Why was playing such a dream? Jeff asks him. "As a kid, you grow up and you want to have a family and you want to have a wife and kids and I got it, and it's amazing. But at the same time, I want to win *Survivor*. I want to play *Survivor*. I got so close! Thirty-seven days."

Survivor is about *Survivor*. The sheer quantity of words—real information, informed opinion, deluded demands—out in the ether is beyond me; I can't even locate it all. The producers didn't expect the show to become its own universe—because who would have?—but boy, they grabbed that golden ring when it went by. *Survivor* has simply absorbed its fans like an amoeba. The application form asks you how much of the show you have watched; the possible answers are "none," "a few episodes here and there," "a full season," and "I have never missed an episode (I'm a super-fan!)." The show has pitted *Fans* versus *Favorites* until a few of the fans become favorites themselves. John Cochran, who played as a fan twice and then became a mentor, said before his second season, "I bring virtually nothing to the table."

Cochran won a million dollars.

THAT'S NOT HOW YOU PLAY THE GAME

Before people knew how to play the game, they didn't know they were enemies. Tribes cheerfully shook hands after a challenge. There was almost no talk of strategy, let alone the labyrinthine machinations of later seasons. The word "alliance" wasn't breathed until the fourth episode on Borneo, when Richard Hatch had an inspiration—a *Huh, maybe that would be a good idea* moment. You can see people feeling their way into the idea, what an alliance might mean, and whether you should talk about it or not. Was it right to be in an alliance? Did that violate the spirit of the game? What *was* the spirit of the game? Players were unsure of when the game ended and real life began. (Many still are.)

Burnett said in an interview last year that playing now "takes deep thought," because people know the game and have become better players simply by watching. Players know the tribes will merge at some point. They expect a chance to win flint, an auction where they can buy food, a reunion of some kind with loved ones. They know how the game is played; *how the game is played* is a key theme in countless chat rooms and fan forums. Players come with strategy prepared. They know (or think they know) how idols work and when to make a move and when to hold off. They know to find some goats—those players who can never win. A lot of time is spent in transparent strategy sessions now.

On season 29, *San Juan del Sur*, one tribe targets Nadiya because she was on *The Amazing Race*. People who saw that show or heard about that show or heard someone else talk about that show think she was a backstabber on that show. In *Survivor* they base their play not on how they think a person may play *Survivor*, but on how they think she played another game. Nadiya is voted out first. At the beginning, there was a lot of talk about *integrity*, but the novel discoveries of the first season are standard practice now, and may be the only way to win. Everything that for years was either ignored or considered somehow unethical or impolite or "not in the spirit of the game" is now clearly the game. Time and again, players turn to the camera with sighs of frustration, to wonder aloud, "Don't they know how the game is played?"

Knowing how to play the game makes it harder to play the game, because knowing how to play the game changes the game. Playing with confident, strategic players changes the game. (It should make you a better player, and yet there is no end to bad ones.) You are playing with different people every time; what you know about playing the game may not have anything to do with the game you're playing *this* time. Knowing how to play the game changes the game you think you know how to play, making it a new game no one has played before. And as soon as you know how to play, you don't, because everything you know will change how you play the game and that will change the outcome. It's the Heisenberg principle of reality television: *Survivor* spirals endlessly up into "the game we know how to play," always just out of reach.

Many reality shows promote the idea that anyone can win, that unlikely people can overcome, bullies can be beaten and superior forces vanquished, and an ordinary person might be the last one standing. But these are not ordinary people. Probst likes to say that "anyone can win," but the players come from the pool of people so eager to be filmed that they've gone to a great deal of trouble to apply. They will be chosen only if they fit the roles to be filled. (The players in the first season in Borneo, says Burnett, included "a Gilligan, a Skipper, a Mary Ann.") In a recent interview, Malcolm (no last name required; he has played three seasons) said, "Jeff used to say everyday Americans are cast on *Survivor*. It's not everyday Americans. It's a bunch of wackos who are on reality TV. So it's not a normal, balanced group of functioning humans. It's a bunch of people who are supposed to kind of go nuts and not get along because that's why people keep watching after twenty years." Richard Levak, the psychologist responsible for screening contestants in the early seasons of *Survivor*, said that people who succeed on *Survivor* are "supernormal in terms of resilience and self-confidence." He added, "The question is how can you put interesting people together, rather than putting people together where there's prurient value. And that's a very, very tight line." I'll say. Look at the situation of players *before* they went on the game: Clay Jordan, who played in *Thailand*, had filed bankruptcy with debts of almost a half-million dollars. Kelly Wiglesworth had a warrant out for felony credit card theft at the time of filming and pled guilty after the show aired. Altogether there are so many minor crimes, DUIs, bankruptcies, and soft porn in the backgrounds of contestants that it really raises the question of what all that background checking is *for*—that perhaps it is done to find such players, rather than eliminate them. Players must convince their family members, spouse, roommates, and, in some cases, parents and children to also sign contracts with CBS. In general, players are told not to tell anyone who doesn't have to know what they are doing, and the producers offer counseling for how to "safely" tell family members and employers that one is about to play *Survivor.* This is mainly for secrecy, but it's also a warning about exposure.

In early seasons, we saw images of the players in their regular lives at home and work. They stood in place for the rest of us: just plain folks marooned in an extraordinary place. The producers work at this. In the second season, Rodger Bingham called himself a farmer and high school shop teacher, which was true; the producers didn't want him to mention that he was also CEO of a bank. Reality shows then make the ordinary, private life of a stranger into a commodity by virtue of its ordinary, private state. With celebrities, we long to know what their private life is like because we already know the public one. But ordinary people put in the public eye are mysterious. We have no foundation for what their life is like. The fact that they appear before us means their status is unclear. But because they are "ordinary" people, we are seduced by the promise of something "more real" than what we are used to seeing on television. We are "situating the truth of personhood in that which has not *yet* been captured," says Misha Kavka, a media studies scholar, "in the intermediate space of capture-in-process." That capture appears to be spontaneous, unscripted, unpredictable; it may be involuntary; it appears to be happening right now, as we watch. This public revelation then changes the private life being revealed in the moment of it being seen. The ordinary person is ordinary no longer. The real person we wanted to meet and get to know is extinguished in the process of getting to know them.

The players are dislocated representatives of a dislocated audience. Those of us who like to watch may be imagining ourselves in those conditions; we imagine how we would *be*—an ordinary person in an extraordinary condition. I'm curious how I would fare on the show, but I'm no good for it. Too old, too fat, too introverted, way too snarky. (There's a reason I'm partial to the stocky, older women who get the chores done.) But when I think of what it would be like to be *on* the show, I just cringe. I'd play the game, but only on the condition that it *wasn't on television*.

Gilligan, Skipper, Mary Ann. Diversity on the show is largely a matter of typecasting. Season after season includes several bland, interchangeable, conventionally attractive people, and I can never remember their names. I can't even remember what they look like sometimes, because they look the same—vaguely pretty, fit, with little in their faces. For the most part, these are the redshirts, not destined to last. There will be a few silver foxes, one or two plain or tomboyish women, a few older folks, and a few confused Raisinets scattered in. It's an important conceit of the show, that anyone can win the game. I know the players are not ordinary people. They are stage actors, so the voices are louder and the gestures are broader. They have to be, because our seats are hidden below the lights. But they are acting out our concerns: Who do I trust? What are the consequences of greed? Of need? Where do I belong?

Contestants have included professional athletes, actors, a Super Bowl–winning football coach, Olympians, and veterans from other reality shows. Celebrities already deal with being other than they are perceived to be. Then they play *Survivor*, where they try to hide their identity. Cliff Robinson, a former NBA player on the Trail Blazers, went on the show. The Trail Blazers are my local team and so I was inclined to root for Cliff. And indeed, he was likable—too likable. (He was also identified out of the gate and never had a chance of winning. But he made some baskets when they were needed, and was a delight to watch in a simple challenge requiring one player to hold on to a pole while two people from the other team try to pull them off and drag them across the beach. Just try to pull Cliff Robinson off a pole and drag him across the beach.) Alan Ball, one of several former NFL players to play, used a strategy he called "full tilt sprint out of the gate"; his was textbook paranoia from the start. Former TV star Lisa Whelchel played and her entire season felt like psychodrama. The screenwriter and actor Mike White calls himself a *Survivor* "obsessive-fanatic"; he said he'd rather win the game than get an Oscar. Though he looks like a David, he played as a Goliath on season 37—a savvy, charming game. He came in second. In *Guatemala*, Gary Hogeboom, a former NFL quarterback, wasn't recognized, and he didn't mention his career. Who's going to give a million dollars to an NFL quarterback? He told people he was in landscaping. Another player, a sports radio host, outed him again and again, but he kept denying it, even while climbing a pyramid with a pot balanced on his head. "I'm totally going to deny that I'm Gary Hogeboom until the end," he said, and he lasted well into the game. Then he earned a new—and in these circles, more exciting—fame by being the first player ever to find and play a hidden immunity idol. Tyler Perry hasn't played, but he's a big fan. He says, "I love everything about it. I love everything *America* loves about it!" Perry has been known to text Jeff in the middle of the night with ideas. Now, *that* is CBS All Access.

Survivor hides actual famous people on the show, creates new ones, and rewards eccentricity—an overt kind of non-ordinariness—

with screen time. What happens when the ordinary person becomes a celebrity by virtue of having been televised as an ordinary person? What happens when a celebrity tries to pass as an ordinary person? What happens when a celebrity is discovered among the ordinary people, having already passed as ordinary?

One reason we watch reality television (and one reason we cringe when we do) is the promise of seeing private acts. Why is amateur pornography so popular? Because we know enough about sex to recognize that professionals are following a script. But what we don't know is what we each do in private. And many people long to know. With reality television, we think we are seeing people behave as they do in private, and how else can we see this? The fact that so many contestants seem to forget they are being filmed is one of the rewards. Misha Kavka wrote that in artificial conditions like a reality show, people "cannot but perform intimacy." All they have is each other. "The impossibility of a 'raw' performance does not discount the very real possibility of a *raw performer.*" After all I've written about *Survivor*, how can I describe any of it as raw? But the moments are there. They may be produced; they've been designed a bit, captured and edited and shifted in time and sometimes I'm watching the Dream Team or a planted tarantula, but the moment, the words, happened. Slipped out. Slipped through. People say the things they say. All these things.

During World War II, Allen Funt started a radio show called *The Gripe Booth* so servicemen could make anonymous complaints. In 1947 he turned that concept into *Candid Microphone*, which *Time* called the end of "the last threshold of privacy." This became *Candid*

Camera. The origins of hidden camera shows lie with those irritated soldiers, identical grunts lined up for disposal. But after the war, American society was marked by the pressure for conformity and fears of surveillance. This was the fruitful world in which Erving Goffman wrote about the ways we perform for each other, scripting and surveilling ourselves.

In 1965, *Candid Camera* posted signs along the highway saying that the state of Delaware was closed for the day and had men in uniform wave cars away. People accepted this and turned around. In another episode, the producers posted signs in a shoe repair shop with a checkered floor: "Please step only on the black squares." People valiantly tried to obey. In one famous scene, a man gets on an elevator with several people in it. As soon as the doors close, everyone turns to face the back of the elevator. The new rider turns around, too. The others turn to face front. He turns around again. And so on, a series of mostly gentle pokes at the urge to be in the crowd, to not stand out. At one point, Funt tried to get into the White House and talk to the president but ended up being interrogated by the Secret Service, which of course recorded the interview. *Candid Camera* so disturbed the culture's idea of what was real that when Funt's family was on an airplane that was hijacked to Cuba, the passengers refused to believe the hijacking was real until they landed in Havana. Funt recalled someone shouting that they must be on *Candid Camera*, and "people began cheering and stamping their feet . . . [until] the skyjacker stuck his head out of the cabin. This only made matters worse because 150 people gave him a big round of applause."

The contracts signed by players on reality shows are exploitive to a startling degree. One can argue that many human relationships are both exploitive and transactional, and I'm not sure celebrity is possible without both. *Candid Camera* pioneered the use of a release in which people give away their right to privacy; it may have been the first time that people agreed to be secretly filmed. *Survivor* takes this so much further. A crucial part of the contract is the name and likeness release. There is no room for negotiation, and the signing away of the heretofore fundamental right to control one's own image lasts for at least three years after the show ends. On *Survivor,* as on most reality shows, people "play" themselves. They *act* themselves. Perhaps this is not so shocking in a culture driven by Instagram and TikTok, where our most intimate and most mundane experiences are equally recorded and shared. But those platforms are at least nominally controlled by the performers. "The individuals on *Survivor* are 'raw materials' used by CBS to construct celebrities. CBS invested the labor and thus owns the results," writes Debora Halbert, a political scientist. "CBS has the power to narrate the lives of its contestants in any manner it chooses," and those contestants are not allowed to "offer an alternative narrative" of their experience. In other words, they aren't supposed to say what really happened during the show if it contradicts what is shown on the show. By contract, the players on *Survivor* can never write a book about their experiences or give away secrets of production, and they aren't supposed to explain what happens off camera. (This rule has been broken a lot.) When Bob Crowley, who won *Survivor: Gabon,* wrote his autobiography, he was forbidden to mention even that he had played the game.

People consent to be filmed in circumstances that in any other context could be an actionable violation of privacy. The network may create a domain name for players and a fictionalization of the player to be used as the network sees fit, including for "a humorous or satirical effect," and these versions of the players belong to CBS forever. The contract makes the point that you may be subject to having information of a "personal, private, intimate, surprising, defamatory, disparaging, embarrassing, or unfavorable nature that may be factual and/or fictional" broadcast on television. Players' personal websites and social media accounts must be closed for the duration of the show, and they are not allowed to comment online about anything (not just the show, but anything) during the course of the broadcast. They must undergo psychological tests and lie detector tests, and the results of these tests may be published by the network. They give away the right to anything they create on the show, from a song to a pose to their own words, in perpetuity and throughout the known universe, in known and not-yet-invented media. They are placed under an exclusive talent contract to CBS for a long period after the show. Many players are surprised to discover who they play on television. The first player voted out of the Swedish show *Expeditie Robinson* was a Bosnian refugee named Sinisa Savija. He feared how he would be represented and killed himself before the series aired. (The show was temporarily banned and a producer resigned.)

Dirk Been, the 24-year-old son of Wisconsin dairy farmers, was portrayed on the first season as a dour, boring Christian virgin. He was definitely Christian and maybe a virgin, but he claimed not to be dour or boring at all. Since the show, he said, "Everybody thinks I'm just a shy, nervous, dry stiff." Phyllis Rose, a fan of the show, wrote, "You would think that if a contestant on *Survivor* learned anything, it would be the constructed nature of reality." Been couldn't sue about his loser edit; the contracts rule out virtually any kind of lawsuit. But he complained that the show wasn't as real as he thought it was supposed to be. In this post–Van Doren era, there is a federal statute requiring that contests on television requiring "intellectual knowledge, intellectual skill, or chance" not be rigged. (Does

Survivor require those things? An argument can be made either way.) Been claimed that he heard a lighting technician say that Mark Burnett had put fish in the contestants' traps and that they had planted tapioca and sugarcane on the island ahead of time. He also said that he and another player, Sean Kenniff, had been approached by Burnett, who suggested that they vote against Stacey Stillman. So Stillman, a lawyer, sued. She wanted $75,000 because she was not given a real chance at winning. CBS countersued for defamation and breach of contract—that she talked about what happened off camera. The lawsuit revealed the gag order in the contract, and went far enough before a settlement that Burnett admitted "he would occasionally grill contestants about their votes to prime them for entertaining responses during later on-camera interviews" and that he had reenacted some scenes using stand-ins "in order to provide better camera angles of certain events." But Burnett denied coercion. The case was settled out of court.

I can't imagine a similar lawsuit now, not just because our fundamental concepts of truth, fairness, and the American way have changed, perhaps forever. Such a lawsuit wouldn't happen now because the contestants know the drill. They're fans; they know the rites and catechism of the game, and they may be playing on a season called *Heroes vs. Villains* or *Fans vs. Favorites*. Everyone knows there will be a goat or two. (One of the many academics who has studied *Survivor* notes that no matter how much the producers create heroes and villains, the players "all believe they are the hero of their own journey." Why bother? The Hero role in *Survivor* is largely a powerless one; in many cases, you are the Hero *because* you are powerless, because you sacrifice your own position for another, or don't connive, or don't create divisions. Having power just makes you a Villain.)

*   *   *

On most reality shows, players agree to a non-union shop, and this extends to themselves. Players cannot renegotiate, and can be summarily dismissed without cause (but not allowed to leave). In many cases, quitting has to be done on camera; I assume this is to allow for public shaming. A lot of performance and professional contracts include *morals* clauses; actors can be fired for behavior that violates conventional standards. There is no morals clause in most reality show contracts, for obvious reasons. It's a little Panem. You agree to go on a show that might kill you, will almost certainly hurt you, with no guarantee of reward, and thank you very much, I'd love to.

I write in general terms, not just because there are so many shows in so many places, each with its own variations, but because almost all such contracts are secret. A few people have said they were able to negotiate changes when they returned to the show, but gave no details. The one leaked *Survivor* contract is ten years old. Is this the exact language of the *Survivor* contract now? How could I know? The release for applicants for *Australia* leaked, 18 years ago. But it's instructive. This was merely the release for people being called to a late audition, before casting. *Before* casting. It included a clause allowing the network to "use and reuse" the "voice, actions, likeness, name, appearance and biographical material" of a player, including the right to "alter or modify" any of it, that they may "portray me and my Life Story either accurately or with such liberties and modifications" they prefer, including just making stuff up, and granting CBS the right to use their audition video "and my Likeness in any and all media now known or hereafter devised, worldwide, in perpetuity."

People line up to sign these contracts.

Look, these terms have worked out just fine for a number of people. Boston Rob and Queen Sandra play versions of themselves on the show for a nice chunk of change. They are basically brands now. Things haven't worked out quite so well for others. Richard Hatch won that first season, as most of the TV-watching world knows. A writer named Peter Lance interviewed him extensively while the show was being broadcast, before anyone knew who had won. Six days after the finale, the two men signed a book contract with St. Martin's for $500,000. But Hatch didn't tell Lance that he was bound to show everything related to *Survivor* to CBS and that the contract included a "life rights" provision preventing him from gaining any monetary advantage from his status as a *Survivor* player for up to three years after his appearance. What was he thinking— that CBS wouldn't find out? When the inevitable happened, the book contract was withdrawn. Both Hatch and Lance later wrote bad books; Lance's was self-published and microscopically detailed, an excoriating hate letter to the first *Survivor* villain.

As far as CBS is concerned, the non-disclosure agreement is the most sacred of idols. Helen Glover made it to the Final Four on *Thailand*; two years later, she was hired to write a column about the *All-Stars* season for the *Providence Journal* in Rhode Island. But CBS shut it down fairly quickly, claiming the columns violated her confidentiality agreement because it was less than three years since she'd played. A fan's minute dissection of the few columns she published made it clear they contained no surprises, describing events and methods that were already widely known, such as the fact that booted players were kept under wraps at a resort while the game played out. CBS didn't care. You are not supposed to describe your experiences and that was (in fact) all she wrote. A blogger was sued by CBS in 2010 for posting spoilers for a couple of seasons, for "misappropriation of trade secrets" and "tortious interference with contract." He said he was getting his information from Russell Hantz, one of the more notorious players in *Survivor*. The charges were later dropped. There's no evidence that Hantz was sued, but CBS released an odd statement, complaining about the "fervent activity" of fan sites. If nothing else, such a lawsuit shows CBS's complete lack of a sense of humor when it comes to the show. A player in *Survivor: David vs. Goliath* posted a photo of himself with another player on Instagram, before the season's premiere. He was uninvited from the reunion and lost all his appearance fees.

Players are bound by these agreements for years—but not forever. Long after their season, players tell the stories that CBS never tells. Several people claim the producers discuss hypothetical voting scenarios and have given players small amounts of food, and that crew members have sometimes lit fires for them. (CBS did respond to these claims, by saying that they "never interfere with reality.")

The contract stipulates that there may be severe mental stress during the game; that players may be injured or contract diseases, including HIV and herpes; that they may die. The producers may change the rules of the game at any time, even in the middle of a challenge. There are elaborate rules in place for handling ties, from drawing colored rocks to an attempt at consensus. Fire-making is also a common tiebreaker at Tribal Council. (Could Jeff Probst build a fire? He's watched it a hundred times, but he's never needed to do it.) Players generally can't skip a challenge; this has been allowed only a few times, due to injuries. Tribes aren't supposed to visit other camps unless it's part of a challenge, though many exceptions to this have happened. Players are not allowed to "defame or disparage" the network or the producers or to do press tours without permission. Players in the American game cannot vote for themselves (this has happened in Australia) and they may not refuse to vote. (On the first season, one tribe voted out Jeff Probst.) They are not allowed to help each other during an individual challenge. There is a lot of "Producer's sole discretion" language in the contract. Even the money is given by discretion and can be withheld. Malcolm said in a recent interview that the producers don't tolerate pushback. "It's kind of like a mob threat. Like, you will be taken care of. You will not be sticking around for long if you keep fucking with us."

The rule book is secret, but one was leaked with all the drama of the Pentagon Papers in 2010, and portions were published on the *Survivor Wiki* site. Since then these fragments and a few others have taken on the status of a holy relic, the words endlessly parsed, the pieces examined in the light of each new clue. Since the contract states that the fine for violating confidentiality is $5 million, this analogy is not entirely absurd. Players are not allowed to damage the environment and are limited to hunting only for food and using only approved materials for shelter. They must abide by local laws. When Colby Donaldson took coral from the Great Barrier Reef during a reward in *Australia*, he broke both the contract and the law (although he was never charged). CBS stated that he was fined about $50,000. CBS formally apologized; whether the hefty fine was paid is unclear. (In the same season, the producers were fined the same amount for letting helicopters fly over seabird rookeries.)

Contestants may not hurt other contestants, though this last is worded a bit vaguely. During the show, they are not allowed to steal personal possessions from each other, including the hidden immunity idol, but there is no rule against searching each other's belongings, and this often happens. Players have destroyed items of clothing belonging to another player, without apparent punishment. Russell Hantz burned a contestant's socks in one season; in a later season, Sandra burned his hat. Players meet before a season starts—at least, there are photos of various casts together. But at some point near the beginning, they are supposed to stop talking to each other. Each season starts with the players being transported, by boat, sailing ship, truck, and plane, to the remote site where they will play. We watch their suspicious faces as they glance at each other in silence. Sometimes we hear their thoughts in voice-over. Shallow thoughts.

Players must wear "producers' choice" clothing, sometimes of similar colors. Finding this out explained so much! Why would you show up to play *Survivor* in heels and a sundress? Or a blazer and cowboy boots? Because you're told to do so. Why did Chris have to wear an ugly red wifebeater tank top through his season? Because he was told to do so. Cochran was dressed in sweater vests, apparently because he was a stock character called Nerd. He'd never worn one before. It's hard to see how this isn't a severe disadvantage to women, but there you go. Why do certain women have several different bikinis? Now I know. Season 7, *Pearl Islands*, begins with the players dressed up for what they think is a publicity shoot. But then Jeff announces that the game is starting. One woman is wearing a strapless, tight sheath dress, another woman is wearing a scoutmaster's uniform, and one man is in an Armani suit. "Those suitcases, so carefully packed with essential outdoor clothing?" he says. "Worthless." He takes away their jewelry, watches, and passports, gives the woman in high heels a pair of tennis shoes, and makes them jump off the boat.

Then there is the rule against sharing. Players can't share their prizes or even talk about sharing their prizes. The 2010 contract says, "Contestants are prohibited from sharing or making an agreement to share all or any portion of the Prize (or from making any other similar *quid pro quo* agreement whereby one Contestant receives a benefit or some form of consideration [whether monetary or otherwise] after the series has concluded) with any other Contestant or any relative of any Contestant or any representative of or person affiliated with any Contestant in any way." This includes deliberately throwing a challenge in exchange for "consideration of any kind." The rule prohibits even talking about splitting the winnings. Breaking this rule can lead to immediate expulsion. I am obsessed with this rule. You are telling me that I cannot give a particular person or their cousin any money, *ever*? How about a car? How about a toaster? Players, including winners, have become romantically involved with each other. Do they have to split the bill for every date? How can this possibly be enforced? I spend some of my viewing time wondering how players could sort this out, how and when two people could have a conversation so private it wasn't overheard. Could two players ever trust each other enough to work out a way around this? The rule of *not sharing* is so central to the anatomy of the show and how people think the game is played that all strategy depends on it. I fantasize about a season in which this rule is revoked midway through. Absolute chaos ensues!

People do get hurt. A player died of a heart attack in the 4th season of the Bulgarian version. On the first day of filming in the 2013 season of the French version of the show, a 25-year-old player died of cardiac arrest. The season was cancelled, and the staff physician later killed himself; his note said that his reputation was irrevocably ruined. But in all the countries where the game is played, over all these years, serious events have been rare. Rashes, cuts, and diarrhea account for most of the problems. Medical care is available to keep the players healthy enough to play, but not to make them comfortable. Stitches, yes; Tylenol, no. At times, the beaches have been sprayed with insecticide. The players are told to be careful about water intake, but on occasion the paramedics have given people IV fluids. The contestants are supposedly given sunblock, tampons, insect repellant, and contact lens solution, and birth control is available on request. No one talks about constipation. The players do not get toilet paper and are encouraged to use the ocean for their bowel movements. "Once you aqua dump," said Malcolm, "you never go back." No one mentions menstruation, morning erections, or vaginitis. But where else can you see three women sit on the beach and compare armpit hair growth rates?

On about a dozen occasions, players have been evacuated for medical reasons; in a few cases, tribemates have accused their fellows of malingering. (When a player sprains his ankle and volunteers to be voted out, his tribemates won't do it, because "that's not how you play the game.") A few have quit because of illness or injury despite being medically cleared, and a few have left or failed to start after a psychological breakdown. Bad weather led to one medical elimination, when the boat bringing players back to camp slammed down on a wave and one person got a serious back injury. The bad weather turned into a cyclone and the tribes were evacuated overnight. They returned to find the camps in shambles.

On the Cambodian island called Kaôh Rōng, Jennifer appears to get an insect trapped in her ear and she seems to be really suffering; everyone, including the medical team, look on impassively until the bug emerges. Later, the players do a digging challenge in hot and humid weather. Three people collapse, and eventually a dozen crew members are giving intravenous fluids and oxygen. Caleb is evacuated. A few days later, Jeff and the doctor arrive on the beach because so many people have open or infected wounds. The doctor tells Tai, who has gashes on his inner thighs from climbing trees to harvest coconuts, that he's okay and can stay. He looks a little disappointed.

Aubry is given antibiotics for an abscessed wound. But they pull Neal from the game over his protests, because of a knee infection.

The success of *Survivor* helped create a new trend of "real" survival shows. I watched Lloyd Bridges wade out of the ocean and Marlin Perkins track down elephants, but the new shows are participatory. What we want from real survival shows is much the same as what we want from fake ones: the idea that anyone can do it, that maybe *I* could do it. In some ways, these shows are not that different from the structured reality of *Survivor*. In *Survivorman*, the host, Les Stroud, strands himself in different places for ten days—a desert island, a rain forest, a snowy mountain road. Stroud sometimes deliberately makes mistakes to show the ways people go wrong in the wilderness, to show that *you* could survive a Norwegian winter stranded or getting lost in the jungle just like him. In *Out of the Wild*, a group of nine people is left in a remote area to find their way out together. There is no elimination and no prize. They must cooperate, which means moving at the rate of the slowest and least fit among them. The strange show called *Naked and Afraid* puts a man and a woman, strangers to each other, alone in the wilderness with no food, no water, and no clothes. This show often seems more about masculine pride than anything else: Will he let her use the only knife? Will he bully her into drinking unsafe water? We quickly forget they are naked and just feel like we're watching our neighbors fight. The History Channel show *Alone* is the antidote for too much *Survivor*. *Alone* is a serious-minded competition between people with deep survival skills, left in a harsh environment to last as long as they can in solitude. These are not citizens stranded in their car. They are tested and trained in full-on survival skills, given a few hand tools and a couple of small cameras. The contestants each have a radio in case of accident and get a brief medical check once a week—nothing more than weight and vital signs. The crew is genuinely far away, and the dangers are real. Days are hard and plain. Some people build little lean-tos and spend the day fishing; others build awesome cabins and ingenious traps. But the show always devolves into a starvation game eventually.

In a season 4 episode of *The Office*, Michael is hurt because he wasn't invited on a camping retreat with other managers. He decides to go on a personal quest, taking only a knife and some duct tape "deep into the Pennsylvania wilderness." He tells Pam, "When I return, I hope to be a completely changed human being." He lasts about three hours, during which time he is beset by heat, cold, loneliness, insects, and hunger. When he returns, he says, "Man became civilized for a reason. He decided that he liked to have warmth and clothing and television and hamburgers and to walk upright and to have a soft futon at the end of the day. He didn't want to have to struggle to survive." He doesn't need fresh air, he adds. "I have the freshest air around—AC."

THE HOST

I love *Project Runway*, but only in its Heidi Klum and Tim Gunn phase. Early Tim Gunn is the gold standard of reality show hosts (and yes, I know he was the *mentor* and Heidi was the *host*, but we all know that Tim was the center of the show). Tom Colicchio is interesting and Ted Allen acts like a grownup on *Chopped*, one of the battier cooking shows. But for every Tim Gunn, there is a preening Tyra Banks; for every Colicchio, there is Kelly Wearstler on *Top Design*. It wasn't just her apparent difficulty with spoken language, but the fact that she was judging a design competition while appearing to have been dressed by drunken Muppets. Nicole Byer is having the time of her life on *Nailed It!* and so we do, too. Alton Brown anchors the highly entertaining *Cutthroat Kitchen* with sadistic glee and an iron fist; he's also a skilled chef, even when he's dressed like Beetlejuice.

The meta-Survivor, the most famous player in the game, is Jeff Probst. He is host, referee, therapist, and local god. He is in control and clearly adored by almost all the players; perfectly competent adults turn into simmering teens in front of him. When Troyzan wins immunity on *One World*, he's really excited. He's wanted to play for years, but he admits that a lot of his excitement in getting the necklace is because "You're touching me, Jeff Probst!" Probst has won five Emmys for the work and has been a producer since 2008. "His job," said Burnett once, "is to entertain millions and millions of people." He campaigned hard for the job; he wanted "meaning," Burnett wrote in his book on the first season: "The deep-thinking on-air personality wanted to do something that mattered." On Paramount+, where you can watch every episode, the photo is not of the island or the tribes or the shelter or the beach, but Jeff Probst, looking trim and neat in a safari shirt with the sleeves rolled up, leaning on a palm tree. The guy who once shared a few beers with the players and stammered a bit at the Tribal Councils now roars by in a speedboat, his gaze moody and distant. He hosted his own variety talk show, but it only lasted one season. In one of the many, many interviews he gave before the 40th season, he was asked how the show had changed him. He's more compassionate now, he said. He's a better listener. "The biggest change in me is that in the first season, I thought I was the center of the universe." Now he knows he's just "a grain of sand."

This grain is paid several million dollars a season, which probably contributes to his relaxed demeanor. He's in on the joke. Sometimes there are shots of Jeff standing casually on the strut of a helicopter as it banks and flies away, apparently keeping his balance with the sheer force of his personality. He takes the urn full of votes for a winner, leaps on a jet ski, and races up the dark Amazon River. Then he is sliding up to the Statue of Liberty, bouncing across the Hudson to a dock, walking along a Manhattan sidewalk, onto a subway train, up to Seventh Avenue to the CBS studios, and out onstage. Or the helicopter lands in the middle of the street and Jeff climbs out, whistles down a taxi to take him to Central Park; he gets a receipt from the cab driver before walking onstage. He leaps into a sport boat in Fiji and reaches Los Angeles a few moments later. The show filmed a sequence requiring Probst to paddle a canoe into Venice, California, and then do skateboard tricks. But he couldn't master the tricks, and they gave it up. In the Philippines, Jeff gets the votes, walks down the stairs and into the night, and comes out onstage in Los Angeles, still wearing a safari shirt and khakis. He smiles at the audience's mad clapping, then calls for a minute of silence in memory of the families who had just lost children in the Sandy Hook shooting. Ugh, that sure kills the buzz.

He's confident enough to date a contestant for a time: Julie Berry, who lasted late into the *Vanuatu* season. I didn't remember Berry. When I watched the season again, I could barely find her; she seems to be one of the crowd of good-looking young women in bikinis who spend too much time lolling in the sun. When she merged into a tribe with a majority of men, she sunbathed in the nude. At one point in the season, Jeff said that she "worked her best assets," so I guess he was able to pick her from the crowd. Did she end up UTR on the Edgic scoreboards because of Jeff, keeping things on the down low? They dated for three years after the show, which feels off somehow. It breaks the frame.

When *The Atlantic* ran a systematic ranking of the first 27 seasons of *Survivor*, they used a "Jeff Probst Annoyance Factor" in the scoring. ("So many man-crushes in one place, it's a wonder Jeff didn't pass out from the vapors. -1." "He's been worse. -2." "Nothing major sticks out, but just to be safe: -1.")

Jeff, who seems to be contractually required not to be quiet during a challenge, shouts things like, "You got *nothing* else going on in your life right now but this *challenge*, in Fiji, for a million dollars!" During challenges that require a lot of concentration, he just keeps talking, quietly but without cease: about how important it is to win, how crucial this challenge is, how it could be *a million-dollar challenge*, how *you want to be the one who wins*, how you need to *dig deep, dig down, concentrate*. My favorite: "Don't think about anything. Nothing, nothing, nothing but this. This is it right here. Balancing that little ball on these pieces of wood is all you should be thinking about right now." Shut up! During a later immunity challenge, a ball-spinning-while-standing-on-a-sloping-balance-beam event, Jeff walks around, hypnotically repeating himself. *Don't let the ball hypnotize you. It's going round and round. Round and round. You're getting sleepy, sleepy.*

In season 28, in a challenge requiring the tribes to collect heavy chests on a cart, disassemble and reassemble the cart, and then solve a puzzle, the Brains tribe fell apart. Jeff talks smack. "Whatever brains they had have clearly evaporated 72 hours into this game. Unbelievable how far behind they are!" yells Jeff. "One of the worst performances out of the gate in the history of *Survivor*!" He transparently favors certain players and disrespects others. "My *nephew* could throw it harder than that!" he shouts in season 24. Jeff absolutely denies this partiality. He says, "It's rare that I comment on someone personally." Has he watched the show? Jeff manages our view, trying to influence the game. Or rather, to *appear* to influence it. It's part of the game that he denies doing this, and we see only what he allows us to see, but we see enough. "This is what you call a disaster," he'll say of a player's performance in a challenge, and suddenly we see that player a little differently. And perhaps the other players do, too.

Probst has a cheerful, mild-mannered style most of the time, but he's always manipulating the game. He came to camp in the middle of the night in *Cambodia* to tell Terry Deitz that his son was seriously ill and that he needed to leave the game and go home. (Terry's son eventually had a heart transplant.) Jeff had his most serious face on, and kept returning to the drama all the next day, asking the other players to imagine what it's like to know your kid is sick and not know what's wrong. How awful it would feel *not to know what's wrong*—as though Jeff didn't himself know, as though he'd gotten the call and made the arrangements and bundled Terry off home without any idea what had happened. Of course he knew.

Jeff rules at Tribal Council, which functions as a combination of trial and sacrificial rite. The Councils usually last for hours, though in the show as broadcast we may see only ten minutes. Jeff sometimes muses on the transformative quality of Tribal Council. Once he said, "The people here will tell you exactly what they think. True or not, we'll never know." Hmm. At Tribal Council one evening he says the conversation started as an attack. He bangs his fists together. "Then it went *deeper*, and it got *personal*, and yet once again we're going to do the thing we do, which is vote, and it will all"—he widens his eyes and swings his arms into a big arc—"ffft, *crystallize* again! An amazing journey." Amazing. Under Jeff's guru-therapist gaze, everyone can pretend that *Survivor* is authentic, that people are having an intimate, life-changing experience. They're all sitting around a pretend campfire because it's time to vote someone out so they can win a million dollars, but it's deep.

He can be scornful when listening to the players, frowning at awkward comments, transparently sympathetic at others. Sometimes people start hatching plans in real time, new alliances are formed, old alliances break up. "Live Tribal" is a way of saying that the discussion is getting lively. In one Council during *Edge of Extinction*, Julia plays her fake idol and then Lauren plays her fake idol and then Devens plays a real idol for Gavin and then Chris plays a real idol. Jeff: "One of the single craziest Tribals I have ever been witness to. I cannot wait to see what comes of it." I am not 100 percent sure that he doesn't already know.

Jeff says he wants a "truthful response" to his questions; does he think he will get one? He will point out a person's weakness or betrayal, ask in an only slightly veiled way about secrets and deals he's not supposed to know about—you know, *hypothetically speaking*, what if certain players were planning to do such-and-such? Sometimes he laughs out loud in disbelief, and it can be the kiss of death. "Now let's talk about Amy's chronic injury to that ankle," he says. Amy protests. She just "tweaked it a little bit." Jeff gives her a hard stare and says, "*Tweaked* it a little?" (Why do they answer his pointed questions?)

Jeff, Jeff. Jiffy. In season 39, Jeff says, "I never want to snuff anybody's torch. It's never fun." If you believe that, I can sell you a bridge. After a challenge on *Kaôh Rōng*, Alecia is in danger, and the three women in one tribe privately discuss the possibility of a secret women's alliance. They could keep Alecia and take out a man instead. At Tribal Council, Jeff just floats a few ideas, just talking, you know, the way people do about "a lot of ways that Tribal could go tonight," and says, what if, you know, three women formed a secret alliance? He does it every season, but do people remember that? No, Jenny just owns up to the secret women's alliance. (The other women look at each other: *Damn. That was a secret.*) Jeff, just so surprised, says, "Wow, just like that, Jason, the game turns!" Then he steps back and lets it run, watching the sudden collapse of defenses into a middle-school playground scandal, and yet they can't help themselves: Jenny and Alecia turn on each other and Cydney says the whole unfolding soap opera is "about being in the wrong place at the wrong time and saying the wrong thing at the wrong time to the wrong people." Is that all?

Jenny is voted out. So much for the women's alliance.

One would think Jeff Probst leads an interesting life, with his scads of dough, exotic locales, and fame. But I suspect he feels he has earned every one of his millions of dollars. The hours of numbing repetition. At the finale of season 37, Jeff walks out with the votes, into the darkness, through the fake jungle and onto the stage in Los Angeles, wearing different clothes. He says this season was "one of the best times I've had in a *long* time on *Survivor*." Like all television hosts, Jeff says exactly the same thing at the same time, over and over. Sometimes he laughs and says, "Never seen *that* before!" with relief. He takes back the necklace or the totem and says, as he always says, as he has said countless times before, "Immunity—back up for grabs!" In season 30, *Worlds Apart*, the players must solve a word puzzle and both teams are stumped. They can't find the familiar phrase, which is *a reward with all the fixin's*. Jeff says, "Start thinking *Survivor*. It's been on for thirty seasons. I say the same two hundred words over and over and over and over and over. I'm in therapy, I say the words so often." On season 37, when a team loses, he says—as he always says, as he has said so many times—"Got nothin' for you," and Mike says, "We got nothing for you, either." Jeff laughs and says, "Finally! Someone says what people have been wanting to say for *years*." Now and then he seems to go over the edge. In the middle of a noisy challenge, Jeff shouts this running commentary: "The big question is: are your tribemates helping you, or are they throwing a monkey wrench into your plans? It's very close. Another hot day in Fiji. My poor brain is fried." At the next Tribal Council, he listens to a confusing bit of strategy and then gets a strange look on his face, a weird, wild-eyed stare. "It's kind of like that moment when they want to get the bad guy, so they get the bad guy by getting his wife!" It's a weird job. Imagine doing play-by-play for building a fire. Jeff uses a sportscaster's low monotone: "Devon now scraping more magnesium. Ben just looking for a spark, trying to get something to light. Devon taking a more methodical approach—"

Jeff knows he is the divine hand. On *San Juan del Sur*, one tribe asks if they can trade their beans for flint, since one of the men managed to lose their flint in the fire. But can they please keep the fishing equipment they've just won? Jeff is amused. "Walk me through from a negotiation standpoint. You're the ones who need to make the deal," he says. "My life is fine. So you come in, survey the scene, see what the reward is, and then offer me the thing of least value." He is unmoved. "That doesn't work on *Survivor*. I got one offer for you, you want to make it, and that is you give up all this fishing gear for a new flint." They say no. Jeff continues, "Now that I know you don't have a flint, when it rains, and it will, and your fire goes out and now you need to make a trade, the payment will be much tougher. This is your opportunity now to seize it if you want it. Because I promise you, to get a flint later will cost you more than fishing gear." They finally agree. It has taken them this long to figure out who's in charge. A few days later, the tribe finds their lost flint. Drew decides to be "balls up" at the next challenge and negotiate with Jeff again, because "that's what a good leader does. You have to make decisions that nobody else has to do." (He's deluded about his position in the tribe.) At the challenge, while his teammates cover their faces and laugh, Drew asks if he can trade their flint for part of the fishing gear they'd given up a few days before. Jeff says, "Well, it sounds reasonable." Drew: "Exactly." Wes: "I feel like you're taunting us." Jeff: "I *am* taunting you. Put the flint back. You made the trade." The other tribe applauds. And it's still not over. The tribes are mixed up, and the new members of this tribe discover that they are virtually out of food. The tribe had been winning so many challenges because they were eating well. After another win, they ask if they can talk to Jeff. "Another conversation?" he says. "This is going to be good." They ask if they can trade something for a bag of rice, and Jeff says he'll drop by. The next morning, Jeff walks down the beach with a big bag of rice. He's enjoying this. "There's never been a tribe in the history of *Survivor* that has needed as much help as you guys have and only fourteen days in," he tells them. "It's not lost on me that the disproportionate amount of food that you have had is probably a big part of the reason that you have dominated in this game so far." The new members and the other tribe are at a big disadvantage because they've been rationing as they are expected to do, eating half a cup of cooked rice each per day. "So in fairness of the game and in fairness to the Coyopa tribe, who is playing the way you should, the penalty for that has to be just. So I have enough rice to last you the rest of the game, but it's going to be a stiff penalty." He takes the tarp, hammock, blankets and pillows, the hatchet, hammer, one pot, and the extra flint. They are left with only a machete, a pot, and one flint. "You are starting over." As he drags all the stuff away, he says, "Let's hope it doesn't rain."

Any shift in this power dynamic is satisfying. In *David vs. Goliath,* the immunity challenge required players to balance on a narrow perch while holding a handle behind their head. They have to keep both feet on the perch and both hands on the bar. Jeff offers food to people who are willing to quit, and three people do. But the rest last and last in the hot sun while insects crawl on them and everything hurts. After 95 minutes, three are left. Jeff says they have a "zero point zero" chance of being comfortable and Christian takes issue: "You're reporting an excess of precision that you don't actually know." After two hours, Gabby is contorted and crying, whimpering, "It's *so hard*!" Alec swears he won't quit and whispers to Gabby to drop out, and she does. But Christian just smiles. Alec tells him, "You're not going to win," and Christian gets a big grin on his face. He tells a long story about building a robot. Then he keeps talking. And talking and talking. After more than five hours, Christian looks over at Alec with a smile and Alec quits.

"I won immunity and it had nothing to do with algorithms!" Christian exults. In an interview after he was eliminated (late in the game; he came in seventh) he says he'll always cherish the memory of Jeff as a "captive audience." It was his favorite experience in the game. "I will remember the three-hour mark of the crazy-long immunity challenge with Alec. That's when I remembered that I was free to talk to my heart's content. That's also when I realized that once I started talking, I felt no pain. It was transcendent. From that point on, I had no temptation to step off from the pain, because it weirdly didn't exist. I have no idea why. I felt like I could have stood there through the night, reciting my doctoral dissertation to a captive Jeff Probst."

Jeff says, "I *was* captive. I couldn't go anywhere."

LOSERS (OR, THE THINKING SEAT)

In the opening moments of season 10 on Palau, the contestants struggle to get their boat to shore. Wanda Shirk, a 55-year-old English teacher from Pennsylvania, stands up in the stern and begins to sing. She's written a lot of songs about *Survivor* and she wants the game to be "a big party as long as it lasts." Willard Smith, a lawyer from Washington, later says, "We're sitting there, it's a really hot day, rowing the boat, and this lunatic jumps up and starts singing songs. I wanted to knock her off with the oar."

Such is the "loser edit," what Colson Whitehead calls "the plausible argument of failure." When a tribe loses an immunity challenge, the film shifts into slow-motion close-ups of their disappointed faces—because this is war and they *lost*, because they are *losers*. Certain players are "doomed to perform personality deficits episode after episode," wrote Whitehead. "It has been written, by fate or the producers, pick your deity."

There are a lot more ways to lose *Survivor* than to win. Far more ways: getting angry, gloating, whining, saying you're tired, saying you don't feel good, saying you're lonely. Choosing to have your bowel movement in the shallow water by camp on the first day, as Darnell did in *Kaôh Rōng*. If you want to win, don't talk all the time. Don't be too loud. Never say, "I'm in control of this game." Don't act paranoid. Don't start a romance. Never say you are the weak link. Don't share your hard luck story. Don't be too confident and never predict you will win. "I was counting my million," says Boo, on *Fiji*. Oops. You will lose for not working and for working too hard and for asking others to work and for not doing the specific work that others want you to do without being asked.

Crying. You do not win by crying. (I cry when I'm angry or frustrated and I know I would cry on *Survivor* because getting angry and frustrated is part of the game. One more strike against me.) I think the crying prize probably belongs to Gabby, on season 37, who cried because she was in an alliance and cried when she thought she was out of one, cried on Christian's shoulder (literally, leaning on him and weeping in one scene after another), cried at challenges and cried at meals, cried when she decided that Christian was "playing up" the role of "comforter" and cried because she couldn't let herself be seen as a victim, and then cried when she sucked up to him later. In a confessional interview, she cried about making a big move. She cried when she tried to make her big move, cried when she was inevitably relegated to the jury, and then she cried when she voted for a winner.

You lose for complaining, you lose for not sharing your complaints, you lose for being sensitive, you lose for being insensitive, you lose for getting emotional, and you lose for being stoic. Don't be annoying. Such a simple, obvious rule. On season 35, one player described Patrick this way: "It's like you've got a newborn baby. You really want to like it, take care of it, but it's really, really annoying, because you've got to watch *every single second.*" Ali takes him aside and tries to get him to play a more social game, but Patrick is convinced that he already has a great social game. He says to the camera, "Ali telling me to cool it is difficult because it takes away from my personality." Exactly. At Council he pleads to stay because he can "make people feel loved and comforted." When they vote him out, he says, "You guys are awful."

You need to at least appear to listen to and care about the others, be moved by their story, but not be dramatic or over-involved. It's a faint line, and many people never find it. Robb, a young bro with big hoop earrings playing in *Thailand*, never shuts up. He grooms himself in his own reflective sunglasses. He cheats during a challenge by choking a member of the other team, and he comes back to camp in a loud, sour mood. He makes fun of the man he choked, calling him a "backwoods hick" and a "weak little whiny punk." He's disgusted that the other tribe won. "We lost," he adds, "but we lost by a bunch of rules." One night, after the tribe has won a bit of alcohol—Robb won it for them, almost single-handedly—the tribe stays up late. Robb lets it all hang out: how the game has changed him, how he's been selfish and immature and he's sorry and it's all confusingly about his father in some way, and it goes on for a long time. On some level, I think he's sincere; on another, his confession feels about as immature as everything else he's done. But Tribal Council is designed to take advantage of such moments. After Robb explains his change of heart, Jeff says, "Clearly you guys have experienced some real spiritual growth." Then Robb is voted out.

Sometimes there's a health nut who disdains white rice or a vegetarian who refuses to eat a snail and collapses from hunger instead.

You can't be a picky eater and you can't get sick. People are looking for targets, so the smallest things get latched onto and blown up until people can rationalize their way to the vote. A single word turns into "he's whiny" and a single look becomes "she's mean." Or so it appears; who knows how many words and looks are left on the editing room floor?

In the season called *Worlds Apart*, where tribes were divided by perceived social class, Nina claims during Tribal Council that she's on the outs because of her deafness. Her tribemates claim that she's on the outs because she's not chill enough. Nina can't just "take life as it comes" and doesn't "ride the highs" and "ride out the lows." Hali says, "Nina doesn't have that same *flow* going." She's always begging for reassurance that she's not on the outs because of her deafness. Jeff says, "There's something that happens on *Survivor* where perception becomes reality. No matter what perception the group has, it is real and it is true, to them." This deep thought does not just apply to *Survivor*, but it certainly applies there. Nina is voted out.

Don't be too pushy. Vince, on *Worlds Apart*, spends a lot of time asking other people for reassurance.

"He's got a lot of issues," says Joe.

He certainly does. Before the game, Vince described himself as a "pillar of support." During the game, he is all over Jenn like a cheap suit, hugging and petting and stroking and *ick*. He tells her that he always forms very strong attractions to women, apparently thinking she will be flattered by this. Within hours, he is asking Jenn for "evidence" of her feelings for him. "I know how to handle him, I think," she says, and does; he is voted out first.

One of the tropes of the game is the *big move*, which often involves taking out an alpha player, so it works only if you don't tell everyone that's what you're doing. A big move is part of *jury man-*

agement, which involves *building your resumé,* not showing up with a *blank resumé.* You can't be game-y or "strategic," but you'd better play strategically.

You can't be disloyal, at least until everyone else is. Leslie Nease, the Sunday School teacher who so annoyed Courtney in *China,* admitted to her tribemates that she had bonded with the "other Christians," who happened to be on the other team. In writing about office politics, Erving Goffman considered how people surreptitiously attempt to create intimacy with a member of a rival group or a superior. Goffman calls "catching the eye of a member of the other team" a "betrayal" that is both common and dangerous. If you're invited into such an intimacy and refuse, you offend a rival who may come after you. If you accept, you risk everything. Leslie was voted off third.

All through the season, every season, I see a train wreck, a loser, a saboteur, and wonder, why is *he* still there? And then I remember. Who would I rather sit next to, facing the jury, than a train wreck? (Would I be sitting there at the end, blithely unaware that *I* was the train wreck?) Good players are wise to protect the unpopular, the lazy, or the mean player for this reason. Shane, talking about Courtney: "She's a dream to take to the final two. *Anyone* could win against her. *Anyone!* She's a dream." Believe me, so is Shane. At one point, he threatened to kill Courtney "in her shitty little apartment" if she ever voted for him. Not a winner's arc.

You don't want to be a goat, though goats can make some serious bank. A goat may be crazy, weak, or passive. There's a goat in every season, and the goat never, ever knows he is a goat. Not knowing is the nature of goats. On season 37, Dan, a SWAT officer, says he used to be a fat kid (he tells his tribemates this many times). He is a little anxious all the time. During a challenge, he whispers to himself without ceasing: "All day, baby. All day. Focus. Keep telling yourself how awesome you are. You are the man." Such insecurity can never win. Linda Holmes, a culture writer for NPR, said that having a goat nearby "is like sitting next to a bag of rotting dead leaves: You may not enjoy it, but you won't lose a popularity contest to it." Boston Rob bulldozed over the entire cast in *Redemption Island*, hauling famous goat Phillip to the end, essentially to use as a pillow.

On *Island of the Idols*, Dan says of Noura, "It would be statistically improbable to get on *everybody's* nerves, and she's accomplished it." Cut to Noura flailing around, laughing, shouting advice at a couple of the men about the fire, and saying, "I'm gonna be the biggest train wreck of *Survivor* ever. Just kidding." Noura has too much confidence, too little insight, schemes constantly, and can't keep a secret. She spends hours working out "what-if" scenarios, to the point where she uses leaves to act out possible votes. At one Tribal, there's a lot of whispering between alliance members, then Noura just blurts the plan out loud, shows the idol, and totally screws it up.

Yet she thinks she's in a great position to win: "My game has been *bold, zesty, flavorful, interesting, unique, healthy, fun, different*," she says as she checks each word off on her fingers, and that kind of talk is part of the problem. At the final Tribal Council, she describes her strategy, talking loud and fast: "Don't be bland, don't be bossy, don't be lazy, don't be annoying, don't be not trustworthy, and don't be dead in the water at a challenge." Be *zesty*. The entire jury interrupts her and tells her to stop talking. At the finale, when the votes are read and she gets none, her eyes well up. She thought she had it in the bag.

Goats don't understand what's going on. But dumb is different. Dumb is just dumb. On *Fiji*, Mookie, Alex, Edgardo, and Dreamz formed an alliance they called "The Four Horsemen," apparently confusing the Musketeers with the apocalypse. Maybe it's just me, but *Kaôh Rōng* had more than its share. Caleb says he is "murderalizing" a tree with an ax; Alecia, trying to make a fire, says, "We had an embryo, but it went out." Nick, a chiseled male model on the Beauty tribe who isn't half as clever as he thinks he is, announces during the immunity challenge that one of the three remaining Brains will be voted out. But meanwhile, he tries to manipulate Aubry into joining a Beauty alliance and he directly asks Julia if there's a women's alliance. You can see her light up. The women's alliance didn't exist until he suggested it. Nick and Kyle are expecting the vote to split between Aubry and Debbie, but *boom*, blindside, Nick's gone. You can see it in his face as his torch is put out and he walks away— *"Damn. Didn't see that coming."* (I like Aubry, who says in a later season when her tribemates are hugging, "I hate *Kumbaya Survivor.* It's the worst.")

In *Africa*, on day 28—day 28!—Frank starts talking at great length about gun rights and liberal stupidity, just in time to piss people off before Tribal Council. Even his longtime pal and ally, Teresa, votes against him, the way a person in a shipwreck will push away a drowning person trying to drag them down.

You can survive for a while by finding a hidden immunity idol, the talisman that protects you from being voted out once. Men find idols more often than women do; they spend more time looking and look more frantically. (Tony Vlachos single-handedly raised the frenetic level by 50 percent.) In *Game Changers*, Tai found a hidden immunity idol. When the tribes got switched, he thought, what the heck, and used the same clues to find the second idol in the new camp. But just looking makes you a target. People standing idly at the campfire look around and say, *Hey, where's So-and-so? Are they looking for an idol?* Saying you have an idol makes you a target and denying you have an idol makes you a target. (On *Blood vs. Water*, people are given clues to hidden idols after the *Redemption Island* challenges; one after the other, they publicly drop the clues into the fire. No target on me, thank you very much.) People search each other's bags for idols, offer to let others search their bags for idols, and drop their trousers to prove they don't have an idol (but only after burying their idol under a rock). A lot of people have been voted off with idols in their pockets. Once in the hand, the idol's power seems to cloud the mind. If you find an idol, you should never tell anyone. This is a fundamental fact of the game; everyone knows this. Never tell. But people have to tell someone; they can't stand not telling people. Sometimes they tell everyone.

Having an advantage in *Survivor* often isn't an advantage; advantages make people nervous, and nerves show. People lose their balance. In *Game Changers*, Culpepper (Brad, former NFL player) promises to take Tai to the end if Tai will give him an idol. Culpepper's real plan is to vote Tai out once he is idol-less. Tai puts his head on his knees and cries from the pressure. But he smartly holds on to the idol and Culpepper is furious. Somehow he has become the victim; he says, Tai "done me wrong." This kind of twisted-panties revision of history is one of the most common delusions of the game. (The most common has to be the idea that you're in charge.)

On *Worlds Apart*, Rodney, a contractor from Boston, was mouthy and sarcastic, easily offended, playing as (or simply being) a type of profane, misogynistic, hot-headed party hound of no more than average intelligence who still lives near his "Ma." Rodney has a tattoo for his murdered sister. "I knew I could get to any girl's heart with that story," he says. "My strategy from day one, get the girls. Girls, they want to sit back and let a man take the lead and all. So I want to get the girls, I want to be their leader, and I'll take them to the merge with me."

To the camera, he says, "I don't start nothin' wit' nobody. If you just start one fight with somebody, you're 100 percent target on your back." Then his team doesn't win a reward challenge, and he's really upset. "It's my damn birthday," he complains. He begs one of the three going on reward to give it to him as a gift. They refuse. "They've just turned me into the psychotic person that I am," he says later. "Bunch of scumbags who neglected me on my birthday." He won't let it go, pacing around camp and grumbling, cursing, throwing things. "Rodney is slipping off into that abyss," says Dan. He won't stop bitching even after the winners return, the rain is pouring down, and everyone is stuck cheek to jowl in a leaky shelter. Not much later, Tribal Council ends in a tie between Carolyn and Rodney, which means they must compete to make fire. Rodney goes out swinging. "I wish I coulda gone to the final three. It woulda been a breeze, I woulda easily won this game." (This is so not true.)

A player claims to be an "Federal Secret Agent" or seems to think everything is real or simply believes she is running the game up until the moment her torch is extinguished. In Panama, Shane supposedly was a marketing executive but acted like the lifer you avoid in the prison cafeteria. He says to the camera on the first day, "I don't really fit in with the older guys, they *just want to work all the time*, and I'm exhausted and I haven't had a cigarette. I've smoked three packs of cigarettes a day for twenty years and I haven't had a cigarette in, like, thirty-one hours. I mean, I'm just at the end of my rope, I'm fried. I'm not in a good place, man. I've *got* to get through this detox stuff. I can't lash out at anybody, I can't, I can't, I can't." Shane chooses a rock as his "thinking seat" and starts shouting at everyone to leave it alone: "No one else sit on my thinking seat. Please. You want this one? *I'll go get another one! I want one, this one! If you want this one, I'll go get another one!* I just want *mine*, this one!" Later, Shane takes Aras aside and unloads his intense resentment of Cirie. "I'm *disappointed* in her in a *big* way," he whispers intensely. "It was *wrong* yesterday. It was *wrong*. Listen, I'm not worrying about anyone but *me* now. That's why *everyone* is in big trouble. You and Cirie may believe it's still the three of us, but I'm turning the whole game. *Look at me. Look at me.* Game on. I'm in the game now. Everyone's got a *big, big problem*." Aras is listening as though Shane might have a weapon; he nods solemnly, because that's what you do when the crazy guy has hold of your shirt.

Coach may be the most delusional player ever. Season 18, *Tocantins*, was a good season, in part because it featured the first perfect victory with one of the most charming winners. The season also introduced the world to Tyson, the king of *Survivor* snark, described by one critic as "a four-tool player in a three-tool game." You could tell that playing with Coach made Tyson happy. Call him Coach or Coach Wade or let him call himself Dragonslayer. He really is a soccer coach, but his autobiography includes being related to Pocahontas, surviving a hurricane, getting abducted in the Amazon, being attacked by both a shark *and* a crocodile, and holding some kind of world record in long-distance kayaking. For most of the season, he believes himself to be in charge of the entire game. When Brendan gets nominated to be the tribe's leader, Coach takes it hard.

Coach calls Tyson his "assistant coach," and instructs him carefully about voting. Tyson says, "He has a little schoolboy crush on me. So if I just keep plugging away, I'll eventually make Coach. He may promote me." Tyson, who says, "*Survivor* has been my profession," has played four times and won once. In *Tocantins*, Coach is a great foil for Tyson's wit; he has neither wit nor irony himself, and misses most of the jokes. He confidently makes weather predictions that are completely wrong. Erinn says, "I think Coach really truly wants to be this, like, Survivorman. I would not be surprised if, when this game is all said and done, Coach said, 'Gotcha! I'm an accountant! I've never left Nebraska.'" When he screws up the cooking and burns most of their remaining beans, he says, "No need to blame anybody."

The editors knew they had gold. One episode opens with sunrise on the beach and the theme from *Carmina Burana* swells as a shirtless Coach performs some kind of yoga–martial arts–tai chi amalgam with his eyes closed. He tells the others that he can't teach it to them because you have to learn it in a monastery where it is only "passed down verbally." When he's done, Sierra tells him he "looked hilarious." But no, he doesn't get it.

One evening he decides his tribemates need an example of perseverance and determination, so he decides to "share a piece of my life" with them, and tells a long story about kayaking on the Amazon. "*National Geographic* wanted to come with me," he notes, but he turned them down because he wanted to do it alone. But then, *zut alors!* He is kidnapped by savages who plan to kill him in a primitive ritual until he miraculously escapes. Everyone sits around the campfire, silent, not meeting his eyes in fear they will burst out laughing.

Coach decides to vote out J.T.—*everyone's* favorite person—and thinks this is a game-exploding, mind-boggling big move. They should call him the "orchestrator," he says to the camera. "I feel brilliant!" In his confessional, he lets loose with a guttural shout. "The battle has already been won. Victory is mine."

Coach says again and again that he wants to compete against the best, the strongest, the "warriors" in the tribe. He wants "iron that sharpens iron." (This is how Coach talks.) But then he drops out of an immunity challenge in order to eat pizza. That night he tells Jeff he wants "to walk the path of the noble warrior and finding that great competition that you can pit yourself against." (At which point we see others laughing, rolling their eyes, because he's been trying to vote out every strong player all along.) Coach has played the game three times now—like I said, gold—but he's terrible at jury management. When he calls himself the "chosen one" and starts quoting Jesus, even Jeff can't stop laughing.

Like all self-appointed leaders, he tries to bully people who won't do what he wants. When the plan is to vote out Sierra, he tells her, "In love and war, it's kill or be killed," which would alarm me if we were dating, for sure, and then, "The honorable thing is to accept your fate." This is because she had voted for him. "The samurai warrior, if he did dishonor to himself or his family, you know what he would do? He would fall on his sword. Death before dishonor." Later he says to his supposed ally, Debbie, "People who don't play this game even half as honestly as me, even *half* as bold as me, like we saw tonight, *Pisses. Me. Off.*"

Debbie: "You gotta let it go."

There's a point, of course, where it all starts to feel sad. As he finishes a challenge one day he shouts, "Dragonslayer!" and strikes a pose. Later he asks J.T. in a little-boy voice, "Did you hear me say 'Dragonslayer'?" When the loved ones arrive, his reunion is not with a sibling or parent or girlfriend. It's with his assistant soccer coach. Instead of taking a walk or having a heart-to-heart talk, they do stretching exercises. Coach says, "Hey, man, guess what they're calling me out here? Dragonslayer. 'Cause I'm slaying all the dragons. I'm running this fricking show."

Tocantins included Exile Island, the barren camp where one or two people are sent to survive alone for a day or two. When Stephen is sent, Coach tells him, "Be the wizard, Stephen. Be the wizard." Most of the other players have been to Exile Island; Taj has been four times. When it's Coach's turn, he suddenly mentions that he has asthma and a bad back, and asks them not to send him. "J.T. and I are *eager* to send Coach to Exile. He's been *so* skittish about it. He's been selling out everyone, trying to get them to Exile before him," says Stephen. "I'm not entirely sure Coach can build a fire and cook this food by himself. I think he's scared."

J.T. says, "I'm ready to test him, and also we plan on sending Coach at the next Tribal Council, so it would be nice for him to come very weak to the next immunity challenge." J.T. easily wins the challenge and it's time to pick someone for Exile. He says, "Let's be noble, Coach." With no way out, Coach says he's "going to take the monastic approach. I'm not going to build a fire, not going to eat. Just gonna meditate."

He is, of course, not really alone on Exile Island; there is a camera crew. As he climbs the dune (the one that the women have all climbed, most of them more than once), the music swells. He says, "This is gonna be like a vacation," since he's away from "all those wishy-washy people at camp with no character. Coach Wade's foundation is built on a rock. I could stay out here for a week without food." Coach Wade claims indigenous heritage, and adds, "I will not have anything to eat. It's going to be like the ancient American Indians that are my ancestors." Then he prays out loud.

I puzzled over where to put Coach in this book. He fits in with delusional players, obviously, and with bosses. But he is also a good example of the show's colonial mannerisms. The ponytail, the long feathered earrings, the Asian character tattoos, this reference to vision quests. Of his supposed ancestors, he says, "They used to go out into the wilderness for 48 hours and they would commune with the creator of the universe and they would become men. Well, I'm already a man, so this will just make me more of a man." Jason Concepcion, writing in *The Ringer*, put it best when he said, "Coach is one of those people who is so performatively woke that it feels racist."

When Coach Wade returns from Exile, he tells people it was an experience of "no sleep. Starving. No food. Very little water. And it was fricking awesome. It was a great experience to be out here and once again test myself." As the other players have done several times. "I've been in the Amazon, the Congo, the Orinoco, the Darién Gap. Chalk another one to the list. The dunes at Exile."

Then he quotes Marcus Aurelius and refers to himself as "the last of the Mohicans."

He's a great goat. No one would ever vote for him to win. But he's used up all of their patience. At Tribal Council he explains that Exile was harder for everyone else than it was for him, because he had past experiences to draw on. The others are laughing, and so is the jury. Then he quotes Mark Twain. Just as Jeff calls for the vote, Coach says, "One more thing! I wrote a poem for everybody to hear. 'With friend and foe, we march to the battle plain. Some to seek success, others to seek fame.'" People on the jury actually have their heads in their hands now. "'We play with honor, for the love of this game. And with armor or without, we will toil in vain. So that someday, someone, somewhere, will remember our name.'" Jeff says with a poker face, "I can't think of a better way to lead in to the vote."

Coach is voted out.

In an episode of *The Office*, there are rumors of downsizing. Dwight somehow thinks that it will be based on popularity. He suggests to Jim that they form an alliance to "help each other out." He's very serious, standing too close, on the QT. Jim keeps a straight face:

"Abso*lute*ly." To the camera, he smiles with surprised glee. "At that moment, I was so happy."

Dwight wants to figure out who is "safe" and who is "vulnerable," and insists they keep the alliance a "total secret." Jim sincerely agrees and immediately tells Pam. He pretends to spy on people and then gets Dwight riled up about loyalties and betrayals stirring. "Toby and Kevin are trying to get Angela kicked off," Jim tells him, though they had actually been discussing sandwiches. And so it goes until Dwight is hiding in a sealed box in the warehouse for hours, hoping to eavesdrop on a nonexistent alliance meeting, and finally has to cut himself out with a jackknife. For some reason, this made me think of Coach.

Players do quit. The first time this happened was in season 7, *Pearl Islands*. The season starts with the players jumping off the boat and swimming to shore, fully clothed, then buying supplies in a nearby village. They have only a little money, so Osten sells all his clothes, keeping only a pair of underwear. This is not wise. Within a few days, he's ready to leave. He's big and strong, but what do you know, he's *cold*. At Tribal Council on day 19, he calls himself "a bag of atrophy" and asks to be voted off. There is no vote; Jeff impatiently snuffs his torch and drops it to the ground, more or less telling him to get lost.

Two players quit in *All-Stars*: Jenna, because her mother was dying and she couldn't stop feeling that she should be home, and Sue, who had a meltdown after being bumped by naked Richard Hatch. Neither seemed to bother Jeff very much; I assume he could see which way the sympathies were likely to roll. In season 28,

Cagayan, Lindsey was upset by a devious play and got into a fight with one of the other women. She goes down to the beach alone and after a while, Jeff shows up for a therapy session. Lindsey says she's afraid she'll lose control on camera and would rather quit than have her family see that. Again, Jeff doesn't seem particularly upset; he almost seems to admire her concern.

Colton, a contender for Worst Person to Ever Play *Survivor*, was evacuated from the *One World* season out of a concern for appendicitis. He returns to play with his boyfriend, Caleb, in *Blood vs. Water*. He wants to play differently, he says; he's a changed person. But he can't; he is relentlessly hateful toward the others and tries to sabotage them. "Hopefully, this camp will erupt into chaos, because if there's one thing I know, I can rule in chaos." But instead, he quits, on day 7. This time, Jeff is angry: "The first time you feigned an appendicitis. Turns out you didn't have it. You want to own that one, now?" Colton says he was really sick, and he's tired of being hated by everyone. Jeff has no patience for it. "Lots of people like to *watch* adventure," says Jeff. "It doesn't necessarily mean they really should get up off the couch. And I'm now convinced that Colton is the guy who never should have got up off the couch. We brought a quitter back and we got a quitter again." He refuses to let him throw his buff in the fire—one ritual of farewell—and Colton leaves without much in the way of goodbye.

The rules now state that contestants who quit for any reason other than a health or personal emergency may not be on the jury or receive any consolation money. This rule came into play after *Nicaragua*. On day 28, both NaOnka and Purple Kelly announce that they're going to quit. (Day 28—just over a week to go.) They say the lack of food and sleep is too much. "My body is wearing down and tearing down," says NaOnka, who has been a handful all along. At Council, Jeff is clearly annoyed. "You're *this* close to being able to say, 'I did it,' and you're *this* close to being one of those others, the quitters that nobody remembers. Think about it." NaOnka defends herself by saying that she wanted to "go out with a bang" and that she knew she could have won. (One glance at the jury's faces and you know *that's* not true.) Jeff asks, with clenched jaw, because this is not how the game is played, "What do you think should be done with your torch? You guys are quitters." As he snuffs NaOnka's torch he says, "You want to go? Go." He leaves the dead torches at the Council as a reminder.

Back at camp, the others name their chicken "Kelly-Nay." Then they kill the chicken.

Russell Hantz, a persistent and creepy saboteur in a tank top and fedora, started out as a notorious villain. He has become a hero to some fans, who see him as a great strategist. He has been voted fan favorite twice, winning $100,000 each time. I hate to use the word "notorious" because I'm sure that's exactly how he wants to be described. He's about as subtle as a hippo and has never had a sliver of a chance of winning, but seems not to know this. His strategy in three American seasons and one in Australia was to be so nasty that no one was willing to cross him. He dumped out his team's water, burned another player's socks in the campfire, and lied about being a victim of Hurricane Katrina. Hantz said, "If I can control how they feel, I can control how they think." One almost feels a tiny bit sad for him when the votes are read, when he realizes he won't win, won't even get a vote, won't get a single vote, when the thought flashes across his face: *It's not fair!* He's so sure he's played the best game. He never knew he was the goat all along.

Hantz's nephew, Brandon, played twice; he concealed his identity as a member of the Hantz family the first time, not wanting to poison the well. But he was cut from the same cloth, playing with a kind of panicked paranoia so intense that I wanted to medicate him. Brandon is an evangelical Christian and he struggled mightily with lust in the first season, surrounded as he inevitably had to be by semi-naked women. The second time, he got so angry at a tribemate that he dumped his own tribe's entire food supply. His tribe was so angry in return, they forfeited an immunity challenge so they could go to Tribal Council. They needed to vote him out for their own welfare.

The Hantz family aren't the only saboteurs. On *Kaôh Rōng*, Kyle and Scot are angry about the way the women voted. So they decide to engage in "psychological warfare" by hiding the machete and ax so no one can get food. When someone calls him immature, Scot pours all the fresh water on the fire, announcing that every time they start a fire, he'll put it out again. No fire, no water. No food. Scot says, "It's time to make life as miserable as possible for everybody else." He knows he's turned into the villain. "I came into this game not wanting to be the Russell Hantz, kicking over the rice and pouring water on the fire like I did. I didn't want to be that guy. But I had to make a point, that we were the providers and they weren't going to succeed without us." This is hard to figure. If he wanted to make that point, he could have just stopped providing, left the women the machete and ax and fire to see if they could do it. There's no better way to show how much they depended on him. But destroying the *means* of production doesn't prove anything about *his* production.

The 32nd season introduced the world to Debbie Wanner, who identifies as a civil air captain and a server at Red Lobster. She brags about her survival skills, especially fire building. Then she can't get a fire started. She announces that she can judge the quality and safety of water "just by looking at it." None of that boiling nonsense for her. She flat out refuses to use a saw, chopping vainly at the bamboo with an ax.

"Debbie has a whole different level of craziness," says Neal, who runs an ice cream shop and is wearing pants covered with cartoons of ice cream cones. Peter says that when he first met her, his question was, "Does she have thirty cats or forty cats?" He flatters her shamelessly, because she's good to have along. She "is not exhibiting much game play whatsoever, so she's the person you want on your team. That's exactly what you want."

Two seasons later, Debbie is back—still odd, still stringy and lean, this time calling herself a chemist. She's still confident: "I have military training in summer and winter survival, shelter building, fire making, food procurement, torture training and a superior will to survive." At one challenge, she flips out, refuses to do what her teammates suggest, can't shut up, and complains and sneers and bitches loudly throughout the entire thing. One reward challenge— for peanut-butter sandwiches and milk—requires tossing, digging, balancing on a beam, and a puzzle. Debbie volunteers for the balance beam, claiming that she used to be a gymnast. "I'm really good at balancing," she explains. But she is, in fact, not. They lose. Back at camp, she goes on a wild rant, claiming she was ordered to do it, shouting and screaming and doing push-ups ("That's why I look like this and have an eight-pack!"), and suddenly it all feels a lot like watching Donald Trump give a speech toward the end of his term.

They lose, Debbie gets sent to Exile Island, and everyone heaves a sigh of relief. But this time, Exile Island turns out to be a luxury sailing ship with tons of food, a bed, and a shower. She eats and sleeps and says, "This is a tribe of Debbie." Then Cochran shows up. Cochran is a self-professed super-fan; when he was in law school at Harvard, he wrote a paper comparing the American justice system to the juries on *Survivor*. He has played twice and won the second time. Perhaps his best quality in the game has been that he seems more like a viewer than a player; he doesn't ever seem to be trying. Cochran could hardly be a more different player than Debbie Wanner.

"I've met presidents, prime ministers, and I'm not very often awestruck," Debbie says later, "but to meet one of my favorite *Survivor* winners was an honor and a privilege." He's there to help her talk out and think about strategy, and so he tries to advise her about "swallowing her pride" and being more humble. To the camera, he says, "She claims to be an expert in everything, so I have my work cut out for me. One of her fatal flaws is overconfidence." She tells him that she's very secure and unworried and has *a total plan*. She ignores all his advice, saying grandly that she is controlling *everything*. "There is not a line drawn in the sand. There is a line drawn in *concrete*." When she votes, she says with great satisfaction, "There are people who *give* orders and there are people who *take* orders. It's called a democracy." Well, that's not actually what a democracy is, and Debbie is voted out.

I could never play the game—those cameras. But I like to pretend that at least I would be better than this. I might be as good at untying knots underwater and tossing sand bags at targets as most other players. I have been in lots of boats and I'm a good swimmer. I can read a map and throw a softball and I like puzzles. But I know I couldn't play the social game for long. I'm a little bossy. I find it hard to resist a cheap joke and there's no end of cheap jokes on *Survivor*. I don't suffer fools very well and there is no end of fools. There's a chance I could find myself claiming a rock as my own. *No one else sit on my thinking seat. Please. You want this one? I'll go get another one! I just want mine, this one!*

I watch in part because of such havoc, because of the walking disasters: the people who cannot shut up, who can't get along for five minutes, who won't look for food, build a roof on a leaking shelter, make a plan. There are always contestants who look more like food than anything else. I watch people get terrible sunburns and heat exhaustion and dehydration just sitting around at camp, with shade and water a few feet away. "What schadenfreude this show provides—that joy you're not supposed to have when things go wrong for other people," wrote Phyllis Rose about her love for *Survivor*. "It's a very specialized kind of escapism that wafts you to a Pacific island for an hour and leaves you feeling happy you aren't there." She called *Survivor* a lesson in true democracy, because even idiots and racists get to vote. ("This is not a democracy," said BB in *Borneo*, declaring that he could wash his T-shirt in the cooking pot with the last of the fresh water if he wanted to. He is voted out the next day.)

Don't be a smart-ass. And never sing show tunes. Coby said, "At first I thought, 'Oh, that's so cute, look, Wanda's singing, and oh, goodness, she kept going and going and going, and everybody's just like, 'Is she going to *stop*?'" Wanda was voted off as soon as they reached the beach.

HUNGER

You can keep the oysters and the snails," says Rob on *All-Stars,* as he eats his daily allotment out of a broken coconut shell. He laughs. "*This* is what *Survivor* is all about. Rice, baby, rice." Most of the time, tribes are given enough rice at the beginning of the game for each person to eat a half cup per day. People lose a lot of weight on *Survivor.* The hunger is made more peculiar by the fact that elaborate crew tents with plenty of food are nearby. (During season 16, players supposedly broke into the crew quarters and stole food. Security is tighter now.)

Such hunger is a new experience for most people playing the game. On *Tocantins,* when a few people start eating termites, one of the women says, "I'll eat one at a challenge if I have to, but not in real life." After two weeks, a player on season 24 shouts, "I haven't had soda in, like, forever!" On season 35, when his tribe is completely out of food, Devon says, "This is a lot more real than I thought."

Smart players eat termites, snails, and roots and rats and snakes. There is a rule in the extensive contract that players are only allowed to eat food approved by the producers. Tyson said in a recent interview, "They don't want anybody dying. That would be poor for a lot of reasons, to have someone die on your TV show. I mean, I don't know how the entertainment industry works per se, but." Malcolm caught and started cooking a poisonous eel during one of his seasons, and a producer did step in and stop him. "They're not really trying to kill us," he said later, "even though they're kind of trying to kill us." On *Game Changers*, a tribe catches a nanny goat and her kid. The group debates killing them, but there is a lot of resistance—except from Sandra, who is all for killing them both. They're afraid of Sandra, but finally, the goats are spared—at least, they are on television. In a postgame interview, Sandra claimed otherwise. In this game of survival, killing a cute little goat was too much for the editors in the end.

Hunger is used as motivation, as reward, as sacrifice, as punishment. People are hungry, they are weak from being hungry, they may be too weak to look for food and too tired to win a challenge where they might get fed. If you want to win the game, don't hoard food—or, as NaOnka did in *Nicaragua*, steal food and bury it in the jungle just to punish everyone else. Never eat more than your share. In season 3, in *Africa*, a tribe opens a can of cherries to share, passing it around and taking one cherry at a time. Ethan says of Clarence, "I saw him take two. Which is an issue." Later, when Clarence and Diane are left at camp alone, the two eat a can of beans. The others do not let them forget it.

On season 35, Cole takes food whenever he wants and then licks the spoon. He catches a fish and eats it by himself. Jessica says, "He eats food *alone!* You can't do that in *Survivor!*" Cole insists that he needs to be fed more than the others because he's big and strong. Even after 40 seasons, people misunderstand strength. Big, muscular men require a lot of calories and are often the first to collapse after days of little food. (On the other hand, I swear some of the women go on diets before the show, painfully aware of the cameras to come. Only a few savvy people gain weight; they have staying power.)

Food is used to sow chaos and disruption. Reward challenges almost always include food. An individual winner is often allowed to pick one or two of the others to share. They can't avoid angering everyone left behind. Judd wins a steak and lobster feast in *Guatemala* and invites Bobby Jon and Stephenie to share it. Then they are seated in front of their hungry, gaunt tribemates. The feast goes on for hours, with cocktails, cigars, and dessert, while Judd gets falling-down drunk. Sometimes the winner is told that the whole tribe will get a little food if the winner gives up their feast. On *Game Changers*, the players are excited to get food when they merge tribes. Then Jeff says they will feast only if one person from each tribe volunteers not to eat. We watch the silent, painful contemplation of sacrifice for a long time before anyone speaks up.

"It might be truly said, that now I work'd for my bread," said Robinson Crusoe. "'Tis a little wonderful, and what I believe few people have thought much upon, the strange multitude of little things necessary in the providing, producing, curing, dressing, making and finishing this one article of bread." Bread is gold on *Survivor.* Most seasons include an auction—the commodification of hunger, capitalism at its best. The players are each given $500 and allowed to bid, but some of the items are not revealed until after the bidding ends. You might get a steak dinner and you might get a raw clam. The auction ends without warning; many people wait tensely for their fantasy meal to appear and then leave with nothing at all. On season 24, the items included peanut butter and chocolate, nachos, a BLT, some cocktails, doughnuts, and iced coffee, but also a shower, letters from home, an advantage in the game, and finally a whole cake that the entire group must eat in 60 seconds. They dig in like hyenas on a baby zebra.

The hunger on *Survivor* is real. It hurts. But Jeff makes it hurt so much more. Whenever he describes a food reward, he whispers, seductive. Sadism is important to storytelling. Every murder mystery has a corpse; every thriller requires an innocent in danger. Fairy tales have ogres and sometimes the hero dies and then Jeff brings a single slice of pizza and cuts it into nine tiny bites, just so they can have a taste. He says, "You can be so close to a cheeseburger, and not taste it if you don't win." Jeff can have a cheeseburger anytime he wants, though he looks more like an egg white and kale omelet guy to me.

Late in a season, players may get a letter from a "loved one," the term invariably used for family and friends. Sometimes it's a video and often, it's a visit. In the drawn-out scene, the loved ones are called out one by one: "It's your mother!" "Here's your wife!" and the players weep and clap for each other. Later the winners tell their relatives how much they hate everyone else. Usually the players get to greet their loved one for a few moments and then separate, because loved ones are doled out like food. Jeff lets them take a small bite, then pulls it away. (At this point, they may have been playing the game for two or three weeks, perhaps away from home for a month or a bit more. The drama, the buckets of tears, the near-hysterics are a bit much.) To win more time with their loved one, the players must win a challenge—they must "win love." Also, food. Sometimes the loved ones have to participate in the challenge, awkwardly throwing balls or scooping water while the players shriek in frustration at their incompetence. The loved ones are well fed, wearing nice vacation clothes, a bit pink from the tropical sun. *They* aren't used to being filmed all the time, but they gamely walk the plank or crawl in the sand. At the end, after one person has won and chosen a couple of others to join, Jeff says to the rest, "Got nothing for you. Enjoy the afternoon."

A frequent food-related challenge on *Survivor* is a race to see who can eat the most disgusting local food fastest. On the fifth season, *Thailand*, the loved ones appeared after 31 days. Jeff brings the visitors in, and then tells the players that the winner will get 24 hours with their relative. "For the losers, nothing," he adds. "Hear me clearly: not a kiss, not a hug, not a handshake." Then he says that the winner will be decided in the disgusting-food challenge. The players are ready: bring it on, we're starving, we'll eat anything, let's go. Jeff says, "I believe you guys. I believe all of you would do just about anything to win this reward. But that's not the question. The question is, would they?" Will the well-fed, just-arrived loved ones eat insects to see a person who is going to be home in just over a week?

The loved ones don't look happy about this.

It takes only a few plates of ants, water bugs, and live grubs to eliminate most people. When only Helen's husband and Jake's wife are left, they must eat a boiled tarantula in one minute. They both do it, with difficulty. The tiebreaker is a boiled scorpion. Whoever is first to finish will win. Helen's husband wins, and Jake's wife turns around and pukes.

I'm not disturbed by the players' hunger; they scavenge for coconuts and catch the occasional rat or fish. They suffer as much from the monotony of what they do have to eat as the lack of calories.

The disturbing part, to me, is the enforcing of hunger and the constant reminders by Jeff of this enforcing. I am disturbed by the dangling of food in a hungry country, in places where getting enough to eat is the central task in life. Human history and culture are founded on the search for food, and on these islands, hunger may be a daily beast in a village that is more or less over the next hill.

I can't watch *Alone* and then *Survivor*. I can't go from the serious consequences of true survival to no real consequences. *Alone* is partly about interiority and reflection. *Survivor* is about exteriority and manipulation. On *Alone*, catching a single mouse is a real thrill; on *Survivor*, Oreos and potato chips are handed out like treats for eager puppies. I am aware that I have a kind of class bias here. I identify with the composed, careful intelligence of *Alone* contestants, despite being completely incompetent to do what they do. I resist identification with the scheming duplicity and clueless inertia of many *Survivor* contestants, even though I'm perfectly capable of doing those things. I see one as a superior class; I know which one I'd rather be.

One kind of hunger, endured to satisfy another. Is *Survivor* a microcosm of social divides, a miniature political system? The season called *Worlds Apart* divided players into three tribes by class. Jeff described the White-Collar tribe as the ones who "make the rules"—that tribe included a talent agent, a corporate trainer, and a Yahoo executive. The Blue Collars "follow the rules" and included a postal worker, a hairdresser, and a state trooper. The No Collars, who "break the rules," had a jewelry designer, a sailing instructor, and a coconut vendor.

"None of us know how to make fire," says Joaquin, a marketing director. "Why would we? White Collar. We hire Blue Collar to go make us a fire." And Blue Collar does make fire, for itself.

Meanwhile, No Collar is struggling with its hang-loose vibe. Joe and Vince clash on how to build shelter, and the clash is as much about process and trying to avoid being a boss on a tribe where people don't like bosses as it is about shelter.

Survivor more or less created the popular form of elimination show where a group of people is whittled down to a single winner. Every three days, someone will be voted off the island. The tribe has spoken, and sometimes it's your closest friend and trusted ally who speaks. (The whole elimination thing has come full circle with *The Great British Baking Show*, where the weekly loser is announced with a teary eye and a catch in the host's voice. It's so hard, she says, because "we get to know you a little bit more. And we are incredibly fond of you. We don't want to lose anybody. But the journey has to end this week for somebody." They *could* just change the rules.) But *Survivor* digs its cruelty. How about that schoolyard pick, when the numbers are uneven and one person will be left out? *Survivor* can only exist in a market economy, because stoking envy is part of the game. Mark Burnett called the lies of the first season "queasy-making"; I get a little queasy thinking about how much money Burnett made elevating Donald Trump's profile. I get a little queasy thinking about how many times gazillionaire Jeff says the magic words: You have a shot at *a million dollars*. This is potentially *a million-dollar challenge*. You're in the game for *a million dollars*. This could be *a million-dollar decision*. One mistake can cost you *a million bucks*.

The show has made a lot of money for CBS and the VIPs. But, with a few exceptions, the players are middle-class or working-class or just plain poor. It's another *Queen for a Day*, a competition of need where we watch factory workers and waitresses starve for money. If you are voted out, if you are one of the 15 or 18 people who don't win the single prize, you've failed. When Ben made a mistake in the final immunity challenge, he says, "It just hurts that a silly mistake is going to cost my dream and my family's dream. My kids' college. Retirement. I just let it slip away. And that hurt." I don't blame Ben, or even *Survivor*, for that concern. I blame capitalism for that. (And when it was all done, Ben won a million dollars. He isn't a failure after all. Everyone else is.)

It's times like that when I hate the game. Reality television, which is definitely television and a kind of reality and most of all a kind of shared fantasy about reality, can be as depraved as a Roman arena. "The spectacle is the moment when the commodity has attained the *total occupation* of social life," wrote Guy Debord in his manifesto against capitalism. "Not only is the relation to the commodity visible but it is all one sees: the world one sees is the world."

MIRRORS, CAMERAS, BINGE-WATCHING, AND MAKING A SCENE

Three thousand years ago, the Olmec of the Mexican lowlands wore mirrors made from iron ore around the neck. The mirrors were so polished they could reflect pictures and start fires. The Scythians, proud of their elaborate hairstyles and manicures, always carried mirrors. The Etruscans made mirrors the way Americans make hamburgers and game shows. Toddlers recognize themselves in mirrors. How? So do apes, it seems, and there is evidence that dolphins, whales, and elephants do, too. What does it say of the nature of a brain that it can recognize its own encasement? To look in a mirror is a profoundly human act, even when it is the orangutan doing it. One is forever haunted by the question of what one is.

What is the nature of the self that knows itself to be a self? A solipsistic, infinitely regressive concern, what one is, who one is, the wonder and fear of it leading brilliant minds into tiny corners from which they seem unable to escape. I am me because *I know myself* to be me, but how? The urge to claim a space for the self collides and colludes with the urge to construct a self to fit the space. We are not entirely in charge here. Even in our most intimate meetings, we are presenting a version of ourselves; to interact is to script. We are literally putting in an appearance every time we meet; there is a fragment of me that has never relaxed around another human being. How can we know, how can we *be known*, when all this knowing and striving to be known is done by fragile beings in the midst of arriving and departing? For the briefest of seconds we meet, and then are lost again. The immutable opacity of *relationship* is as rippled and broken as the pond into which our ancestors gazed. Self-consciousness is the human condition.

The philosopher Walter Benjamin was deeply struck by a key moment in the early 20th century. Theatrical performance was a living art, never the same twice, experienced in the moment and then consigned to memory. The nascent technology of film changed everything. Was performance still the same when it was captured? Is a film of a play still live theater? Benjamin saw the way the camera controls and manipulates the actor. Onstage, the actor has control; nothing is done without the actor's consent. With film, the audience has control—invisible control, which is power. He wrote, "The representation of human beings by means of an apparatus has made possible a highly productive use of the human being's self-alienation." An actor can't help but feel estrangement from the camera "of the same kind as the estrangement felt before one's appearance in a mirror." Film captures—everything. "Now the mirror image has become detachable from the person mirrored, and is transportable," he wrote. "The screen actor never for a moment ceases to be aware of this." Film calls into question every value of the stage, deforming the frame created by a stage. Film invokes new boundaries, placing the *viewer* (perpetually now a single person rather than the group) inside, holding the edge of the fourth wall closed but never forgotten. I suspect that Benjamin would find reality television frightening in its ability to create a consensual fantasy. He thought film functioned the way fascism does, inserting itself into a culture so quietly that one barely has time to notice that everything has changed.

There are people who feel real only when they are being watched; perhaps this has always been true. In our current age, this means only when they are being filmed. Hannah Arendt said, "Our modern identity crisis could be resolved only by never being alone and never trying to think." From Benjamin to All Access and YouTube may be a long path, but it is a pretty straight one. We are saturated not so much by screens, though constant surveillance is now a fact of public life, as we are by the awareness of screens. I am not at ease here; I put masking tape over the camera on my laptop. How ill at ease? I read user agreements. When a friend says to me, "Your privacy hackles are really up," my only response is, why aren't yours?

We are conditioned not to do or say certain things *in public*. Cameras are everywhere. *Everywhere.* To have privacy means to carve a small space out of the public sphere because otherwise we conspire in our own surveillance. But what I see are people who simply engage in private behavior in public, unconcerned with making a space for it. I see people who aren't alive except on camera and I see people who do seem to be entirely relaxed around others. Perhaps they have perfected the appearance of relaxation. (Such is the nature of acting.) In ordinary life—whatever that means anymore—the camera we think about is the one in our hands. We don't forget the endless gaze because we have become each other's camera. I look at you; you look at me; we record ourselves looking. I can never look at me, but I can imagine what you see when you do. And that image is always removed from what I really am. I can never know *for real* how I appear to you. We may not always know the words, but we know it, this flinching from the longed-for closeness of another. We know our struggle with both the mask and its slippage, with the sense of being caged in a body—caught, mute, the perpetual loneliness locked inside. *How do I look?* is nothing more than *Where do I belong? And to whom?*

For several years, I visited the online world called Second Life almost every day. I have always recoiled from Facebook in faint horror, at the me-me-me of it. I tend to turn from even the friendliest of cameras, forever a little disappointed by my captured self. If Facebook is an endless parade of me-ness, Second Life is a world of not-being-me-ness. How do you present yourself when you are anonymous, when you can be anything you want? Second Life is not a game or a story, though it contains both. It is just a place where you can do whatever you want. And you can look any way you want, so I was amused by the fact that many people chose fantasy selves resembling the ideal bodies we are shown in magazines. I was often struck by the startling creativity and playful wit in Second Life, by landscapes of dream, unpredictable music and hallucinatory art and a tiny dancing ferret lecturing about the current state of trade tariffs. I found liberation in Second Life's infinite masks. I came to see, though, that after a time most people moved in, the same way they would move to a new home in real life— settling on an avatar not so unlike themselves, building a house, growing relationships. Going to the same places at the same time and saying hello to the same people and the same Ents and ferrets and queens, day after day.

*   *   *

The cameras are always on, watching the players, and the players are always watching each other. This is the obvious surveillance, done to create the third layer of surveillance to come, when the show is broadcast, which slides eternally into the fourth layer of criticism and analysis and reinvention by people who will never play the game. *Survivor* is hollow; it is tabula rasa of a kind. On *Tocantins*, Debbie, standing on the beach, says they should build a bonfire: "We could pretend we're at the beach somewhere." In *Marquesas*, Sean wins a local feast; looking it over, he says, "This is better than *Gilligan's Island*." Even today, when epistemology begins to seem like a quaint hobby and people have come to believe that objective truth is malleable to one's needs, fans will argue about what they saw and didn't see, about whether something actually *happened*, whether what they saw was true. It starts to thunder during Tribal Council and Jeff looks to the sky and says, "Is this a reminder of how *real* it all is?" Early in the first season on Borneo, Colleen describes the challenge requiring players to answer trivia questions. "I was thinking, it's going to be just like a game show!" she says to the camera. "That's going to be so cool. Then I thought, wait a minute! We're *on* a game show!" A real-life game show.

I am binge-watching *Survivor* until the casts, the places, and the winners are all mixed up. I follow the shifting alliances and dwindling tribes through a season, watch with real attention, and when it's over the entire season dissolves.

Streaming has its advantages. You can zip right past irritating people ("I'm sure she's really nice, but the bottom line is," John K. says of Eliza in season 9, " 'Oh, my god, would you *please* stop talking?'!").

Binging on *Survivor* may be the closest thing to being there. It's so repetitive from one season to the next. The days are all the same. Same challenges, same discomfort. Same people. Not infrequently, the stream bounces me around an episode and I discover that it doesn't really matter. I can figure things out because I've heard these conversations before. Baylor is crying again. Missy is babying her again. Before every season was available for streaming, I had to get DVDs out of the library. When I got to the penultimate episode of season 10, *Palau*, it stuck just as Jeff was going to read the votes. I started over, found the place, and it stuck again. I kept reaching the point where Jeff is lifting the first piece of folded paper out of the box, and just as in the game, time stood still.

Survivor persists—thrives—in part because it has mastered the addictive combination of the familiar with the novel. It's like an Agatha Christie novel or a new Taylor Swift album: brand new, but exactly the same as the last one. We know we like Agatha Christie and Taylor Swift and *Survivor*, so we happily partake again. We are comforted by the duplication, by the traditions. It's familiar and yet I can't predict what will happen. Who expected that the gambler Jean-Robert, in *Survivor: China*, would reveal several days into the game that he can speak Mandarin? Or that Denise, the lunch lady, has a black belt in Kenpo karate, and her hobby is ax and knife throwing? I didn't. The show can be exhausting. But I keep watching, because I never know what's going to happen, not really. In season 39, Dean needs to suck up to one of the women for a while. He says, "Do I want to sit there and hear her yap the whole time? Absolutely not. But do I want to be taken to the final three? Absolutely." So do I.

Survivor renews itself by disruption, what Goffman calls creating a scene. "An individual acts in such a way as to destroy or seriously threaten the polite appearance of consensus, and while he may not act simply in order to create such dissonance, he acts with the knowledge that this kind of dissonance is likely to result," wrote Goffman. He was discussing office behavior, but he might have been a *Survivor* fan. "The common-sense phrase 'creating a scene' is apt because, in effect, a new scene is created by such disruptions. The previous and expected interplay between the teams is suddenly forced aside and a new drama forcibly takes its place. Significantly, this new scene often involves a sudden reshuffling and reapportioning of the previous team members into two new teams." Exactly. If the players don't do it, the producers will. They create scenes in exactly this way, by reshuffling tribes. And there's always a person like Shane to fill the role of the lone gunman, sowing mayhem: suspicious of everyone's motives, planting toxic seeds of doubt. Sandra stole all the sugar and told everyone she was sure Michaela did it. When NaOnka lost a sock, she stole Fabio's socks just for the heck of it. (NaOnka is #3 on a "most annoying players" list. She's probably on every such list.)

None of the disrupters have been as entertaining as Greg in the first season. Greg (identified on camera simply as "Ivy League graduate," which is funny enough in itself) was the original meta-contestant. He was a funny, smart guy who was clearly in on the game. He alarmed his tribemates by making a "jungle phone" out of a coconut and walked up and down the beach on elaborate business calls, arranging deals. Greg slept in a nest in the forest rather than the crowded shelter and hid behind bushes to jump out and scare the camera crews. During confessionals, he rambled on about the voices guiding him. He caused no end of difficulties; one story told is that he made so many bizarre jokes at his tribe's first Tribal Council that the producers had an emergency meeting to figure out how to handle him. Jeff was furious; Greg was pulling all the attention and deforming the entire game. He obviously didn't care about winning—a perfect saboteur, there only to amuse himself. As a jury member, he created a terrific scene when he told the final two players that his vote would go to whichever one picked a number closest to the one in his head. He later said that he intended to vote for Richard all along and was just making a comment about the fake seriousness of Tribal Council. But his teammates were maddened by it; that's *not*, several said, how you play the game. (To this day, people complain about it.) After a contestant is voted out, they make a private confessional speech, wrapping it all up. When Greg was voted out, he burst into hysterical, phony weeping, and this continued during his post-elimination interview, where he referenced the Death Star and the Rebel Alliance. (You can watch part of this on YouTube; the rest I take from Mario Lanza, who captured the transcript at the time.) Then he suddenly stopped, and shifted into a posh English accent. "Excellent game, well manufactured. Well thought-out. A microcosm of humanity," he said, then lowered his voice. "I hear noises in the jungle now." Burnett couldn't accept the possibility that Greg really didn't care. Instead, he wrote, "Greg was like a patient undergoing a very long psychotherapy session . . . the hard work of diving inward to touch his soul had begun. *Survivor* was his slow journey to the truth. He called it a game only because calling it anything else would have been too painful." He calls him a "child," but also a "genius," who understood "even, I must admit, before I did—*Survivor*'s potential as a Peter Pan–like world where what was real and what was imagined were all in the eyes of the beholder." After the show, Greg modeled for a bit; of course, he signed with Trump Model Management. But then he started a renewable energy company and has steadfastly refused to come back and play again.

HELL IS OTHER PEOPLE

On *Alone*, solitude is often the most difficult part. People who are doing just fine at survival quit out of loneliness. "I've been craving human companionship like it's water," says one man just before he gives up. Solitude is hell to many, but the lack of it is one reason I would struggle on *Survivor*. In China, Todd says, "We have been in the jungle for 23 days now, and these people are driving me *insane*." On *Edge of Extinction*, Aurora and Ron are allied even though they can't stand each other. "We are literally dating each other when all we want to do is break up," says Aurora. Ron says, "I have made it a month with Aurora. If I have to go 39 days with her, I have to get $2 million." When Cirie gets to go to a local village as a reward in Panama, she says, "I was ecstatic just to be around people other than *these* people." On *All-Stars*, Rob, who has been unflappable throughout, says to the camera, "At this point, you get so fed up of being with the people that you're with. You don't want to hear their stories anymore. You're just drained, you're tired, you're cranky, you're hungry, you're not sleeping at night, and it's just like, 'Shut up. Don't talk to me.'"

Exile Island was added as a twist in the game in season 10 and has been used several times since. It's usually a barren spit of land where a player is sent for a day or two to survive with just a machete, flint, and canteen. (Also, a camera crew.) The player can't be voted out and usually gets a clue to the hidden immunity idol—something helpful, like *it's back at the camp somewhere.* When exile is to Redemption Island, the player voted out must compete with other eliminated players in a faux-gladiatorial arena.

In season 10, Janu, a Las Vegas showgirl, is the thinnest and most anxious person in the group. She really looks like the first to go. In a challenge that requires players to stand under a metal grate in water up to their necks while the tide rises, she quits after a few minutes. Then she is sent to Exile Island. Janu has never made a fire. She's never done much of anything; for three weeks she's been lying in the hammock. She spends hours trying to start a fire, long into the night, and when she finally does, she twirls dramatically around the beach, doing the *Castaway* fire dance. She is all alone, surviving. And we get to watch.

In *Panama*, Aras, tired of dealing with the grating personalities of Courtney and Bruce, says to the camera, "To be perfectly honest, I kind of want to go to Exile Island." A little while later, Bruce says, "I want to go to Exile Island, just to get away from Courtney." Instead, Sally is sent, just as she is about to be voted off. "Exile Island is my saving grace," Sally says. "It's not hurting me one bit to be away from the rest of my tribe."

When the *Edge of Extinction* twist was introduced in season 38, Jeff said he had begun thinking "that we should try to get a little deeper psychologically, a little deeper spiritually. Let's see how far people want to go. Is there a possibility of the spiritual death and rebirth that you seek in life, where you realize something deeper about yourself? That's where this idea was born; what if you play the game, and you get voted out, but you also have an option?" I've noticed a change in Jeff over the last several seasons. The host who was visibly annoyed when people cut up at Tribal or talked back in a challenge is a lot more relaxed; there's an air of *bring it on, let's see what happens*. Jeff Probst, of course, doesn't have much to lose now; he's revered by the players and as built into the game as the torches he snuffs. He can stretch a little. But does he really believe this? Does he think *Survivor* is a kind of religious experience? "On *Extinction*, you will have to work for everything. And with no certainty that you will get back in the game, it comes down to one question: how badly do you want this? How far will you want to push yourself? How curious are you to see what you're capable of?"

With *Edge of Extinction*, the player voted out is given a choice, to quit or go into exile. Those who choose the latter are ferried through the dark by a silent boatman in the role of Charon, the player's torch a lonesome light in the black ocean. The numbers on Extinction grow and they have occasional challenges, but little to do most of the time. No one knows what happens next, so there's no way to strategize, and if they can't use the other players to further their own game, what's the point of allying? What's the point of even talking? Or standing up? We see slow scenes of people sitting on a log or kicking through the surf, staring out to sea, silent, melancholy, dull. We get it, Jeff. They want it badly.

One of the lessons of exile in every form is how much we

actually share. There have always been hermits, nomads, loners who prefer no one's company. The players in *Alone* struggle to survive in daunting environments. These places have supported people for thousands of years. But they support people who live in extended families and villages, who travel together gathering food through the warm months and then settle in well-built houses for the winter. We form tribes for many reasons, but one of the most obvious is how much easier it is to do the hard work of surviving together. In *Palau*, the Ulong tribe lost challenge after challenge and shrank way past the point at which tribes usually merge until only Steph and Bobby Jon were left. The Koror tribe had shelter and food and lots of players. Steph and Bobby Jon, worn, hungry, and demoralized, had to compete in every challenge, while Koror only had to play two people at a time. Meanwhile, over in the other tribe, they were driving each other crazy. When Bobby Jon was finally sent home and Steph was the only one left on her tribe, she could barely move the outrigger on her own. She had to make fire and gather water and food alone, climbing palm trees for coconuts and spearfishing off the boat by herself. (When Steph survived to be the last member of her tribe and was sent to rival Koror at last, she joined a cohesive group. There were tiny cracks, but she couldn't find a way in. The fact that she was there at all was a problem. If anyone deserved to go to the end, it was her. Ian said, "I get concerned about the whole eleven tribal councils in a row, and Stephenie's still surviving. I just feel like it's a story developing that we need to put an end to." The story of Stephenie is the story of the Final Girl, beating all the monsters. Can't have that.)

In even extreme environments, there are traditions requiring one person to go out alone: a vision quest, a search for resources, wisdom, power. But such marathons of solitude are undertaken for the tribe, for a chance to return with greater strength. On *Survivor*, any time spent in exile is spent preparing to battle the tribe, not help it. The stillness, the time alone, eats away at people. But this, I could do. I don't know much about snares or shelters and I've never started a fire without a match. But I can do solitude. I can do *alone*.

BOSSES AND LITTLE OLD LADIES

Natalie, playing as a Goliath in *David vs. Goliath,* made enemies effortlessly. Can they really edit a person to be this off-
putting? She didn't want to be the boss—she wanted to be CEO.
She lounges across a log while everyone else works on the shelter,
now and then calling out instructions. She sits by the fire pit, giving
directions: You, use this piece of wood. You, blow on the flames.
This isn't *just* editing. In her pre-show interview, Natalie said that
her pet peeves were "People who are negative; people who talk too
much and listen too little; people who tend to say no before they
consider 'the yes'; people who are quitters as they are too lazy, igno-
rant, or a combination thereof to do better; people who lack motivation but want others to make things happen for them; sagging
pants on young men; when my employees make silly errors that cost
me revenue and lastly, when people sign up for things and are not
fully committed, thereby negatively impacting results. That's all . . .

not much." I would say forewarned is forearmed, but no one was warned. She could be a good goat to take to the end, but the others can't bear it and vote her off after 15 days.

The issue is leadership. How many challenges are lost for the lack of it? Tribes need to know their own strengths and weaknesses, who to put forward and who to sit when there's a chance. Do they make good choices? Not very often. Haven't they spent a few of those empty hours around the campfire talking about how to handle different challenges? Tested their skills, practiced running races on the sand or throwing coconuts at a target? Or, for god's sake, swimming? Few tribes really cohere into a single group for long, derailed by internal trickery, self-conscious posing, and backroom deals. Over and over again, a strong tribe loses because they are incapable of simple tasks like rowing a boat. Instead everyone yells, a young woman in a bikini sits in the stern doing nothing, a big guy loses his temper, and the few people actually rowing are at cross purposes, so that, as Jeff noted once, they seem to be "paddling to another island." People wish for a leader but resent anyone who attempts to lead. People hate the leaders even when they know they need one. Tribes tend to divide into people who favor dictatorship and those who favor democracy, but generally, the anarchists triumph.

One of the most enduring conflicts on the show is the one between the worker bee and the sloth. The arguments are ceaseless and repetitive. Many players seem to prefer a trashy camp with a leaking shelter to having to do chores. Seriously: it happens every season. "Would you mind getting some water?" one person asks. "You're not the boss of everyone," someone yells back. "Don't be giving me orders." People refuse to get the water they need to drink to prove a point most people finished proving in middle school. On *Worlds Apart*, Rodney says to the camera, "I'm the leader. I'm gonna be the leader, no matter what. I'm the Tom Brady here. If I step on the field, right, all business aside, I'm Tom Brady out here." But he won't work. Instead, he complains. "I'll do work when I want to do work. How's that? Ain't nobody my daddy out here. Let me tell you that right now." Mike answers, "Stuff has to be done." And then they're off and rolling into the same you're-not-the-boss-of-me, *just chill*, we'll-lose-if-we-don't-eat fight that happens every season. Most of the tribe joins in until everyone is calling names and throwing shade and Lindsey is screaming at Mike about God *and fuck you, too!*

On *Survivorman*, Stroud cautions people to conserve energy. "If you don't have to stand up, sit down. If you don't have to sit down, lie down. If you don't have to be awake, sleep." But he's talking about not dying. On *Survivor*, this equation is not so clear. Should you rest and go hungry or tire yourself out finding food? If you let others work, you risk looking useless. If you work, you risk looking like a show-off. (Or, worse, the leader.) Those who do work are ridiculed for any failure by those who haven't tried. During season 2 in Australia, one of the young men tries valiantly to fish for hours a day, without luck. One of the young women sits on the beach watching. She has made no effort to fish or do anything else, but she doesn't hesitate to snicker at his empty line. "He's not a fisherman, obviously. He should keep his day job." (He's in the Army.)

On the Pearl Islands, Rupert is sent to the opposing tribe for a few days. Their shelter is about to be washed away. He explains to them that the full moon is bringing rising tides. Osten says he'd rather "wait until it becomes a problem and then deal with it." Meanwhile, waves are breaking within a foot or two of where they sleep. "These guys work very hard at not working," says Rupert. Later in the season, Tijuana complains that people who expect her to work are interfering with her "personal freedom" to just *be herself.*

In every season, several young people will spend most of their time sunbathing while the rather more grizzled players fish and gather firewood and grumble. (Sunbathing. In the tropics. Without sunscreen. I don't get it.) The tension between older and younger contestants plays out like family therapy. On *Cook Islands*, Jonathan, the oldest person in the tribe, gets up early and goes fishing while the others sleep. They've lost several challenges in a row, in part because they're hungry and uncomfortable and not organized. When Jonathan comes back with fish, the others are sitting around a dead fire looking haggard. He suggests someone get water, but the young people refuse.

Jonathan: "It's like a dorm or something."

Nate, off camera, says, "Shut up, fool. We all know what we're doing. We're not knuckleheads around here." They are a real bunch of knuckleheads.

Season 28, *Cagayan*, features dopey Morgan. She said in her pre-show interview that her main reason for competing was to "show everyone that just because I have huge boobs and a pretty face does not mean I am dumb, it just means I look better when I am winning." Yes, she said that. She spent most of her time on the island sunbathing while her tribemates worked, and at one point says that such is "the privilege of pretty." She's picked as weakest on her team in the first few moments and you can tell she's never been dissed like this in her life. Tony describes her as "the girl that you can't tell if she's a pillow or a person." She doesn't last.

The younger players frankly dismiss older people with phrases like "over the hill" and "low-hanging fruit." In *One World*, Kat is visibly upset because she is beaten in a challenge by an "old" woman, Kim, who is 28. Many of the attractive, athletic, middle-aged players get nicknamed Mama or Papa or, in *Marquesas*, "Pappy." In *Pan-*

ama, the tribes were divided into four groups: "young men," "older men," "young women," and "older women." One of the young men immediately named the female tribes the Spice Girls and the Golden Girls. The average age of the Golden Girls was 40. Vince, painfully competitive from the first moments of the game, says plaintively, "I was young once, too. I'm 32 now."

In season 18, in the Tocantins region of Brazil, the tribes arrived on trucks; while they travel, you hear their thoughts in voice-over. One young man says of his tribemate Sandy, "We have the strung-out old lady, and it *is* kind of encouraging to have her, because you know you're not going to be the first to go." He has fallen for a common myth. Sometimes the first player voted out is the oldest, but this is actually uncommon; many older players go a long way. They are more composed and usually much better at manipulation. In 40 seasons, the average age of the winners was 31; the oldest was 57. On *Kaôh Rōng*, Joe, 71 years old, makes it to the final five. The reward challenge—best reward of the season, a night at a spa—is a run-into-the-jungle-and-get-sandbags-to-throw-at-targets challenge. Joe is far behind everyone in the running section. He's still gathering sandbags while everyone else is throwing at the targets. But they all miss too many times. Alone, he tosses, and gets the last target with his very last bag. (Karma is a bitch. At the spa, Joe gorges on meat and rich sauce. He comes back to camp sick and is pulled from the game the next day by the doctor.)

The bias toward youth is often posited as a need for strong players to win challenges, but age doesn't mean weakness and youth doesn't mean strength. In *China*, Courtney, 26, was almost unable to lift a machete, and frankly didn't seem to be trying very hard when she had to, grimacing and whining and looking helplessly at her teammates as she ever so slowly sawed through a rope that everyone else ripped through in seconds. Back at camp she complained that the machete gave her blisters. The common misperception—even now, after 40 seasons proving the opposite—is that strong men are better players. But strong men often have lousy game. They need too many calories and aren't used to cooperating. They may be completely unable to do a puzzle, walk along a thin balance beam, or squeeze through narrow tunnels. Muscles just get in the way if you're trying to balance eight people on a very small platform. When this challenge was run on *Kaôh Rōng*, the feet of Scot Pollard, a former NBA player, were bigger than the entire platform. (He was just able to hold everyone on his team for the few seconds they needed to win.) On *Tocantins*, a challenge required players to simply hold an increasing amount of weight on a bar across their shoulders. The record, from *Pearl Islands*, had been set by Rupert, a really large man who was able to hold 220 pounds. But J.T., slim and wiry, also manages 220 pounds. In the end, two women are left, and Taj wins. She is 37 years old and holding 100 pounds on her back. (Both records have since been broken.) In *Survivor: Nicaragua*, a challenge simply required people to lean over water while hanging on to a knotted rope. It was won by Jane, a stringy 56-year-old dog trainer. In *Marquesas*, Paschal, the oldest player at 56, won the last challenge you would expect, a daunting one requiring players to dive multiple times to retrieve shells and then race underwater with a 40-pound rock.

In *Palau*, the tribes were clearly unequal in physical strength. They faced a challenge that seemed to be all about strength and stamina. Each tribe was roped together, given heavy bags to carry, and then set to chasing each other through shallow water while the tide rose around them. The big, strong guys look smug; *this will be quick.* But they are carrying their own weight as well as the bags, and slogging a lot of mass through the surf. It took a while, but the weaker tribe—thinner, smaller, and much more efficient—won.

One immunity challenge, "a *Survivor* classic," in Jeff's words, is called "Get a Grip." It's a simple hang-on-a-pole-as-long-as-you-can event. The weird scene is unmistakably *Survivor.* A sunny white sand beach, tropical greenery, lapping ocean, and a line of poles about 25 feet tall, each painted a different color with thin black stripes to mark tiny ridges in the wood. On each pole hangs a person, arms and legs wrapped tightly while the sun beats down. On *Game Changers*, Tai, a tiny Vietnamese gardener, went up against Ozzy, 17 years his junior and perhaps the best athlete in the history of the game. Ozzy had already won this challenge twice in previous seasons. But Tai hangs on, and at a little over 90 minutes, Ozzy slips.

The tenth season on Palau was divided in such a way that one tribe, as Ian put it, was "the wise tribe," with "a little bit of the old folks," and unfortunately "we're up against the young bucks." The first challenge was an obstacle course; each team had to choose which heavy boxes of supplies they wanted and then carry them through and over a maze, fences, walls, and a swamp. The winning tribe got to keep whatever they carried. The young tribe grabbed everything. The older tribe—the wise tribe—chose just one box, the fire supplies, and they won easily. In a later challenge, players had to swim out to a shipwreck and dive down to release bottles. The older tribe won again, methodical and calm, while the younger tribe grew harried. Ibrehem, easily the strongest guy in the game, couldn't figure out how to untie the knots.

On *Thailand*, the game begins when the oldest man and the oldest woman are forced to pick tribes. Jan, the woman, is terribly flustered, in tears. (Let's face it, Jan's an odd one. She cries at the nod of a head, has a breakdown when she finds a dead embryonic bat, and buries the chicken's feet and head in her "pet cemetery.") Jan picks older people for her team, by and large, leaving the younger and fitter players to the other tribe. The men are dismayed. "I don't want to be on the little old lady tribe!" one complains. Mark Burnett wrote later, "We had analyzed the scenario a hundred times but had never considered that anyone would be crazy enough to choose all the older, unfit, and slower players." Even Burnett falls for it, assuming that the team would be destroyed and it would "make for somewhat pathetic television." When they arrive at their respective beaches, the younger tribe, called Sook Jai, swings from vines and climbs trees rather than trying to make camp. Robb is triumphant. "That other team, they're definitely inferior to our youth and our strength, and we definitely've got all the hot chicks, or most of them, and we definitely got the young, strong guys, which is huge." They go skinny-dipping and stay up half the night. When it starts to rain, they have no shelter. They seem to have given no thought to shelter at all, or to fire, water, or food. (One of the slogans of the actual survival show *Survivorman* is "You're either dealing with weather, or you're preparing for weather." Not building shelter is always a dumb move.) "We're horrible campers, we're terrible outdoorsmen," says one of the women. "We are *starving*!" They win a fishing net but can't get fish. "Nobody's ever lived on the beach, nobody's ever been around the water," says Jake. "We don't really know how to work it." But the little old lady tribe does; they're doing okay.

In a reward challenge, the tribes must race to steal supplies from each other while getting past other players. This seems like a strength challenge, one the youngsters should win going away. But the young men are too aggressive; they flout the rules, get kicked out of the challenge, and the tribe self-destructs. As the season wears on, the entire Sook Jai team is eliminated before the end of the game: the hot chicks and the young, strong guys are all gone. The final four are 34, 46, 47, and 53 years old. The little old lady comes in third.

On *Palau*, Ian is a 23-year-old dolphin trainer; Tom is a 40-year-old firefighter. They have been friends as well as allies, but there is a strong element of parent and child in their friendship. Ian confides in Tom; Tom puts a paternal hand on Ian's shoulder now and then. It's a brittle alliance. Ian says, "If I win the challenge, Tom goes home. If I don't win the challenge, all of a sudden, Tom's my best friend again." One day, Tom tosses off a throwaway line about how Ian is immature, that he doesn't yet understand commitment. Tom knows exactly what he's doing. It's a firecracker in the ammunition dump of Ian's mind.

Tom, Ian, and Katie, the final three, compete in a last challenge: standing barefoot on a tiny platform on a swaying buoy in the bay. Katie lasts a few hours, and then falls in. But Tom and Ian go on and on. Through the sun and the rain and into the night. After almost 12 hours, Ian offers to step down. He'll give up the chance at immunity, at winning the game, just because of what Tom said.

"I'll give up the million, to get back you guys' friendship," he says. In the dark above the water, under the starlight speckling the ocean, he talks about how he's dug himself a hole of deceit and he can't get out of it. Swaying, feet numb, back aching, he says he feels like a traitor and can't figure out what to do, how else to get back his integrity, how to escape the machinations of the game.

Jeff, sitting on the dock with Katie, says, "Nobody would have predicted *this* move."

Then Ian leaps into the water, and Tom wins immunity and takes Katie with him to the final. Katie is not well liked, and Tom sits beside her with confidence—the man who won challenges over and over, who fed his tribe, who stayed cool and got to the end. Tom was a master of a game of subtle manipulation, the old man who knew exactly where the buttons were, exactly how to push the young man down. A certain cohort of viewer really dislikes Tom for this, as though it was unfair for him to use what he knew about Ian to beat him. But I think it was nearly a perfectly played season. "Tom Westman won with honor," Jeff said later. "He gave Ian a life lesson."

The third season, called *Africa* (it took place in a part of Kenya), involved a bitter struggle between older and younger players featuring one of the most unpleasant players ever. Is she really like this? Is she a designated villain or a negative edit? To be honest, I don't know where to put this. Lindsey could go under the *annoying players* heading or the *clueless young women* heading or the *lazy sods* heading. Or here.

Frank, 42, seems to be the odd man out at first. He sets a blistering pace on the way to camp, yelling at people to "pick it up." Someone asks him what branch of the military he was in and he says, "I was in the American branch. It's called freedom." I can already see he's risking friendly fire. He says to the camera: "I spent nine months of softness in my mother's womb. Everything's hard when you come out." Frank sees meat everywhere he looks; I can imagine him doing okay in the Donner Party.

Frank is on the Samburu tribe, which is divided from the beginning, with four young people who are shown sleeping in and sunbathing while four older people do chores. (Sunbathing. In the grasslands of central Kenya. I don't get it.) Lindsey says that the older players—average age of 44—are "sucking up to us a little bit. So, yeah, if they'll go get the water and we don't need to help, why not? We want to save our strength." Brandon says the older folks are "conniving, miserable little people" because they want the others to work. Lindsey and Kim make friendship necklaces for their own cohort while Carl tries to fix the essential water jugs alone. Kim says, "It was flaunting right in your face, it's the four of *us*, and then there's the four of *you*. And yeah, it was definitely a slap in the face." Burnett compares the show to the workplace, but sometimes it feels like a ninth-grade breakup. *You're my best friend but you went to the mall on Saturday with Denise and you told me you weren't going to go and that was really mean and now I can't even talk to you anymore.*

In her pregame interview, Lindsey describes herself as having a "happy-go-lucky" personality. In the game she decides to be "shameless" in resting, "no reason to exert myself." One day she sunbathes until she is so dehydrated that she vomits. When she gets a few votes from older people at a Tribal Council—one in which the younger people are voting for one of the older people—she's furious. "They picked *me*, those *bastards*! I just got really *angry* and I just wanted to lash out, just being mad at those people for voting for me." At the campfire after Tribal she says, "I'm *seriously* pumped and trust me, when I'm pumped, you don't want to fuck with me."

I know that many people (and sometimes, I am one of them) watch this kind of thing with the fascination we feel as we slow down by a car wreck, but I found this season painful to watch. Some seasons go as quickly as a beach read, while others drag; *Africa* felt like it lasted for months. I wonder just how difficult it was to edit these character arcs; the actual players gave them a lot of material with which to work.

After several days, Frank has had enough of their laziness and decides to stand back and see what happens. See "how they run a household." Now that Frank isn't leading the walk to the water hole, they run out. "We were all dehydrated from the challenge severely," says one of the younger players, "and, I'm sure to prove a point to us, Frank and Linda and T let the water level get completely gone."

Then another water pot breaks and they have no way to boil the water. "My plan of attack," says Frank, "was, you know, to let the comfort level drop completely low, and I know they would break down. You could see that things were falling apart." At this point it is no longer a conflict between young and old. It is between toddlers and parents.

Then the producers create a scene. Three players from each tribe are switched, and the toddlers no longer have the numbers. The parents who have joined them aren't a bit happy with what they find. Frank has gone to the other tribe, but there's no relief for the kids. The new parents are just as pissed. While the parents get to work on improvements, the remaining toddlers take a nap. They can't see the freight train bearing down.

In episode 6, Lindsey has a blinding moment of insight. "When we had the upper hand, we treated Frank and Teresa poorly," she says. "Especially me. I gloated and I was excited and I felt like I was the queen of the land, which was a bad move on my part. And I think they were definitely out for some kind of revenge." And they are. Lindsey is voted out. An article on *E* at the time said, "She may be gone, but her screechy whimpering will forever live in our darkest nightmares."

SEX

Men have won *Survivor* about two-thirds of the time. (They also find more idols, because they look harder.) But there have been women in the final three in all but one season. Small women with no athletic skills often go far in the game, while strong young men do not. I doubt if this is the dynamic the producers expected; they seemed to anticipate some kind of natural selection that would root out women early. But women slide under the radar and manage the social game better than men. As time goes on, writes one academic, "The contestants have stopped underestimating women and now see their social skills as a threat."

I'm not so sure; the men still seem to underestimate the women all the time. On Season 35, one of the challenges requires players to throw a ball. Patrick blows the lead for his team by throwing and missing, over and over. He refuses to let Lauren have a chance. Lauren played outfield on a softball team for 25 years and "can hit a catcher in the forehead." But she's 35 and he says he can tell just by looking at her that she can't throw a ball. Their team loses. When the players on season 24, *One World*, discover that they are sharing a beach but in tribes divided by gender, the men are chill. They're sure that "they need us more than we need them." Then the women catch all the chickens, win a fishing kit and a canoe, and sneak over in the middle of the night to steal fire from the men. The season is a bit of a slog, thick with heterosexual bickering and flirting that climaxes, so to speak, in the bikini-clad women racing down an oiled slip-and-slide. I imagine a room full of editors guffawing at nipple shots and making fart jokes. When the tribes are mingled, a few of the women prove good at turning the men against each other, playing on their competitiveness and insecurity. *So-and-so said you weren't strong in challenges.*" "*Oh, yeah?*" Chelsea tells Troyzan (yes, that is his name; he's billed as a swimsuit photographer) to "take it like a man," and he goes into a sexist rant. When he wins immunity, he beats his chest, shouting, "This is my island!" And you can guess what happens next, how the season goes. The final five are all women.

Is the gaze always a male one? It is intrusive; it claims possession. But we are all gazing out of our own bounded bodies. The writer Andrea Long Chu claims that femaleness is the state "in which the self is sacrificed to make room for the desires of another," and that seems a pretty neat description of our relationship to screens these days. That means, Chu adds, that we are all female.

Survivor is deeply heteronormative. I used to imagine a season divided by sexual orientation, but there would be way too many tribes. Gender in *Survivor* is an ontology of convention. Between women, gender tension is about age and appearance. "Kass, she's just a bitter, ugly old lady. I think she hates me because I'm cuter than her, and I've always been cuter than her," says Morgan on *Cagayan*.

Kass is a perfectly attractive 41-year-old attorney. Between men, the tension seems to fall along conventional lines—competition for territory and power, with a side of homophobia. Hardly anyone can make fire, but for some reason making fire is still seen as masculine. In season 39 when Chelsea quickly gets fire going, Tom says, "You just ruined my male ego for the rest of my life." It's become abundantly clear that most men can't fish (and few women seem to try). Dr. Mike, a pudgy urologist who specializes in sexual dysfunction, is thrilled to catch a little fish with a spear gun. He says it's a moment that proves "I can do anything I put my heart and mind to." He's "providing for my tribe." "Do you feel like a man?" one of the women asks, with a studiously neutral expression. He takes her seriously and says yes. Then he accidentally drops the fish in the fire.

Are the sexist comments really so common, or are they simply cherished by editors? Brian is pleased to see his female tribemates washing dishes. "It's interesting to me, being out here in the wilderness," he muses to one of the men, "even after hundreds of thousands of years, the girls are still doing a very domesticated thing, and they enjoy it! Which I think is great. Kind of resorts back to the good old days, where the men just ate and the women did all the cooking and cleaning. It's quite an observation."

In *San Juan del Sur*, the men try to get rid of the women all season. Drew tries to throw the immunity challenge because he wants to vote out the "girls." He's confident because he's "a badass and the manipulator of this game." He says to the camera: "I don't know if they knew I was throwing it, but I could care less, because we need to start getting rid of some of the snakes on our tribe." He talks to a couple of the men. "Think about it, guys," he purrs, "I'm telling you. Let's get Kelley out tonight and then all these bitches don't know what to do other than come to us. Trust me, guys."

Kelley is standing a few feet away, listening to the entire speech. That night, Drew is voted out, and as he leaves, he says, "I knew all along those girls wanted me out of there." 'Cause he would have *beat* them. At the end, three women remain, looking at all the men on the jury.

In the same season, a boyfriend and girlfriend compete against each other and she wins. Jeff asks him how it feels to lose to his girlfriend. The man is John Rocker, a former Atlanta Braves player who got in trouble for making racist comments. He says, "Remove the friend part. I'm losing to a *girl*. I just got beat by a girl." Way to endear yourself to half the players, John. He's already been recognized by one of the Black players, who remembers the controversy. At the challenge, John body-blocks Natalie, an Indian woman, and she calls him a racist. He yells back that she's a "mouth" and needs to shut up. "If you were a man, I would knock your teeth out." He's voted out third.

In *Guatemala*, season 11, the players are given a compass and map and a few supplies, and sent on an 11-mile trek through the jungle. They bushwhack their way for almost 24 hours. Several of the young guys fall to the wayside. They vomit and faint. One man messes up his shoulder; another tears his bicep. The women are holding up fine. It's a good season to consider perception versus reality, because the men remain convinced that the women *just aren't strong enough to play the game*, while the evidence shows something else entirely. On one tribe, Lydia is a dog of work. She's never sick and usually wakes up first to do chores. The young guys (who are sleeping in and puking in the bushes) want to vote her off because she's "not athletic."

Judd says, "I'm just a freaking doorman from New York, man. I never even went camping." He is glad when the tribes are rearranged because he's gotten away from the other alpha males. Now he can let loose. "I know I'm the big gun around here, man. I know it. You feel like you're King Kong, man." Judd says whatever comes into his head, loses his temper, and insults the women. When he is voted out, he turns to the last five players—four women and Rafe, who calls himself "a little gay Mormon"—and spits, "Scumbags." Lydia comes in fourth.

On *Vanuatu*, another season with tribes divided by gender, things begin with a greased-pole-climbing-spiritual-mana-rock thing only for the men, leaving the women without an advantage. Then Chris, the lone chubby guy on the male team, almost single-handedly loses the first immunity challenge for the men. He is the symbolic female all season, hapless and weak. The women go on a winning streak but their alliance dissolves, is revived, dissolves, and shifts again. I am falling for it; I watch and wait for the weak, chubby guy and the oldest women to be voted off, as of course they must be. The final three players are the weak, chubby guy and the two oldest women.

Chris wins a million dollars.

On *Pearl Islands*, one alliance of men becomes convinced that the women have no strategy. When there are only two men and three women left—notice the ratio?—the men still feel absurdly confident. They are sure the women haven't even thought of ganging up on them, so they go on a reward together and leave the women alone. The "girls" don't have the men's "intellectual advantage" and have been "riding coattails the entire time," says Burton. When they return, he checks with Sandra: Hey, are you secretly planning to vote me out? She clutches her pearls and says, Oh, of *course* not. I trust *you*. I would *never*. He asks her to show him her hands, so he knows she's not crossing her fingers. Since Burton is convinced that women are not "good liars," this is enough for him.

Jon, with his trademark smirk, says to the camera, "All three girls are dumb. There's no 'they share a brain.' I don't think they even share a whole brain, or obviously they would have figured out, 'Hey, we can get rid of these guys.'" This is Jon Dalton speaking and he is deliberately playing a villain; he said he wanted to be the most hated player ever and he may have succeeded in that, so one doesn't take him at face value. But. He says it. "I'm the king of men and they're women. There's a huge difference. If it's a getting-pregnant contest, they can probably win. But other than that, no." (At this point, one of the women has won immunity three times in a row.) "I think it's downright foolish that they didn't talk, but I felt and will continue to feel that I'm smarter than they are, anyway. Kind of par for the course." Of course, the women have had a plan the whole time; they've even staged fake arguments as a smokescreen. That night, in what proves to be a very popular episode with viewers, the women vote Burton out and leave Jon high and dry. He gets taken to the final three as a perfect goat and Sandra wins a million dollars. It's a satisfying conclusion, except for the fact that Dalton won some money. That's a shame.

Lust is a useful tool, wielded properly. Many players are wonderfully fit—dumb as oxen, some of them, but nice to look at. The Rarotonga tribe in *Cook Islands* has a lot of beefcake. Four shirtless young men sit by the fire in a fog of entitlement. J.P. hollers for a drink of water and a piece of wood. Parvati, lithe, barely clothed, laughs her throaty laugh and complies. "You have to find the best way to infiltrate," she says. For her that is sex, the scent of sex, the promise. Parvati constantly flatters the men in small ways, touching their arms, laughing at their jokes. It's like water torture; drop by drop, she breaks them down until they can't think straight. It's all painfully obvious to the viewer, but many of the men seem bamboozled. It works; J.P. is the fourth one voted out, and Parvati lasts until day 36.

Survivor functions with a weird inverse equation, in which people who are the most desirable sexual partners seem the least capable of survival. It's anti-evolution. "I want to smack 'em with a fried pineapple," says Rocky about two women who keep talking about makeup and fashion. In Thailand, Penny tries flirting when the tribes come together. Says Clay, who is long married, "She thinks her looks and her little talent can get whatever she wants out of men. Well, I'm 46. She ain't getting shit from this one."

The *Cagayan* season began with three tribes, named Brains, Brawn, and Beauty. Early on, the Beauty tribe wins three chickens and a rooster. The following conversation ensues.

"Does, like, the rooster have to get it on with one of the hens to make eggs?" asks Alexis.

"I was wondering that," says Morgan.

A guy says no.

"So the eggs keep happening?" Alexis asks. "So what's the rooster for?"

One of the guys says, "To make chicks."

Later, to the camera, Alexis says, "There's been some talk about how this egg chicken process works. But I really think everyone is just pretending to know and they don't know."

The show cuts back to everyone standing around the chicken cage. Alexis says, "So are they, like, asexual? What makes them make eggs?"

Jefra says, "They have to be in a thing, like a—heat lamp." She sounds uncertain.

Cut to LJ, alone. "Nobody knows how a chicken is born. I don't understand—" He starts laughing and can't stop for a minute. "I can't even believe that some of this stuff comes out of people's mouths."

Cut back to the group around the cage. LJ asks one of the young women, "Don't you carry eggs?"

She answers, "Oh, so like another—*ooohhh.*" Something begins to dawn on her face. Cut back to LJ alone: "We have the stereotypical Beauty tribe, and it's just so unfortunate."

The Amazon was the first season divided by gender. The ploy was a headline story at the time. "It's a huge risk," Burnett said at the time, "but you have to be brave and just do it." He worried that the show relied a little on sexual tension and assumed this would be missing on same-gender teams. (He doesn't know from racism, and he doesn't seem to know from sexual tension, either.) At the start of the season, Jeff explains that the Amazon got its name from a female tribe of warriors. Then he repeatedly refers to the women as "ladies," somewhat undermining the point. A few players are disappointed. Ryan, a model, had a "game plan" that's useless on an all-male tribe where it's "one big sausage fest." Jenna, also a model, feels the same. "You can't use any of your womanly powers on women." Where have these people been living?

The editing was pretty ham-handed, with lots of time spent making the women look incompetent and squeamish and the men look tough and strong. Rob C., whose luxury item was a Magic 8-Ball, laughs about how the women must be so discouraged since they didn't have "any idea they'd be doing this on estrogen alone, over there in Camp of the Vagina Monologue." The men spend a lot of time talking about sex and dissing the women and assuming, in Rob's words, they're "all crying, panicking, trying to build a cell phone so they can call their boyfriends and help them build a shelter." The women scream about tarantulas and Deena fulfills the symbolic dyke role when she kills one. The players aren't supposed to swim because of crocodiles, but some of the young men consider this cowardly and bully each other into swimming anyway. I found myself hoping for an attack. Alas.

Okay, I hated this season. Lots of viewers enjoyed it for all the reasons I did not. All this awfulness—Shawna collapsing in tears because they don't win Coca-Cola; the men suddenly realizing they could try *baiting* a hook—is what the editors choose to leave in. What was left out? The story line of weak women and tough men is a setup. This way, when the women beat the men in the first immunity challenge, it's supposed to be a satisfying surprise—in one commenter's words, the show was "fulfilling a modified bourgeoisie nightmare." The women go on to win four of the first five challenges and half of the challenges before the merge. The first person voted out is a strong young man; so is the third one. Then a new story line emerges, that of the men being afraid of being beaten by the women.

The older women work and get annoyed with the younger women, who are in turn annoyed at being woken up by the sounds of wood chopping and fire building. Heidi says that her tribe has "the bigger women that have more fat to live on that, obviously, can put out more effort, as far as manual work. Then you've got the smaller girls, that are like the stay-at-home women." Heidi was thin to begin with and has lost so much weight that her breast implants look like hybrid grapefruit stapled to her chest. (Supposedly Heidi had the highest IQ of the season. She certainly wasn't edited that way.) JoAnna tells her, "Beauty will fade with time, but only your virtue and your character is what's going to last." Heidi's response: "I'm really not sure how that quote fit in with anything, except maybe she was just trying to pick on the fact that we were cute girls."

Jenna says to the camera, "Don't be mad because we have good bodies. It's not our fault. Get over it! Me and Heidi are definitely the skinnier of the group, and better looking, but I think it's definitely a liability." The three young women go to the swimming hole to bathe, stripping down and admiring each other. They talk about how nice it is to be alone, be private, be able to let their hair down (that is, their bikini tops) and not be "judged." All of this is in front of the cameras, of course.

Soon they form new tribes, mixing men and women. A group bathes in the pond together. Washing involves a lot of what Deena, who is a decade older, calls "monkey grooming." "This is how they work them," she says. "I know where the players are playing, and I know where the players *aren't* playing."

I can barely keep describing this season; it seemed to go on forever. One of the best moments occurs late in the season when the shelter burns down. Most of their food, bedding, and clothes are lost, along with their luxury items. Even the Magic 8-Ball is lost. Jenna, for reasons I don't feel like articulating because they are painfully obvious, had her sorority pledge crown and jacket with her in the Amazon jungle, and she's heartbroken by the loss.

Yet Jenna will win. This is the season in which spoilers became a big deal. ChillOne did his research and correctly predicted that the final two players were Jenna and Matthew, a quiet, odd man with a formal intelligence. Many people have speculated that the spoilers forced the editors to give Jenna a negative edit to throw viewers off the scent. I was rooting for Matthew to go all the way, but Jenna won a million dollars.

The low queer quotient leads to the inevitable. In *Pearl Islands*, the two bros, Shawn and Burton, tease Rupert, a big, goofy man wearing a tie-dye shirt. He tires of them quickly. "It's like high school. The pretty-boy jock-ass idiots all got to pick on me." When the young men finally manage to catch a fish, they strut around camp. Rupert takes the spear gun and comes back a while later with six fish and no comment. (Rupert's done okay. He's played three times. The second time, on *All-Stars*, he won the fan favorite award in the "America's Tribal Council" vote by a landslide, which included a separate million-dollar prize. The producers immediately saw the mistake in such a big reward; players could just be charming or eccentric instead of trying to win. That's not how you play the game.)

In *Nicaragua*, Shannon demanded that Sash admit he was gay during the second Tribal Council; later he said he did this in order to "protect his butthole." He was promptly voted out. In *Palau*, James is beaten by Coby in a wrestling match on a raft over a lagoon. "It feels terrible having my butt whupped by a homosexual, you know," he says in a Louisiana drawl. "But a lot of gay folks are strong, man. They all working out at the gym and all, you know. Damn." During the first season on Borneo, Rudy, the elderly Navy SEAL, said of Richard Hatch, an out gay man, "The homosexual is one of the nicest guys I met." On *All-Stars*, Richard catches a small shark by hand. Colby asks, "Is it possible to call a gay man a stud?" It seems that every time people mention Hatch's name they also mention that he's gay. In *San Juan del Sur*, a gay couple is split between tribes. The youngest woman immediately approaches the man on her tribe and asks him to join the women's alliance because he's like a "girlfriend," halfway between the men and women. He is obviously offended, but she's oblivious.

On *Fiji*, Anthony is always on the outside. He's a Black video game aficionado who lives with his grandmother, and he's on a tribe with four young frat-bro types. One of the men calls him a "little bitch." Anthony calls himself the "Black male Cinderella." He isn't invited when the other men go out to fish, and speaks to the camera in a creaky Western voice: "Ol' Cookie's been left by the fire, to tend the fire and make the water while the boys go out huntin'." He tries to call one of the men out at Tribal Council that night, and gets a nasty lecture about acting like a man. It works: Anthony is voted out.

On *Game Changers*, the players included Zeke Smith, a 29-year-old asset manager who first played in *Millennials vs. Gen X*. In that season, Zeke appeared to be a fairly relaxed, intelligent guy with a degree from Harvard in religious studies and not a lot of baggage. On *Game Changers* Zeke makes an alliance with Jeff Varner, a 51-year-old real estate agent, also gay. Then Varner starts undermining Zeke. At Tribal Council, with a stunning lack of judgment, Varner declares that there is a lot of deceit by certain players, and outs Zeke as transgender. The group erupts with indignation at this—not at the fact of it, but at the spilling of a personal secret. Varner backpedals, saying, "I thought he was out and proud and loud," but Jeff catches that. Look, he points out, either you can say he's out and it's okay, or you can say it's deception, but it can't be both. Varner then claims that he thought everybody in the world knew Zeke was transgender *except* the people sitting at Tribal Council.

By the end, everyone but Varner is feeling warm and fuzzy. There are tears and hugs and the whole show is self-actualization-and-personal-growth-enhancing for everybody. After a few nods, Varner is out when Jeff cuts to the chase and just asks for a show of hands. Then he declares that it was "ultimately a beautiful night that will never be forgotten."

The mainstream media erupted the day the episode aired—media that paid scant attention to *Survivor* most of the time. Opinion columns (some solicited by CBS in advance) were published even before the show aired. Many of the real-time comments were predictable, from the outraged to the snide, but only a few people noted that Varner didn't out Zeke to the world. CBS did.

In fact, CBS planned for months before the episode was shown. Said Jeff Probst, "The idea of not airing this never came up." Duh. The network claims Zeke never asked for it to be kept off the air, but what would they have done if he had? This is the kind of moment that producers live for (and for which draconian contracts are written). In *Slate*, David Canfield wrote a thoughtful column, noting that *Survivor* is "a heavily, at times deceptively edited program" that still sometimes "showcases raw social dynamics." Canfield knows how little we viewers can know about what really happened, then or at any other time. Maybe the scene was edited to be a lot warmer and fuzzier than it really was. But in the end, Canfield thought it was valuable. "It isn't every day that millions of Americans watch a trans person at the center of their favorite show, playing the hero." Zeke, a self-admitted super-fan of *Survivor*, said later that the show had "integrity," that old trope, helping CBS to toot its own horn about how sensitive the network and the show's producers were to him. ("Gender," writes Andrea Chu, "is something other people have to *give* you.") Meanwhile, Jeff Varner ain't getting any of that love. He's hung out to dry. He got to spend the entire week apologizing in abject shame for "the worst decision" of his life, and later said that he was fired and threatened and is now in therapy.

When the dust settles, the game goes on without much discussion.

P eople end up in their underwear a lot on *Survivor*, and swimsuits begin to gape as the players lose weight. (Why isn't *Survivor* played in cold climates? Duh.) Many scenes have discreetly blurred spots. A shot of one male player's genitals actually made it onto the air in *Gabon*, forcing CBS to apologize for once. Considering all the other ways that people expose themselves, this modesty dictated by FCC rules seems pretty silly. Nudity is common on *Survivor* around the world; the Australians don't hesitate to strip. During an immunity challenge in *Amazon*, Jeff offered the players food if they would quit the challenge. Instead, Heidi and Jenna offered to take off their shirts in exchange for peanut butter and chocolate—which they got. And let's not forget the monkey grooming.

Richard Hatch was renowned for being naked much of the time, but he protested that many other players were, too—they just weren't edited that way. There are plenty of examples to prove his point. (Thank you, Way Back Machine.) On the eighth season, *All-Stars*, Richard Hatch stripped at the start of most challenges. His insistence on running the courses naked is both obnoxious and good strategy, because people stay away from him. But one challenge is a narrow balance beam race where everyone is banging into everyone else and wrestling for control. Hatch and Sue come face to face, and he bangs into her for a second. She doesn't seem fazed other than to say it was "uncalled for." But by the next day, it's become a different story, a traumatic event. She can't let it go. "Why didn't he just walk by me?" "I've been with one partner for twenty years!" "I was sexually violated!" she shouts at Jeff. "I was violated, humiliated, dehumanized, and totally *spent!*" What I saw was a big naked gay guy bumping into her in a rough, physically demanding game. But he said and she said, and I will never know. We will never know for sure. Sue quits. Jeff just calls in the boat.

In *Thailand*, Ghandia and Ted are close from the beginning; they talk, play games, and sleep beside each other. One morning, Ghandia is upset. She takes Ted aside and confronts him angrily, claiming he was "grinding into her" in the night. He apologizes, several times; she accepts his apology and they hug.

But Ghandia starts telling the others that Ted is sexually harassing her. Ted calmly tries to defend himself, but by then Ghandia is hollering, calling him a "liar" and a "cheat." Finally, Ted says he was having a dream about his wife, and got aroused. He says he's not even attracted to Ghandia.

"Your version of what happened," she says, and then creates a real scene: screaming and punching a log. She says to the camera, "I accepted his apology, but I felt that everyone in the tribe should know what he did. The only part I left out is that he apologized." The opinion on all this seems divided along gender lines, and at the next Tribal Council, she tries to further the divide. But Ghandia is voted out. Too much drama.

Several episodes later, in a special reel of "never-before-seen footage," we see scenes of the tribe watching while Ghandia poses like a lingerie model for Ted, who is pretending to be a fashion photographer. They refer to her as "the diva queen." There are more scenes of the two of them cuddling and whispering. By leaving these out of the episode, Ted looks more like a bad guy. By adding them to a special episode, Ghandia looks calculating. The whole Ghandia/Ted thing is a weird version of the *Survivor* #metoo moment. There is no sign that there was ever a legal challenge. (Ghandia is still talking about it; she recently gave an interview in which she called her experience on *Survivor* "one of the worst things that has ever happened to me in my whole entire life.")

Edgicers have shown that women are edited differently from men, based on number of scenes, confessionals, words spoken, questions asked. *Amazon* aired in 2003. Times have changed, though not as fast as some may have hoped. On *Island of the Idols*, more than 16 years later, Kellee makes a point at Tribal Council. There are often worries about a women's alliance forming, she says. No one ever talks about an alliance of men. A final three of women is considered a big deal. No comment if the final three are men. She isn't just saying that it's more common for men to win or that a tribe in which men try to dominate is typical. We *expect* men to dominate, to win, and are only surprised when they don't. But she's also hit on something deeper, something hard for all of us to see, which is that maleness is the default of our lives. When a man does something, the attention is on the task. When a woman does it, the attention is on her. We don't see men as a cohort, and we should.

Jeff tells her that he is aware we're in a shifting cultural moment. He has said he wants the show to reflect the culture, to be "of the moment." After Kellee's speech, there's a lot of mush about what a fantastic Council this has been. So groundbreaking and bonding. So honest. Then it's time to vote. Jeff ends with a little speech. "Well, it's nights like tonight that have kept *Survivor* relevant for going on twenty years. Because you take a group of people and you force them to make their own society, and quite often, that society that you form is a reflection of the greater society and then the twist, you gotta vote 'em out." Because you know Kellee isn't going to last.

There was another interesting moment toward the end of the most recent season, *Winners at War*. At the last Tribal Council, with two men and a woman remaining, Sarah stands up to ask her jury question and makes a short speech. "If a woman in this game lies or cheats or steals, then she's fake and phony and a bitch," she says. "If a guy does it, it's good game play. If a guy does it, they're a stud." This season is entirely winners, players who have already dominated the game. But the imbalance persists even there. Tony has played like a ferret on Adderall and no one calls it out. Sarah Lacina wants the right to play with the same aggression and not have it spotlighted. Jeff says—because what else is he going to say, what could he possibly say?—"We are in a cultural shift, and it's beautiful, and it's powerful." He adds, "I'm certain, right now, if I were to look back at all of the comments I have made over twenty years, I would find the exact same bias in me. And I don't think I saw it when *Survivor* started. I don't think I even knew I was supposed to look for it." Then Sarah tells him to call her by her last name, as he often does with men. In one of his lists of favorite *Survivor* moments, Jeff listed the time when Heidi and Jenna took their shirts off. Would he still?

After the season ended, Juliet Litman wrote in *The Ringer*: "Sarah's speech at the third-to-last tribal council was not a revelation. Anyone who has watched two or more seasons of *Survivor* is aware of the gender bias that frequently leads to a woman, especially a woman of color, getting voted out first. But rarely does a show in its 40th season have the interest or capability to acknowledge one of its most insidious flaws. I've never been a big Sarah fan, but I admire her, and hopefully she'll have a long-term impact on the show. If nothing else, Jeff Probst will start calling more women by their last names. It may be small, but it matters."

Then there's Dan Spilo, on *Island of the Idols*. Kellee's comment about men didn't come out of nowhere. Dan lays his head on the women's legs, plays with a woman's hair, gives neck rubs without being asked. The women only complain to each other, because they "don't want to ruffle feathers." Jamal says of Dan, "Dan has that quick-talking, used-car salesman vibe to him that just makes you feel icky." How do you say no without making an enemy? "You can't make a scene," one woman says to another. Kellee: "You can't do anything about it. There's always consequences for standing up." But of course they can stand up. There are five women and one Dan. (After comforting Kellee, two of the women, Missy and Elizabeth, admit that they had exaggerated their discomfort; their goal is simply to get another player eliminated.) At one point, Kellee is unloading in a confessional and suddenly the fourth wall breaks backward, with a male producer speaking from behind the camera: "You know, if there are issues to the point where things need to happen, come to me and I will make sure that stops." Kellee says, "Much as I feel disrespected by him and feel disgusted by him, I'm not going to make a game decision based off of those feelings. I'm upset by the way he's been behaving, and that is the fair thing to do, but this game is not fair. I'm not playing this game to be fair. I'm playing this game to win."

Then the screen goes black and these words appear: "The following morning the producers met with all the players, both as a group and individually. They were cautioned about personal boundaries and reminded that producers are available to them at all times. Based on the outcome of those discussions, the game continued. In addition, producers met privately with Dan, at which time he was issued a warning for his behavior."

At a messy, unpleasant Tribal Council, everyone unloads on every side of the issue. People are pointing fingers and offering to quit and insisting that people speak up and insisting that no one can insist they speak up. Dan is made to apologize without seeming to really understand why. And for the nth time, someone says, "Perception is reality." At the end of the next to last episode, Jeff shows up at camp to tell the tribe that Dan has been taken off the show altogether and won't be on the jury. A black screen flashes the words, "Dan was removed from the game after a report of another incident, which happened off-camera and did not involve a player."

The network later said that Dan had touched a female producer on her thigh when he was getting into a boat. In an interview, Jeff Probst said, "We all worked diligently throughout the entire process to make the right decisions and portray an accurate depiction of what took place. We have learned a lot and it will inform our process moving forward." He apologized to Kellee as well, saying, "You were right to speak up. You were right to step forward despite a lot of risk and to speak your truth. And I want to acknowledge and apologize for your pain."

After the show aired, Spilo issued a lengthy apology for making people uncomfortable and later told a photographer that he wasn't allowed to comment further: "I wish I could comment, believe me."

Missy and Elizabeth told *People* that they were just playing the game, helping to put a target on Spilo's back. Elizabeth: "If I had felt uncomfortable, I would have said, 'Please stop.'" Not coincidentally, they helped put a target on Kellee's back as well, and voted for her to be eliminated.

With many hours of filming and barely 40 minutes of air time, who knows? What we see are whispered conversations and false assurances and sidelong glances, half-secret malleable plans that conflict with each other, and the season becomes an object lesson in poor communication. The players generate material, but the producers create the story. Perception is reality. And editing is perception for the rest of us.

Jeff Probst announced recently that nudity would no longer be allowed on the show. That'll show them.

RACE

Survivor has a big old race problem. More than 80 percent of the winners are white. The majority of contestants are white and few seasons have had more than one or two players of color. Two people of Asian descent have won, and one Hispanic—Sandra, though she has won twice. In 40 seasons, there have been four Black winners, and only one was a woman. In *Fiji*, the final three were two Black men and a Black woman; it would have been a victory for diversity except for the fact that the cast had been recruited for racial balance. But the recruiting did not sit well with fans (the mostly white fans), some of whom apply for the show year after year. Though clearly some players are recruited—and returning players are individually invited—deliberate diversity like that done for *Fiji* and *Cook Islands* has not been tried again (with the expected result). I understand that racial categories are socio-political constructions, variously defined and often erroneously applied; this doesn't change the fact that most people behave as though it were otherwise. (An awful lot of things are constructed this way, like money, gender, and family.) And no matter how we define or view racial identity, those identified by the vague marker of "white" are a minority. *Survivor*, which in Burnett's words is a "way of providing men and women with an opportunity to discover who they really are," appears to be a world run and populated by that minority.

Most of the time, the episodes as aired just ignore race, in spite of the fact that it remains problematic. On the recent season *Island of the Idols*, Missy says during Tribal Council that no one has even mentioned the fact that two African-American contestants were wearing the immunity necklace at the same time, and this should have been called out. "Women typically are the first voted out," she says. "Minorities are the second." Jeff answers that it didn't occur to him this was unusual and (more to the point), he would have been reluctant to call it out because he doesn't want it to seem like it's anything unusual. Then Missy is voted out.

What is diversity? In *Guatemala*, Jamie, a blandly handsome water ski instructor, says, "We got the most diverse group there. We got a bum—" He points at himself—"We got a police officer. We got a magician's assistant. We got a fishmonger. We got a gay guy, and we got a landscaper." Notwithstanding that gay is not a profession and the landscaper is actually a former NFL quarterback, they are all white and all but one is young. Players of color know more about how this works: the way one gazes out of one's skin, but is gazed upon only *as* skin. Gervase was one of two Black players in the first season. Later he recalled a challenge requiring spear-throwing. "Someone said, 'Gervase, throw a spear.' I said, 'No way is Gervase touching this.' If I won, people would think, 'Ah, that Gervase is a spear chucker from Africa.' If I lost, it's 'How can he lose? He's a spear chucker from Africa.'"

Julia Carter grew up watching the show and says she had a great time playing on *Edge of Extinction* in 2019. But she wrote an essay afterward, calling out the producers on their editing. Carter says that there were multiple episodes of racism, including use of the N-word, during the game, that these were followed by long discussions, that she spoke about the racial issues at length in a confessional and was apologized to by the producers—and that none of this was shown. Instead, her own story arc was shortened until she was shown only in passing.

I hadn't watched *Edge of Extinction* before I read this essay. If I hadn't read the essay, I probably wouldn't remember her name, because Julia is barely seen on camera until the fifth episode. You can see in fleeting glances at the background that she's good in challenges and works hard around camp and gets along with the other players. But her first confessional, a brief comment, happens in the sixth episode. She is seen speaking at Tribal Council for the first time in the seventh episode. She isn't shown talking about strategy until the eighth episode, where she is suddenly being courted as a swing vote. And then she's voted out. I read up on her Edgic score: a few Invisible, a few Middle-of-the-Road, lots of Under the Radar, and one Complex Personality. That is not a winner's arc. But the strange thing about this season is that the actual winner, Chris—a young white man—seems to have no more screen time than Julia, perhaps less. He's voted out early and sent into exile, only to return toward the end. This season drove the Edgicers crazy. I wasn't the only viewer who thought, "Chris? Who?" when he suddenly reappears. And then wins a million dollars.

There was another Black player on *Edge of Extinction*, Keith. He is shown in the opening sequence struggling to swim and is the second person voted out.

Players look around their tribe in the first minutes of the game, thinking about alliances. Who do I trust? And who may already be allied—the two young frat guys? The three young women? The two Black players? With the exception of *Cook Islands*, I've never heard anyone worry about an alliance of white folks. On a tribe with nine white folks and one Black person, there is *always* an alliance of white folks. People of color are almost always the "only one"—the only Latino, the only Indian, and so on. They have to find their way into an alliance like sidekicks.

So when there are two Black players on the same tribe, everyone else assumes they have an alliance. Vecepia, who won in *Marquesas*, is the only Black woman to win *Survivor*, and the first Black woman to win a reality show. Early in the season, Sean and Vecepia realize that they will be seen as allies no matter what they do. Sean says, "When you're a person of color and you're the only one, you have to play, and that's something they don't even have to worry about. See, everybody can just be themselves. We have to be ourselves but then hold back a little bit," says Sean. Vecepia sees it: "I can just tell what people are going to say." Sean laughs. "Yeah, those two ungrateful Negroes. You take them on an island and they still complain."

Toward the end, five players are left: Sean; Vecepia; Kathy, a middle-aged white woman; Paschal, a white judge from Georgia; and Neleh, a 19-year-old white Mormon woman. Paschal and Neleh have been openly allied from the start and have said they will never vote against each other. Vecepia says to Kathy, the obvious swing vote, that she and Sean are not in an alliance. But they might as well be. "They're going to look at us as two African Americans, regardless of what we talk about. They're going to say, okay, those two are in together." Paschal says this is *playing the race card*, that race doesn't matter. But perception is reality. Later Sean says, "From day one, myself and V never had a pact, although some people thought, 'Okay, there's the Black couple, they're definitely together.'" Later he says in private, "Just because V and I are African-American, we share a bond that you won't really be able to understand. Does that mean we're an automatic alliance? No." They assure the others that yes, of course they have a bond over shared experiences, but not an alliance.

Midway through the season, Sean and Paschal win a reward; they go horseback riding and are feted by locals, where they sit under a beach umbrella and drink cocktails. "Who knew that a little Black boy from Harlem would be here with a Southern white judge from Georgia?" says Sean. "I dig the fate in that, the irony in that." But the kindly judge hits the wall. He can't believe Sean and Vecepia don't have an alliance, which means they are lying to him. Of *course* they're in an alliance. They have to be. Just look at them. Paschal says to Kathy, "Well, believe me, it's cultural. It runs deep." *Culture* being a code word. Kathy agrees. "They're telling me they don't have a strong bond, and yet they're both Afro-American and I know that's very important in their culture, to stick together." At Tribal Council, Sean gets angry and says they haven't had a pact. But they will now—the white people obviously do.

Vecepia said recently that CBS has never invited her back to play.

*   *   *

Jolanda, a supremely fit lawyer from Houston who played in *Palau*, said that Burnett and Probst made racial comments during her audition. "The one that sticks out to me the most, this was before casting, 'So TV usually portrays Black women as angry Black women. How would you feel if we portrayed you as an angry Black woman?' I should have known what they were going to do, right? I should have known, because they told me what they were going to do."

Jolanda in *Palau*. JoAnna in *Amazon*. Candace in *Tocantins*. Yasmin in *Samoa*. Alicia in *Australia*. They are all edited as Bossy Black Women, one of the worst stereotypes on the show. Crystal in *Gabon*. Stacey in *South Pacific*. NaOnka in *Nicaragua* is the crazy Black woman. Linda in *Africa* is the bossy, weird, religious Black woman. On the same season, Clarence is the muscular, lazy Black man. Natalie in *David vs. Goliath* is presented as bossy, cranky, unsmiling, critical, judgmental, and lazy. (Unlike many of the Bossy Black Women, Natalie seemed to give the editors a lot of ammunition for this portrayal.) When Jolanda took charge of a raggedy group, she was promptly dismissed as "*not* a team player." On *Fiji*, Sylvia, a Chinese architect, was asked to manage building the shelter; she was voted out a short time later for being an honorary Bossy Black Woman. Nick, in *Australia*, was portrayed as withdrawn and lazy, though he built furniture for everyone. In one scene he is shown sitting on a porch, eating chicken. (One observer wrote, "Words just fail.") When Cirie begins to consolidate power in a quiet way on *Game Changers*, Aubry calls her the "Black Italian godfather." Such is the woke state of *Survivor*.

In 2006, for the 13th season played in the Cook Islands, producers were getting a little desperate for a new twist. Ratings were declining a bit and it was common knowledge that the show had a race problem. So they recruited players and created four tribes divided by perceived race: whites, African-American, Asian-American, and Latino. (Parvati, one of the white players, said, "Different ethnic groups— I mean, is that kosher?") A lot of people thought it sounded horrid and many thought it *was* horrid. But there were interesting, perhaps unintended, consequences. The tribes were divided into two mixed tribes in just the third episode, separating the original cohorts. Then, about halfway through, players were given a chance to switch tribes. The only ones who did were two white players, who left their tribe to join the tribe with the other white players. Were they trying to join their original tribe, which is often seen as the safest alliance, or were they rejoining their race? Perception is reality, and both came to regret it. Their desertion left an imbalance of six players to four. But the four they left behind—an Asian-American woman, an Asian-American man, an African-American woman, and a Latino man, all of them fit and attractive and likable—formed a tight, strong tribe. They won challenge after challenge and ultimately became the final four. Perhaps the producers' motives are suspect and it was a blunt tool, but the result was really satisfying. Not a white player in sight except on the jury. Yul won a million dollars.

Recently, three of the players from that season talked about how it felt, the combined pressure to represent an entire minority while at the same time not having to be the only person of color around. "We're from different cultures," said Jenny Guzon-Bae, a Filipina lumped into the Asian-American group, which included two Koreans and a Vietnamese. "We didn't find that much in common." But she ended up liking the divisions, because "having race kind of peek in every once in a while was good to see because it does happen in our everyday world, too." The outcome was satisfying even for many of those voted out. Nate Gonzalez was called a race traitor by fans because he voted out other players of color, but still enjoyed the result. "The Hispanic dude, the pretty Black girl and the smart Asians took out Team Whitey with the fake brother who sold out his own people!"

I find it hard to believe that Jeff Probst hasn't noticed the absence of people of color in the show he produces and hosts. Really, why has it been this way? A recent photo of the editing team is one clue: almost entirely white men. Do the producers worry what will happen when white players no longer form the majority? When there is a real possibility, not as a fluke but as a given, that the final survivors won't be white? That the few white players might ally along racial lines? The show was posited as a new society. The lack of representation of the population as a whole—which can happen only because of bias toward the producers' own social cohort, subconscious or not, a cold calculation of ratings or not—seems weird for a show that's about starting from scratch. *Deserted tropical island. Simple life. Transformational journey.* Starting over. Let's.

In the summer of 2020, Jolanda Jones and Sean Rector formed the Black Survivor Alliance. At about the same time, J'Tia Taylor (now J'Tia Hart), cofounded The Soul Survivors Organization as "a collective focused on improving diversity, equity, and inclusion on *Survivor*." J'Tia, who played in *Cagayan*, has a PhD in nuclear engineering, but she was portrayed as simultaneously bossy and lazy, a truly negative edit. The first act of Soul Survivors was a petition addressed to the network and production company, as well as directly to Jeff Probst and Mark Burnett. The petition stated that *Survivor* should "reflect and honor the racial diversity of our society—both in front of and behind the camera" and made several demands: "equitable screen time and opportunities to participate in marketing and promotional events" for Black, Indigenous, People of Color (BIPOC), equal compensation and hiring on production teams, that *Survivor* "announce and enforce a 'zero tolerance' policy towards racism" on the show, and that the producers treat BIPOC players in such a way that "their portrayal does not perpetuate harmful stereotypes." CBS agreed to meet with several players and some months later, announced changes.

Many former BIPOC players have been frustrated that CBS made no comment on the calls for better representation in media during the 2020 Black Lives Matter protests. "They've got a big platform and people look up to someone like Probst," said Nate Gonzalez in July of 2020. "There are probably a lot of *Survivor* folks and fans who don't agree with Black Lives Matter. And I don't know, maybe they're worried about that audience more than us." After some time, CBS executives agreed to a meeting with representatives of the BIPOC groups. In November of 2020, CBS finally broke its silence and announced that the casts of all its reality shows would be half people of color in the next season. It only took 20 years.

THE TERRIFYING NATIVES

The first immunity challenge of the first season was a "quest for fire" in which the players race to light a line of torches along the beach, ending with the giant "Fire God." The sculpture is burned down in a late-night celebration under starry skies, as the music swells, like the climax of *Wicker Man*. It takes only a few days for the contestants to start decorating themselves with paint. Jeff Probst begins the season in Vanuatu by telling us that the country has "a fascinating history of cannibalism, where rituals like sorcery and black magic are still a part of daily life." Therefore, the season's opening credits have flashes of scary men with dark skin and tattooed faces and the music is full of guttural noise. As they arrive on the boat, the contestants are met by dozens of men and women in canoes, in traditional costume, yelling at them. They lead the players through a "rite of passage" in which the men must drink kava and climb a greased pole to get a "spiritual stone" that could give them power in the game. This is followed by the slaughter of a pig. According to one of Burnett's books, the players were really scared of the butchery, the black magic, and especially the "wild-looking natives."

A lot of this is tongue-in-cheek, but that doesn't make it harmless. Colonialism takes many forms. The colonial gaze is always on the *other*. *Survivor* routinely coopts the local culture for its own use on the one hand, and erases it on the other. In China Jeff notes that Buddhism teaches one to leave behind "worldly possessions," without noting that Buddhism isn't particularly welcome in China anymore. No matter, it's a good segue. They've hauled their luggage all the way up the long stairway to a temple and are wearing nice traveling clothes and dress shoes. But they will play the game with only what they are wearing. Then he gives each tribe a copy of *The Art of War*. If I take even one step back and look at the whole picture, the show's appropriation of—and third-grade-level understanding of—the cultures in which it films is appalling. *It's only a game*, I know. It's only a game *show*. It's tongue-in-cheek, it's ironic, it's a parody, it's just having fun. It kind of sucks.

The aesthetic is just another version of the fantasy of the wilderness Westerners have cultivated from Defoe through New Age shamanic voyages. In the beginning, players are divided into tribes with sham names taken from a local language. (The word *tribe* offends many Indigenous viewers, and there is a growing body of complaint about that.) On the first season, the soundtrack was largely classical music. But for many years now, the music has been a morass of sampling and world music at its worst: a cacophony of didgeridoos and synthesizer, tweaked to fit the landscape and shot through with grunts, shouts, hoots, and cries meant to evoke the savage. Most of this was composed by Russ Landau, who Burnett calls a "creative genius." (Landau left the show in 2013, but the soundtrack remains.)

The theme music is based on a Russian folk song; for each season he added what he calls "exotic layers." For China, he commissioned an all-female choir in Beijing to sing it in Mandarin, added a Chinese folk song, and then a little Buddhist drumming as well. The music fits right in to the rest of the aesthetic, I'll give it that. Before production starts, housing and other signs of development are removed from the site. Sometimes fake boulders are added. Rented animals—all those spiders and snakes and lizards—are wrangled in. Immunity idols, symbols of privilege so built into the world that they seem part of the fabric, have been rough masks, skulls, and fetishes, crudely carved and often with bared teeth and fierce expressions. Like the natives. Supposedly they mimic local cultural symbols, but only those signaling a primitive and dangerous place. (In the Marquesas, the immunity trophy was supposed to be a traditional statue, but it turned out to be one made specially for the tourist trade.)

At the end of most seasons, the final three players must take part in an execrable ritual to honor their "fallen comrades." Jeff calls it their "final rite of passage." (This is one of the advantages of streaming the show; I always fast-forward through this part.) The three remaining players light torches or make totems or flower arrangements as the awful music swells and quick images of the long-forgotten eliminated players flick by. The finalists know the drill; they smile and nod and bow their heads in respect to the players they beat, the ones they didn't like and maybe hated, the ones they plotted against. They are dead heroes now.

Burnett idealized "the simple wonders of life on a deserted tropical island" in his memoir of the first season in Borneo, but he also defended the fake primitivism. It was a necessary protection for the delicate viewer. "The appropriation of elements from cultural anthropology, religious ritual, and Robert Louis Stevenson mines the common subconscious ideal of island life," he (or his ghostwriter) wrote. "All jungles have ruins and fire and lava and rope bridges and buried treasure and a chief. Without that built-in comfort factor the audience would surely cringe as they realize how truly terrifying life on Pulau Tiga will be for the castaways." Uh-huh. In *The Amazon*, Burnett gave the players "shock therapy" about the dangers of the jungle. As he recalls in one of his memoirs, "they were told stories of the natives, the spiders, the fire ants, and everything else previously unimaginable." Because the natives are unimaginable. (*The Amazon* also happens to be the first season where the crew stayed in a hotel instead of a camp.)

Once aboriginal people are diminished in power, they can be revered as exotic—and milked. In Guatemala, the show was filmed in Yaxhá-Nakum-Naranjo National Park. During the season, Tribal Councils take place at the North Acropolis, a place in the ruins, says Jeff, where "leaders would decide the fate of their people," and so it "couldn't be a more fitting spot." In an ancient ball court, they play basketball, three on three, for a challenge, and Amy sprains her ankle. The players have painted their faces and decorated themselves with feathers to "honor" the Mayans. Jeff says, "Now we're doing it like the Maya did!" I think not, since the Mayans might have sacrificed Amy and all the losing players, and perhaps saved a head or two for a ceremonial game.

Later they attend a ceremony involving chicken sacrifice, and then have to navigate a complex maze based somehow on a Mayan deity called the Seven Macaw. There's no irony to any of it, especially the notion of showing your respect by crudely imitating an ancient culture while racing toward a million dollars. The players are told they can't eat the sacrificed chicken; it is taboo. But they eat it anyway, except for Rafe, who feels that he "learned about sacrifice" in the ritual. Then a huge thunderstorm washes half their camp away, proving that the magic was real.

The actual Mayans who lived in what is now Guatemala built vast cities in the jungle. They had a complex written language and intricate mathematics. Throughout the South Pacific, ocean navigation is an elaborate system based on star maps, the patterns of currents, weather forecasting, bird and fish migration, and the ability to read waves. The Marquesans make sophisticated canoes large enough for 30 people or more. The Hanunóo people of the Philippines can describe 1,625 plants in 890 categories, of which some 500 species are edible and another 400 are medicinal. The Fang people of what is now Gabon memorize as many as 30 generations of ancestors. The Aboriginal people of Australia could travel the entire continent by songlines; an elder might know a thousand songs. But you will not hear these facts on *Survivor*. The digestible tidbits of history dropped in the show are wafer thin, and they tend to focus on the small slice involving Westerners. Wrote Guy Debord: "In societies where modern conditions of production prevail, all of life presents itself as an immense accumulation of *spectacles*. Everything that was directly lived has moved away into a representation."

CBS (all of television, perhaps) erases the actual history of a place to focus on Western experience or ancient history. In season 10, Jeff's voice-over describes Palau as a place where "some of the most fierce battles of World War II" took place, and so the season is rife with WWII wrecks, Morse code, and target shooting; no mention is made of the previous 4,500 years of its cultural history. Ancestors, shamanism, explorers—but not how people actually live. A small part of Kenya is "Africa." A part of Samoa is "South Pacific." A reservoir in the northern Jiangxi Province stands in for all of "China." When locals do appear, they rarely speak. The writer Jennifer Bowering Delisle notes that the kind of acting out many tourists do—joining a dance, filming a ceremony—is a way to justify one's presence in a place. Whether we travel for entertainment, education, or personal transformation, we are always using another culture. We either long for an escape, which requires erasing all negative reminders of the world at large, or we long for something authentic. Something *real*, which often is used to mean *old* or *exotic*, which in turn is used to mean *not like me*. How many travelers get upset when they find signs of modern culture where they didn't expect it? We have also internalized colonialism, just like conquered people have; we routinely default to white and Western as the foundational culture against which these others are measured and compared; their difference to that foundation is a large part of their value. Wrote Delisle, "*Survivor's* 'Third World' locales are thus nostalgically constructed as anachronistic space, as places where one may remember this lost history of simple living. Where, in effect, time has stood still."

Burnett would agree; this is Burnett's goal. The fourth season of *Survivor* was supposed to be *Arabia* and filmed in Jordan. Filming was scheduled to start November 12, 2001, but the attacks on 9/11 changed plans. "On September 12," Burnett tells us in *Jump In!*, his book about being successful, "as I was lifting weights at the Malibu Gym, I got a call on my cell phone from King Abdullah." (That sentence gives you a good idea of the whole book.) The king pleads with him to keep going, to "show the world that terrorists" can't stop them. But they can; it's not safe for Americans in Jordan. "But as the Navy SEALs like to say," adds Burnett, "Failure was not an option."

So Burnett sends out scouts and they end up on Nuku Hiva, an island in the Marquesas. This is the island where Robert Louis Stevenson made landfall, and where Herman Melville set his novel

Typee, the plot of which includes cannibals and promiscuity. Burnett was excited to find "a village that had jumped right out of James Michener's *Tales of the South Pacific*. We were met by friendly island women in brightly colored clothes, and warriors with tattooed faces. This was not tourist-friendly Tahiti, but rather a land with its own identity and a colorful history of wars, cannibalism, and missionaries . . . After all, the ancestors of those same smiling Marquesan warriors had tried to eat Herman Melville only two miles from where I sat." Is Burnett a complex enigma, or is he just what he seems to be? Here's a guy who has been all over the world—admittedly, almost always as a pampered producer on a television show, but still. He acts like a yokel so much of the time.

In the Marquesas, the producers erased all signs of farming and ranching after the government gave them exclusive use of four valleys for seven weeks. Four of the families who farmed there went to court to get their land back. But the government was on the side of *Survivor*. One family got a small cash settlement. The family that owned the land where the Tribal Council was built won only the right to have the set removed at the end. And two of the families were required to pay *Burnett's* court costs. A man named Daniel, who had lived his entire life on one bay, was removed to a prefab and his house, dock, and freshwater system were destroyed. Bulldozed. Fishing grounds on the island were put off-limits. Some local people were hired for "security," but it was offset by inflated prices. Daniel said, "The Americans are quick and rich. They took the bay . . . We didn't want to move, but there was strong pressure." (All this effort, for what has been described as one of the worst locations. The terrain of the Marquesas is famously steep and rocky, and biting insects were so prevalent that the camera crews wore protective gear.)

When one contestant arrived, she said, "It's so primeval."

The cultural anthropologist Kathleen Riley did her fieldwork on Nuku Hiva in the early 1990s. About 2,500 people lived there, all that remained after 95 percent of the Indigenous population was killed in less than 100 years after colonization by French Catholics. *Survivor*, she noted, went further (if less lethally) in creating a *terra nullius*, a world without locals and thus free for the taking. CBS defended its behavior in the Marquesas by saying they were leaving the crew buildings as low-income family housing and donating computers to schools. There wasn't enough housing on short notice, so Burnett rented an entire cruise ship for the crew. The government saw its chance and charged him $440,000 in tax to keep it anchored. Burnett's public "gift" was to let Tahiti Nui Television broadcast the show. Riley wrote at the time, "I suspect the response will be in equal measure hilarity at the Americans' foolish attempts to survive their own machinations, distress that the production has left the Marquesas so little," and frustration that, once again, their culture will be misrepresented. A local friend told her that they've seen it before; that foreigners "come in like refuse on the beach, but are swept out again by the next tide." Except maybe in Fiji, where the show has landed for good.

Africa was filmed in a Kenyan national park called the Shaba National Reserve. In the first moments, the truck stops and a local man with a rifle starts shouting at the players. "Down! Down! Down! Hurry up! Stand there! Down." (Then he jumps in the truck, smiles, says, "Have a nice day! Bye-bye!" and drives off.) The producers rented the reserve in its entirety for four months, denying access to local shepherds and residents. The contracts were, as usual, littered with confidentiality clauses and, also as usual, a no-fly zone was created. Few locals got work, though some were hired to haul brush so the set designers could make huts for the players. The hundreds of crew members lived at a camp with a swimming pool, water processor, and modern sewer. When locals complained about the impact on the land, the location manager, Robin Hollister, to my view, completely missing the point, said, "We are doing less damage than a herd of elephants."

As soon as we arrive in a place, we change it. Looking changes what is seen. The presence of a foreigner means that the behavior of a local is no longer what it would be if no one was watching. The sociologist Dean MacCannell explored what he called "enacted or staged savagery." He specifically chooses the word "savage" instead of "primitive" because he means wild and untamed—which is not necessarily primitive at all. He believed that we (the travelers, the foreigners) in a given place deeply want to believe that what we see (the performance) is real. We want to believe that we are participating in something authentic—that's what we've come for, what we're missing. But even if the culture *looks* the same as usual, it can't be the same while we're there. "Masai could earn a living *acting Masai* in perpetuity," he wrote. But that's not the same as *being Masai.*

One story we who love to travel tell ourselves is that our presence, our viewing of this performance, doesn't harm the savage. It doesn't take anything away from the wild, untamed world. We may even convince ourselves that local people benefit the most, because we are, after all, paying them to do this thing they would do anyway. We pay them to be guides, cooks, dancers, teachers, and stand-ins for our own desires. We want them to live their lives, while we watch. "The touristic ideal of the 'primitive' is that of a magical resource that can be used without actually possessing or diminishing it," wrote MacCannell. They can "earn a living just by 'being themselves.' . . . [But] the primitive does not really appear in these enactments of it. The 'primitivistic' performance contains the image of the primitive as a dead form."

In *Survivor*, the locals are paid, one way or the other. (Denied the access to their fishing grounds for weeks or months, they can instead ferry players from camp to Tribal Council. After all, it's still using a boat, right?) And in the larger question of what is exchanged, the producers shake hands with the Fijian government representatives, stay away from the breeding grounds for the endangered Fijian iguana, cheerfully accept the large tax rebates paid the production, and thus engage in the larger exchange: that we have all profited here, that the players, the producers, and the viewers are not actually exploiting anything. We are *celebrating* Fiji, *honoring* the culture. *Promoting* the beautiful landscape. Stagecraft will "permit the destruction of nature and the alienation of work to be hidden from *view*. But how are they hidden from consciousness?" asks MacCannell. The most important difference between the performing local people and the tourists is that the tourists have more money.

What MacCannell called "reconstructed ethnicity" is what happens when the ex-savage try to reclaim or find their way back to a form of what was lost, in opposition to the tsunami of global monoculturalism. It is a push back against the "ethnicity-for-tourism" in which local people give performances, sell at bazaars, and wear traditional clothing, guides to the hidden mystery of a given place.

The local food is used as punishment: boiled tarantulas, pig intestines, live grubs. What kind of people eat like this? Of course, insects, arachnids, worms, and similar creatures have always been eaten, and are considered delicacies in many cultures. But the point is to make you, the unschooled Westerner, wince. It's a narrow window. I grew up in the rural American West, eating bull testicles, pickled pig's feet, and cow tongue. (Can you say haggis?) In one episode of *Africa*, several tribesmen come to camp, wearing traditional dress and beadwork. They are leading a cow. Jeff explains that they drink cow's blood for nutrition. One of the men nicks the cow in a vein and Jeff fills a vase with blood, then adds milk. This is the daily nutrition of the handsome young men, but for the Americans it is the disgusting food challenge. The tribesmen never speak.

Later, just before the finale, Jeff wakes up the three remaining players before dawn. They do the stupid "fallen comrades" walk, and then enact a traditional cleansing ritual with a shower of goat fat and blood. Tribespeople, clean and beautiful and calm, dance and sing around three privileged, dirty white Americans who kicked them off their land for several weeks. *Survivor* is a great expression of the Western yearning for what the West destroyed: the frontier, the unknown, defanged, the sharp edges sanded down, the distasteful aspects of raw life carefully hidden. The symbols—skull, ax, tattoo, fetish, howl—are used to create a version of a world that never was, and that we, pointedly, never inhabited.

The American franchise of *Survivor* has a decent record for environmental cleanup, in spite of their addiction to huge conflagrations at the end of the fallen peers walk. Burnett has said that his crews photograph sites before building sets and return the sites to their original state. But since the production has moved local people off sites and destroyed their homes, I wonder what this means. Do they rebuild those houses? This inquiring mind still wants to know. Where is Daniel living now? Did he get his freshwater system back, or was the *Survivor* production the end of a life he'd known as long as he'd been alive?

The franchise as a whole has a mixed reputation for how it treats the environment. In the Pearl Islands of Panama, several countries including Serbia, Israel, Colombia, Bulgaria, and Turkey have filmed seasons of *Survivor*. Turkey, in particular, has been called out for leaving mounds of trash and debris. Castaway Television Productions, which licenses the show around the world, requires countries to return locations to their natural state. But policing such a clause is almost impossible. Panama's environmental protection agency, ANAM, is supposed to follow up; they deny the complaints. The American show generally gets high marks for cleaning up (especially in comparison) and Burnett insists that the production leaves an area in pristine condition. But the more obsessed fans who search Google Earth for satellite views have been able to find images of challenge sites both during and after production. In one case on the Cook Islands, it is clear from images taken years later that the damage was not entirely repaired.

Is it all bad news? Not really. Some of the locations have become tourist attractions after the show by catering to fans. The number of visitors to Pulau Tiga in Borneo more than doubled in a few years after the first season of *Survivor* was filmed there. (That isn't good news to everyone.) Some locals make money by leasing land; tourism usually increases. The show spends many millions of dollars (and gets a hefty rebate in time).

Many seasons include a special reward in which players get to mingle with locals. A little enacted authenticity. Sometimes it's a feast or a party where they learn a few traditional dance steps. Sometimes it's a chance to be a "*Survivor* ambassador" and take donations to a clinic or school. In *Africa*, Lex gets to drive a truck of supplies to the local AIDS hospital, some miles away from where the producers are hanging out in their new swimming pool. On *Vanuatu*, four players spend the night in a local village and Ami says they were "as far from civilization as they could go." In season 28, *Cagayan*, when Jeff sends a few people off to deliver school supplies, he calls it "a little nourishment for the *soul*," but adds that they will also get to eat hamburgers and hot dogs. "Not only are you going to fill your bellies with food, more than that, you're changing lives. You're representing *Survivor* and bringing supplies to kids who wouldn't otherwise have them." They are greeted like kings, hand out backpacks and supplies, then go off to eat by themselves.

Jeff Probst could build several new schools without noticing a change in his bank balance. No one ever says this. Burnett could build an entire school system. He could certainly build Daniel a new dock. No one ever says this. The contestants get a little weepy, telling the camera how happy they are to "give back." Okay, I'll give Jeff his props. The show auctions off memorabilia for charity at the end of each season. One recipient is a charity Probst himself founded, The Serpentine Project, which helps young people aging out of foster care. Still.

Let's talk hygiene for a moment. The contestants smell terrible. In an interview for *The Ringer*, Malcolm said, "The cameramen will tell you that you stink. The producers will demand that you boil your clothes, because they're the ones who have to suffer through it." Sometimes reward challenges include an opportunity to shower and put on clean clothes. But not the ones where the players are actually mingling with local people. In the Philippines, contestants get to take school supplies to a village after a mud-wrestling challenge, and they arrive covered in mud and wearing only bathing suits. Players show up to feasts, even to family meals, filthy and disheveled, semi-naked, and smelling like garbage. The local people have swept the town square and turned out in their best clothes. The players are treated like dignitaries and no one wrinkles their nose. Such rudeness is quintessentially Western.

One of my reservations about *The Amazing Race* is that many of its challenges are just the ordinary chores of daily life for many people: plowing, herding, carrying firewood, drawing water. What do the local people think? I don't mean, what do the villagers *say*, to producers, to Jeff, to Burnett, to a reporter. I don't mean what does the government say when the producers file the permits and sign the contracts and pay the locals a bit. And I don't mean what do the villagers say *during* production, when they are teaching the stinking faux-castaways a local dance and killing a pig for the feast, or smiling beside the pile of new backpacks. I mean, what do the people in Fiji and Gabon and Vanuatu say *to each other* about all this? It unwinds endlessly: what would they say on camera, and what would they *really* say? When is any of this real, on or off camera? In a reward challenge in *Africa*, teams have to separate goats and get 20 into pens. The three local men who provided the goats watch, heads together, laughing. I would love to know what they were saying, what trash talk they shared. They are certainly enjoying themselves. Considering how the show affected their daily lives, this entertainment seems the least they should get. A *New York Times* reporter asked a few of the locals what they thought, and they expressed some bemusement at the concept of the show. "A million dollars?" said a local named Mohammed Leeresh. "Just for surviving? If they let me play, I can guarantee you it would be mine."

SWEARING, LOYALTY, BETRAYAL, AND A LIE ABOUT A TRUCK

In the first season of *Survivor*, the players didn't seem to get how to play a game with the motto "Outwit, Outplay, Outlast." They were surprised that "people flat-out lied in front of a national television audience," as Colleen said in disbelief. Kelly, who took second place, claimed to be distraught because "she was trying to live a good life, free of bad karma," and it turned out that trying to win a million dollars by beating 15 strangers might require her to fudge a little. She felt that her alliance had lost their "ethical senses" by agreeing to vote together. "It's not about surviving the elements; it's about surviving yourself. I didn't want to be part of the alliance because I thought it was conniving and dirty and untrue to myself. I kind of feel like Luke Skywalker or something. I crossed over to the dark side." Kelly, who was 22 at the time, decided that the solution to the seeming necessity of pretense was to abandon the alliance but pretend to still be in it. In order to be honest, she lied.

In his accidentally funny memoir of the first season, Mark Burnett wrote that the original Tagi alliance—Sue, Kelly, Richard, and Rudy, the first alliance in the game and the model for game strategy—"violated fair play." Yes, a television producer wrote that. The alliance voted out Gretchen because she looked like she could win—in other words, they were playing the game by the game's rules: one person wins. But Burnett couldn't believe they were actually *trying* to win. "In one bold, glaring, awful vote, *Survivor* had changed. The show's moral compass was gone. Whatever was good, whatever was honest, whatever was right" was gone. When Sue lied to Jenna about who she voted for, Burnett said, it was "queasiness-inducing . . . some of the untruths and half-truths bordered on obscene." But it was almost a million-dollar lie. The nature of the show Burnett half-borrowed and half-invented—a treasure hunt in which people are eliminated by popular vote in difficult conditions and which, by the rules, only one person can win—somehow eluded him.

Instead there was a lot of drivel about integrity. Describing the first Tribal Council, the Ur-Council, Burnett wrote that it was "a tense, dramatic proceeding where an individual comes face to face with what they truly stand for by having their actions and words recounted and questioned before their peers." Jeff's solemn words in one of the last episodes—"Tribal Council is where you are held accountable for your actions"—is followed by a faked action sequence of Jeff leaving the Council circle, cutting through the jungle with a machete, climbing on a prop plane, parachuting out over Los Angeles, getting on a motorcycle, and racing through the city to the soundstage where he will announce the winner, which actually happens months later. It's all very *Survivor.*

On the website Common Sense Media, television shows are reviewed for so-called family values. *Survivor* ends up with a good grade, thanks to the need for cooperation, wilderness skills, and the "terrific wildlife footage." The downside is the fact that it "encourages lying, manipulation, deception, and selfishness." It sure does. The show now routinely includes not only a steady rain of lies, but betrayals, blindsides, and pointedly violent language, as players talk about "cutting his throat," "stabbing him in the back," or "taking her out." Wrote a critic in *Time* a few years ago, "Survivor changed the goalposts on what's okay to say or do on TV to a degree that new incidents of nudity, betrayal or bickering have lost their power to shock."

At some point during every season, Jeff floats the trust balloon. Why aren't people prepared? In *China*, Jeff—who has been through every season, watching the development of every kind of strategy, and helping to create character arcs through editing—asked, "Is duplicity part of this game?"

Over the years, players have said not once, not twice, but again and again and again, that lying is wrong and that they themselves are playing with integrity—unlike So-and-So—and that there will come a time for revenge on the others, on *the liars*. Then they lie. There are moments when people wonder what it means to play a game versus how one behaves in "real life." Occasionally a player actually tries to avoid deception. Yul remained calm on *Cook Islands*, saying, "I'd like to play the game with as much integrity and honesty as I can, and I'm finding it to be very, very complicated." (Yul won a million dollars. He said later, "I tried to play a very rational, strategic game. I used a lot of game theory, I used a lot of math." Also, a little deception.)

The first season was 20 long years ago. Recently Jeff said, "There are no rules—only yours. You do get permission to manipulate, persuade, cajole, lie—whatever it takes." In another interview, he said, "You have to remember that *Survivor* has very few rules. The players decide the tone of the game, the speed at which it is played, the moral code, and the amount of effort they choose to put forth. This is their game." He happily promotes these life lessons now. At the end of season 35, Jeff returns to the live audience after a scene in which players try to fool Devon with a fake idol. Jeff asks audience members what *they* would do if *they* were Devon. "That's why this game continues to entertain us!" he says. Because "you can play along at home!" You can practice lying with a straight face.

How do you win *Survivor*? You win by lying. You lie and you pretend not to be lying, you *swear* that you are not lying. Plenty of players these days shake their heads at protestations of honesty, reminding the audience *it's just a game.* To them, integrity is the integrity of the play, the ability to use strategy and understand the plot as it is unfolding.

On *Vanuatu*, Scout says to the camera, "When I came out here, I was determined to play the game with integrity and honesty and truth, and if that didn't work, then I'd lie, cheat, and steal." Chris, who won his season, said simply, "Lying, deceiving—you ain't got no choice." The problem isn't lying so much as being caught lying. The sin isn't lying when you play the game, but not playing the game well.

These days, lying is bad only if you are lying to me. I can vote for you but you can't vote for me. Almost every season, a player is secretly plotting against a supposed ally and that ally is revealed to be plotting against the player in turn, and the player gets upset. How dare you? This is not a game that has no trust or integrity; *because* it's a game, there's no trust or integrity.

"We all know that we're loyal, sincere, and we're just good people," says Benry to his allies Jane and Holly. "You can't backstab someone who you have lots of love for." Benry has already made a secret deal with Chase to vote out Jane and Holly. Everyone hugs. "I feel guilty for lying," he says to the camera, "but as long as it's not me going home next—" But Benry doesn't know about the other plan. Buh-bye.

In *China*, Amanda shares a reward with Todd, because she wants to talk with him alone.

"Honestly, I don't trust you that much," she tells him over slices of pepperoni. "I just have the feeling that if anyone was to backstab me now, you would." He has certainly thought about it.

"There's one girl in this game that I've been honest to, literally, since day one, and it's you," he tells her. (This is not true.) "I swear on my life, I'm in this to the end with you."

Later, he tells the camera, "I hope she can trust me. I really, really hope so, because I need her right now."

On the last morning, Todd says to the camera, to the audience, "I feel like looking at the jury, I stand an okay shot. I've backstabbed and lied to a lot of them, but I was playing a game. And whether I win a million dollars tonight or not, I feel like I've accomplished a lot. And I'm so proud."

Todd wins a million dollars.

Tony Vlachos has won *Survivor* twice. He is a master of the false swear. At one point, Tony insists that Sarah "swear on her badge" because they are both police officers. Then she makes him do the same. He says, "She had me swear on my badge. Which that doesn't mean anything to me, swearing on my badge. 'Cause I'm here to lie, cheat, and steal, I'm here to drag people's dreams through the mud so

I could fulfill mine. That's what I'm here for. Whatever I have to do, I'm going to do." To Kass, he pledges on his wife and child to take her to the end, even though Woo told Tony that Kass wanted him out. Kass then tells Woo he shouldn't have said that to Tony. Tony then blows up at Kass for telling secrets; he's the Trump of *Survivor* in his ability to project his own behavior on others. Later he tells Woo that it is true, he did swear on his wife and child with Kass, but he didn't mean it—he only did it to protect Woo. But *now* he's going to swear on his wife and child with Woo, for reallies. Pinky swear. Tony even swears on his "dead dad." At some point Tony actually explains to the others that his swears only count under certain conditions, and people still don't get rid of him. After blindsiding Trish, he says, "I'm a little sad that I had to oust one of my best allies. One of my most loyal, most honest, most sincere, most genuine allies." (Sarah, at least, learns her lesson. When they play together again in *Game Changers*, she says, "My word is not my bond." Not this time. She plays like a lean, mean, fighting machine, and Sarah wins a million dollars.)

People swear like mad on *Survivor*. They swear on their life, their mother's life, the Holy Bible, their son's name, their brother's name, and someone else's son's name. When Sandra swears on her kids to Jonny that she's not lying on season 7, she adds later in a confessional, "I swear on my two kids that I'm going to screw you *and* Burton." Swear on Jesus' name. Swear on your police badge. There's no end to it. When Russell Hantz played the Australian version, he swore on his wedding ring. They didn't know he was divorced. (In a peculiar irony, Hantz recently gave an interview in which he blamed his divorce on *Survivor*, saying that he ended up becoming the villain he played on the show. Chicken or egg? Hard to tell.)

But people take swearing seriously. Trish gets furious with Tony for his false swears. "Was it worth it to you, for a million dollars, to sacrifice *your own father?*" In *Vanuatu*, Twila swears on her son's life and later changes her vote. By then, the Mean Girls of that season have all been voted out, and when the jury speaks, they tear into Twila. Sarge asks her if it's "worth a million dollars" to "cast her son's name to Hell."

In *Panama*, Shane was the tribe's wackadoodle. He makes a promise to Bobby by saying, "I swear on your kid." Then he swears on his own son's life, and later he mopes around camp, talking loudly to the others, saying, "I want to get out of my alliance with you guys, but I can't do it unless you allow me to take my son's name back." He is near tears. "I swore on my kid's life. I want to ask you guys if I can take my son's name back."

Later, Cirie makes up to him; here it comes, you can feel it, you can almost set your watch by it: Shane says, "I just, please, please, please, on your children's lives, tell me we're going to the four." Cirie nods. "We're going to the four, on my kids' lives." Shane is nodding, nodding constantly. "I swear on my son's life, we're the four." They are not.

People often seem not to understand how competition and negotiation works. They do seem surprised at times by the ethics of the game, which are not the ethics of ordinary life. (*Real* life.) At the end of *All-Stars*, Lex uses his jury speech to complain to Rob, with whom he was friends before the game. Rob had asked Lex to look out for Amber, with a whispered gangster's promise to return the favor if he could. The time came when Rob didn't feel that he could anymore. The writer and *Survivor* fan Joe Reid called this a "devious, shocking, wholly supportable from a gameplay perspective" move. But Lex hasn't been able to let it go. "The line between game and life is not cut and dried. Life blurs into the game constantly. This game exposes who we are as people to the core. It's like truth serum," Lex says in his jury speech. "You sold out your values, you sold out your character, and you sold out your friends for a stack of greenbacks." But of course, that's the point of the game. Rob does a *mea culpa* of regrets, that he didn't mean to hurt anyone, and as his eyes fill with unshed tears, I think, *Pretty effective, Rob.*

In early seasons, votes cast against players were counted against them in a later tie. In Africa, Lex becomes obsessed with the "cancer," the "snake" who voted for him. He wants to "slit their throat." He can't let up that someone *lied*, that someone is *not who you think they are*, that someone is *a rat*, is going to *hang themselves*. Teresa comforts him, then admits to the camera that it was her. He begins to whisper in the dark. He's sure it was Tom. "I'm going to take Tom and he and I are going to have a man-to-man talk, just the two of us, and I am going to make him *shake* on it, on his son's name, and if he won't do that, then I know what the truth is. I'm not naively going to let myself be led to slaughter." Man, let it go. *Let. It. Go.*

In *San Juan del Sur*, Josh asks Baylor to return the favor he did her by not voting for her and not vote for him, "just out of respect." Baylor's response: "I almost feel like I'm being blackmailed a little bit. To me, that doesn't seem like a guy who comes from a Christian family and a pastor for a dad. I mean, I was taught that you should give a gift without expecting anything in return. So I feel like I don't owe him anything."

Speaking of religion. *God helped us row. God helped me to win. God brought us a feast.* Sean wins a car in *Marquesas*, jumps into Jeff's arms, and screams, "I can do all things through Christ, baby!" A player gets sick and the pressure is on to hold hands and bow your head. *Kumbaya.* On season 37, Davie has to choose between urns, only one of which has an advantage. He asks God for a sign. Nothing happens. Finally he decides that the wind blowing the torch flame away from the urns is God's message that he shouldn't bet at all. In *Palau*, a Muslim contestant named Ibrehem regularly gave credit to the divine for victories, but when his team lost immunity, James, in his blurred Mobile accent, said, "He was meant to go the last time, and by the grace of Allah, he didn't go. And now my God says he is, today."

There is a lot of praying in *Marquesas*. So much praying. Vecepia leads most of it, making the others stand in a circle, eyes closed and holding hands. When she wins immunity, she yells, "Thank you, Jesus!" several times. At the end, Vecepia makes a deal with Kathy in front of the jury, that they will go to the final two together. At the next immunity challenge, she openly betrays Kathy, making the same deal with Neleh. Vecepia explains how the betrayal is not wrong. "In every game, sometimes you have to make a move that you really don't want to," she says. "I've asked the Lord for forgiveness. So, being a Christian, we know we have that ability to go to our Father and say, 'Lord, this is what I did. I know you saw this. Please forgive me, and I will go to my brother and ask them—after it's over with!—for forgiveness as well."

On season 25 in the Philippines, there were three tribes. (In *The Atlantic*'s list of the Jeff Probst Annoying Factor, the Philippines is scored this way: "Pretty high. Fawning over the boys, condescending to the girls. It's maddening. – 3.") Two celebrities played—Jeff Kent, a former MLB player, and Lisa Whelchel, a child star on *The Facts of Life*. From the beginning, Lisa, who tried to hide her television background, has struggled in her lifelong quest for self-worth. She's fragile, a bit of a wreck, quick to please others. It's a perfect setup on *Survivor*. She begins to see a pattern playing out: child star under the control of others to a pastor's wife and young mother, having lost all the money she made on television. She had just gotten divorced from a marriage of 23 years when filming started. She sits on the well. "Maybe I'm not able to play this game," she cries. The game is "too big for me." She's right; Lisa is much more concerned with whether or not she will hurt people's feelings and whether they approve of her than winning.

Lisa's fragility is so plain to see that she is picked for a loved one visit with her brother out of pity. He says, "She always seems to say the right thing, she always seems to do the right thing. She's a really good game player, she's supersmart, very bright, she knows how to win." Except, he adds, if anything "shady or underhanded" is required. "I've been too nice," she says. "If I were to start all over again, would I have betrayed people, hurt people, not told the truth? I don't know."

Her main alliance is with Denise and Malcolm, two calm and careful players who know she can be manipulated. Over the course of a day, with the help of their cheerfully scheming family members, Mike Skupin, playing for the secondd time, and Lisa decide to blindside Malcolm. "I *do* know it's a game and I *love* this game, but I haven't been able to step outside of who I am outside the game, to *play* the game," she says.

Lisa's brother works on her all day long. "I knew that you had to lie to play this game, I knew it was part of the game and everybody who signed up knew that you can't take people at their word." Lisa, so malleable, is influenced by her brother. She finally thinks, Oh. It's a game. I *can* cheat and lie and break promises because that's part of the game. This is how she explains it: "When somebody who knows me is able to remind me of the crystal clear picture that I've gotten all confused and befuddled and foggy, it was like, 'Yay! I can play this game! I can play this game and I can play it well!'" She's very excited at the realization. "I'm going to do everything I can to play the game by *these* rules, to win."

She has already said to the camera that she doesn't believe God takes sides and you can't pray for your team to win. But now she gets them all to pray and ask God to "bless this plan and protect it, and if you want Malcolm to win or Carter or Denise or even Abi, we want ultimately your will to be done." *I swear on my kids.* Her brother says, "I wonder what Jesus Christ would look like, playing this game."

Skupin replies, "Sadly, a little bit like Malcolm."

Then Malcolm wins immunity. "Oh, I'm so bummed!" says Lisa. "I was so ready to play this game and make a big move!" Then she reminds Skupin, "We did pray that if this was not the right way to go, that God would close the door." He isn't paying attention. "And either there's a bigger picture, bigger story, bigger plan that we can't see—" Skupin interrupts to point out a large ant. He is not listening. "So this apparently is His will, for Malcolm to have the immunity necklace. I don't get it, I don't see it."

Lisa does learn how to lie, after a fashion. She realizes that all the weeks of telling people how hard it was for her to lie will pay off now, since no one will believe she's deceitful. She throws off the shackles of integrity and ties for second. (She also won fan favorite and another $100,000.)

Should a for-profit entertainment show have a "moral compass"? And whose compass is used? Burnett wrote after the first season (and this is a remarkable thing to say; I can't get over what an arrogant and entirely disingenuous thing this is to say about his role in the shenanigans) that he didn't know "how to explain a game where the heavyset, slow, minimally educated, and wholly unethical stood the best chance of winning." (This is how he described a group that included a corporate trainer who caught fish all day, a neurosurgeon, a Brown graduate, a whitewater guide, and an ex–Navy Seal.) It's not clear even now what he thought would happen, what ending the show's creators planned. A few people, a million dollars, one winner, and Burnett pockets the profits while complaining about how it turned out the only way it could.

"Creating complicated lies and then sustaining them for weeks under interrogation is very hard. Keeping track of lies and inventing additional layers of lies to 'substantiate' the big lies is just a very difficult task." This is not a comment about playing *Survivor*. This is an anonymous post on a *Survivor* fan forum, complaining about spoilers.

The authors of a statistical analysis of *Survivor* winners found that strong alliances are vital to winning and that those alliances rely on "truth-telling (or at least the perception of truthfulness)." Alliances have nothing to do with liking a person. In *Guatemala*, Rafe says to the camera, "I kind of had this really sad realization. Am I a member of the Axis of Evil?" Sadly, he is.

Erving Goffman said that all relationships develop a "surface of agreement," which leads to a "veneer of consensus." Each person suppresses their truest feelings and needs to create harmony, until another value (such as winning) takes priority. One of the most revered (or despised) big moves in the game took place in season 27, *Blood vs. Water*. Returning players came with a relative; they were then separated into different tribes, but eventually mingled. Most people assumed that players would form voting blocs; Laura assured her tribe that she was perfectly willing to vote out her daughter, Ciera. But Ciera has already figured out that pairs of players will be targets; she votes her mother out first. In a contest of any kind, all ties must eventually break. Alliances imply war, and in a war you attack others; and in a war to the death, you eventually must turn on your closest friends. On *Game Changers*, after the tribes merge, Zeke says, "These are the last moments of people pretending to get along."

On *Game Changers*, three newly formed tribes are informed that only one tribe will get immunity, and two will go to Council. The Tavua tribe wins immunity. Then Jeff tells the other two tribes that they will vote together to eliminate one person. What? Suddenly all loyalty is called into question, because everyone has a long game. No one knows how long it will be before the tribes are merged. A player on the bottom of one tribe could flip and support another tribe in the hope of a new alliance. Once upon a time, Jeff didn't allow side conversations in Tribal Council. But that night, Tribal Council is a mad series of whispering huddles, passing secrets, hand signals, and double-crosses, devolving into a game of Telephone that leaves almost everyone confused. In the end, one tribe targets Sierra, but at the last moment, Tai gives her an immunity idol. All the votes for Sierra are thrown out, and so Malcolm is gone on only five votes. "I'm gonna vomit," he says. When Jeff brightly says, "That's a shining example of why *Survivor* is still so entertaining," it feels like the most obvious product placement of all, for a product called *Survivor*.

Each season, when the tribes merge and immunity goes to only one person at a time, the paper-thin loyalty of a *Survivor* alliance begins to tear. For days after a merge, people may do little more than backroom dealing, sideswiping, shapeshifting, promising, hedging, and deals with the Devil. Every apparent alliance consists of secret alliances working with members of other alliances. When Tyler writes down his vote in *Worlds Apart*, he whispers to the camera, "I have no idea what is going on."

The producers deliberately undermine alliances after the merge, when only individual immunity is possible, by offering a Hobson's choice every few days. When a player wins an individual reward, he or she can invite one or two others to join. A person with three allies must leave one out. But you don't want to take all your allies on a reward, anyway, because then those left behind can conspire against your alliance openly. You need to leave a spy behind the Iron Curtain, but that means depriving one ally of a reward. Who gets to feast, get a massage, sleep in a clean bed? And who doesn't? Why don't alliances talk about this before a challenge? Why don't they come up with a fricking *plan*? Former players say such conversations do take place; the editors choose to leave these crucial parts of tribal strategy out. When it comes to leaving people out of a reward, people don't always recover from this choice, whichever choice they make. Really, it's often better not to win rewards at all.

Sometimes a player can't find a way into any alliance. In an odd scene in season 39, Karishma, the first Indian American to play, wore modest clothing and didn't perform well in challenges. Her tribemates seemed bewildered by her existence. One day she cut her hand to the bone. We see her curled up on the ground, cupping her bleeding hand and crying. Her tribemates make no effort to comfort her or help; they barely pay attention. We know that a medical team is hovering nearby; we know the producers are watching. But for a strange moment, she looks trussed up for sacrifice.

Loyalties fray. In *Cook Islands*, when each tribe was down to six players, two were given a chance to mutiny—to leave their tribe and join the other, with ten seconds to decide. At the last moment, Candice and Jonathan step forward. They are both white and they are moving to a tribe with the other two white players. But racial politics aside, they have just abandoned their tribe.

"Mutineers are the first to die," says Ozzy.

Their new tribe is not interested in welcoming the new members, having just watched them abandon their allies. Now there is a smaller tribe of four, tight and loyal, and a larger tribe of eight, with twice as much irritation and resentment, twice as many secrets. Jonathan starts working it doggedly, fishing and humping firewood and trying to find some way to matter to a tribe that he should never have joined. "I'm leading a mutineer's life, man," says Jonathan. "I made the game a lot harder for myself."

"Like, we gonna cradle a traitor? What is this, like, a refugee camp?" Nate says to Brad.

Season 35, with the awkward title of *Heroes vs. Healers vs. Hustlers*, is a study in betrayal. Every time I thought I could identify a goat, the goatness would shift. After every challenge, people maneuver anew. Spying ensues. Eavesdropping ensues. Deal-making ensues. Fighting ensues. And backstabbing reaches a new level. The hours before Tribal Councils pass in a blur of flattery, flirting, threats, smiling, agreement, deceit, humor, distraction, and confusion. At one Tribal Council, Mike makes a speech. "I am disappointed in my tribe. I believe that *Survivor* represents society. We have to play with justifiable moral and ethical codes of conduct here." But what he's really trying to do is influence votes. Somehow he ends up calling Ben "King Arthur" and himself the "Statue of Liberty" because "America is going to beat England in the end." At which point, Lauren puts her head in her hands. When Joe complains that "no one's playing the game" because there are secrets, several people answer at once, "That's the game."

Joe finds a clue to an idol and searches in the middle of the night. "This is not a vacation for me," he says. "It's work." He finds it, and now has two. But he doesn't have self-control. He gets mad at Mike. "He was the villain, which I was upset because that's my role, that's my lane." At Tribal, for no apparent reason, Joe jumps up and says he has *two* idols and *fuck* you all and I *dare* you and what are you gonna *do* about it, and puts one around his neck. After the vote, he plays the idol, but it's wasted; no one voted for him. (Why would they? He had an idol.)

Meanwhile, Ben is pretending to be in one alliance to hide his real alliance. "I should get an award for the performance I put on after I got back to camp. I'm doing my best double-agent, whatever you want to call it." Ashley says, "Ben's still putting on his Academy Award performance as a very disappointed King Arthur, and he *sells* it like I've never seen a story sold. It's awesome."

Ryan tells Devon, then Ben, that he has an idol. He tells each of them that they were the "only one" he trusted. They both promise him they won't say a word, then they tell each other. Loose lips, man. So Ryan sets up yet another secret alliance with Mike. But Mike believes he's in a secret alliance of five that doesn't really exist. Chrissy tries to set up a secret alliance with Lauren and Ryan without asking Ryan. And finally, Ashley and Lauren form a secret alliance of two within the secret alliance of four that formed within the secret alliance of seven. People are betrayed by their friends and are shocked by the betrayal even while setting up one of their own.

At Tribal Council, night after night, the secrets come out. Lies are thrown against lies. Mike throws half the idol in the fire. Ben is wearing what he says is a fake idol and announces that he's voting for Lauren. After the vote, Ben plays an idol that no one knew he had—all the secrets weren't out after all. Ben gets six votes that don't count and Lauren is gone on a single vote, from Ben.

If anyone can follow this all the way through without a spreadsheet—respect. At the finale, Jeff says the producers deliberately salted in lots of idols and advantages to sow chaos, because "nobody in this game could keep a single secret!" Except for one person. Ben won a million dollars.

*   *   *

Then there is the lie about the truck. Yau-Man says, after the tribes merge on *Fiji*, "At this point, I'm definitely having fun. There's a lot more sneaky conversations, there's a lot more combinations going in my head." He wins a balancing-climbing-digging-hatchet-throwing challenge for the biggest reward of the season, a new Ford F-350 pickup. Then he does something unique. He offers to give the truck to Dreamz. In exchange, if Dreamz wins immunity in the final four, he'll give the immunity to Yau-Man. Dreamz agrees immediately, swearing to God he will keep his promise. Then Yau-Man sends himself to Exile Island. Dreamz just says, "Yau-Man is an amazing guy. I don't get it."

Now, this is an exquisite snare for Dreamz, a 25-year-old cheerleading coach from North Carolina. But it is also a blatant violation of the rule against sharing a prize. Why didn't the producers stop it? Maybe they knew they had gold. It doesn't take long for Dreamz to realize the trap he's in. "I could buy twelve trucks with a million dollars," he says. "The best thing for me to do is to get rid of him before he makes it to the final four. Not that I'm a snake or nothing."

At Tribal Council, with six people left, Dreamz goes on about how grateful he is to Yau, then votes for him. "Sorry, bro, that's how the game goes," he tells the camera. But Yau feels the vibe and plays his immunity idol. Stacy goes home.

With four left, Dreamz wins immunity. Will he keep his bargain?

Cassandra, Earl, and Yau agree to vote out Dreamz after he gives Yau the immunity he promised. But Yau says, "Dreamz, if you change your mind, can you at least not vote me?" Dreamz says, "Why are you saying I might change my mind?" Yau says to the camera, "I think he's a man of his word, but from the very beginning, when we brought him into our alliance, I think he's one of the biggest wild cards. He seems a little bit out of control. But now he is in control and he made a promise and it worries me very much."

Dreamz has a very public wrestling match with his own greed. He says, "It's so hard to give up a million dollars. I worked *hard* to get here. And *lied.* I took out a whole alliance. And I bowed down to a freakin' *car*." Pause. "I want to do the right thing." Pause. "I'm just saying, if I do the wrong thing, you all better vote Yau. Or one of y'all going home." He knows he's in a bind. "After the game, the benefit that I get of giving away the immunity necklace is, uh, people knowin' that I'm really who I say I am. I am an honorable person, I am noble, I am a truth-teller, I am Dreamz." And the benefit of keeping it is, uh, maybe getting a lot of money. "This is going to be one of the most difficult decisions I *ever* had to make." He's convinced he'd win, of course; people always are when they get close to the end. "One million dollars or keep my word? Being honorable or one million dollars? I could use both of them. So I really don't know what I'm going to do tonight."

At Tribal Council, Dreamz talks about how he did want the truck, he still wants the truck, but now he realizes Yau was doing it "out of strategy" and he's talking himself into believing that he's a victim in some way, that all this is Yau-Man's fault for taking advantage of his good nature. Somehow, he's rationalized it all—taking the truck and keeping immunity and leaving Yau-Man with nothing. "That's what makes everything so down to the bone," he says at Tribal Council, bemoaning his dilemma. "It sucks, Jeff."

Yau says his gut feeling is that Dreamz will live up to his promise. "What you do, you have to live with it." Dreamz keeps immunity. He seems to have forgotten that the jury who will decide the winner is listening to all of this.

Does he grasp that he can't get the million that way? Any way? That he lost when he accepted the truck? He had to either give up immunity when he needed it the most, or publicly break a promise to the most likable player in the game.

Yau-Man is voted out, and says, "Sorry, Dreamz. You did not see fit to live up to your end of the bargain. Enjoy the truck."

At the end, when the jury gets to ask questions and make little speeches, Boo calls Dreamz an "immature Christian." Yau says he himself is old enough not to have "testosterone overload and therefore testosterone-poisoned brains" and can admit to a mistake. He gave the truck in good faith. "So now I'm going to give you a chance, to have the gonads to stand up and say why you changed your mind." But Dreamz doesn't. He claims that he didn't change his mind, that he was playing the game all along. "I came here knowing what I was going to do." This is easily contradicted by the many scenes of him holding his head in his hands and musing aloud about what to do. Back at camp, Dreamz is worked up, defensive, a little pissed, claiming that he doesn't care what people think, he has no regrets, everyone else is "snakes, rats, weasels." He's already shifted the blame.

"I'm going to sleep comfortable tonight knowing I got a shot at a million dollars tomorrow," he says. He doesn't.

Shortly after the season aired, Dreamz was sued by his girlfriend for allegedly not paying child support. But Jeff Probst was the disingenuous one. In an interview, he said that he was "sad" that the tribe didn't give Dreamz a "second chance." After all, he said, "Dreamz was just an excited kid who never, ever had a shot at something like this. He didn't know what to do." Gosh, what kind of people would put a kid like that in such a predicament?

WINNERS (OR, THIS IS THE PART WHERE I OUTWIT YOU)

One way to win *Survivor* is to be on a winning tribe. The tribe that wins the first challenge usually gets flint. Then they can start a fire, boil water, and cook food. They'll be in better shape at the immunity challenge, and sometimes one tribe just rolls over the other one for days. Season 14, on Fiji, deliberately created an extreme disparity between tribes. The season started with one tribe and a lot of great supplies—lumber and building plans, tools, food, a toilet. They were divided for the challenge and the Moto tribe won everything: immunity, the nice camp, and crazy luxuries—a couch, a sewing machine, dishes, candles, hammocks, and a shower. The Ravu Tribe was sent to an empty beach without fire, food, or shelter. Moto was at ease; Ravu was licking dew off palm fronds. The rich kept getting richer, the poor even poorer. One day, after Moto wins immunity again, Jeff delivers the real twist. Moto must choose between immunity and keeping their comfortable camp. They choose to sacrifice a member and keep the camp. But then the tribes are merged into one. When they return happily to the paradise of Moto, they discover that everything has been taken away. Suddenly those from the old Ravu tribe have the advantage: they've been living rough all along.

To win *Survivor*, it's good to be helpful but not bossy. A bit quiet but not silent. Likable but not too likable. Do well in challenges but don't be unbeatable. Be loyal but never domineering, kind but not sycophantic. You can win by being the least objectionable among several disliked people. It's good to be a little Midwestern—ordinary and polite. (It's not that good to actually be *from* the Midwest; people from the West and Midwest are more likely to be voted out than players from the South and Northeast.) Successful players get along with everyone, saving their real opinions for a private moment with the camera. They don't argue, do chores without complaining, and don't complain if others don't do chores. They don't express many opinions. They work hard—not too hard—and don't make waves. Conformity wins; one of the strongest predictors of a person's chance of winning is how often they voted with the majority. In *Africa*, Ethan is friendly, doesn't talk too much, has no particularly strong opinions, helps out around camp but doesn't complain. When he wins an award, he is properly thrilled and modest. He is also smart enough to bring back cookies and candy to share with the others. Ethan wins a million dollars.

The longer you can go without having a vote cast against you, the more likely you are to win. On *Fiji*, Earl was on the unfortunate Ravu tribe, licking palm fronds. He's staying out of range, going with the group, and you hardly notice he's there for a long time. In the entire season, Earl receives only one vote against him. But Earl has had a plan all along, influencing decisions, encouraging people to lean on him, to become dependent on him until he is quietly, even gently, directing everything.

Earl wins a million dollars.

Earl is one of the game's cool players. The writer Laurence Gonzales wanted to know why some people survive and others die under the same conditions. He wrote an entertaining book about this called *Deep Survival* in which he says that staying cool proved to be the most important skill. "The first lesson is to remain calm, not to panic." Stop and assess, plan, adapt. "A survivor expects the world to keep changing and keeps his senses always turned to: *What's up?*" Other people—most people—Gonzales notes, "ignore the obvious and do the inexplicable." Then they die.

You see this in the show *Alone*. Can you have a bad day without being crushed? Can you fail, fall down, screw up, and keep going? Can you manage to entertain yourself? The most conventionally masculine contestants tend to fail. They have rigid standards. The guy who swears and complains about every little obstacle is already in trouble. Such people care about how they will appear in the show, what people will think of them. "I don't want to feel like a loser," says one, just before he quits. "I feel like a failure," says another after being injured. The contestants who do well in this show of genuine survival are softer, more flexible. The woman who laughs at the fish and makes a hand puppet will last and last. Women have come in second in two seasons, and both times they were pulled out for medical reasons under protest. In the season set in Mongolia, Sam, a young man playing for the second time, had gained weight ahead of time for "emergency rations." He moves slowly, stays loose. He spends hours carving spoons to bring home as gifts because when you're carving, "you're in your own little world." Good players adapt to the weather and don't worry about looking foolish. In one season, a player makes a point of speaking his gratitude for small moments: "Beautiful meal, beautiful fire. Good, good day." He wins. And Sam wins, after 60 days alone.

All kinds of people have won *Survivor*. But with few exceptions, it is the cool head that prevails. From Richard Hatch through Sandra Diaz-Twine to Yul to Boston Rob and Tyson, winners have stayed calm, stayed patient, kept their eyes open, thinking ahead. As though their lives depended on it.

In *Philippines*, Denise, a petite 41-year-old, was a quiet, steady player who went to and survived every single Tribal Council in the season. She called herself a "little old sex therapist from Cedar Rapids, Iowa." She was allied with Malcolm most of the game, and then betrayed him in the end. Can he complain? She just beat him to it; he was planning to blindside her. She says, "This is the part of the game where I can say, 'Malcolm, you were a great ally. You played a great game, but this is the part where I outwit you.'"

Season 39, *Island of the Idols*, is the full-circle metaphysics. The players have no idea what *Island of the Idols* means—most assume it means there are immunity idols hidden there. Elizabeth is sent first, where she discovers that the idols are Boston Rob and Queen Sandra, living in the shadow of two enormous statues of their heads. They are there to give lessons in how to play *Survivor*. Elizabeth foolishly gets talked into doing a fire-making challenge with Rob, which of course she loses. The real lesson, he says, is that you should always negotiate a deal. When Kellee is sent, Rob and Sandra chat her up for a while, just being friendly; then they quiz her to see what she remembers. Everything counts, and you should get to know your fellow players. "Your lesson started the minute you arrived on this beach," says Rob. When Vince goes, he is overcome by meeting the idols and starts to cry, and his lesson is about staying calm under pressure.

Unbeknownst to the players, Rob and Sandra listen in on every Tribal Council. One night, listening to the waterworks, Rob asks, "Was it this hard for you?" Sandra swears, *bleep.* "I vote you out and that's it."

The final five are taken to the Island of the Idols and left there for the duration of the game. Rob and Sandra leave, but they've planted clues to a real idol. Tommy finds the clues and gets Dean to help. Then Dean finds the idol. "If I were Tommy, I would not have told *me* nothing."

I still don't understand why Tommy wins a million dollars.

In *Fiji*, Yau-Man always knows he's at a disadvantage. He's a 54-year-old, bespectacled, balding Chinese computer engineer. In one challenge, he is paired in a wrestling match against Dreamz, and it's not so much David and Goliath as it is POW versus Mr. Universe. Knowing he was outmatched in such things, Yau-Man made himself useful in other ways. He was born in Borneo and he was the only one who knew how to open coconuts. Two big guys are unable to break open a sealed box of supplies. Yau-Man applies simple physics. It's a satisfying moment, watching this petite guy, half the size of the other men, pick up the box and drop it on one of its corners, wiping the smirks off their faces as it shatters open. Later, in a throwing triathlon—blow-dart, spear, bow-and-arrow—Yau-Man beats everyone. And later still, in a blindfolded, giant-maze-key-and-drawbridge challenge, he handily wins, never letting anyone ahead for a moment. He comes in fourth, betrayed by Dreamz in the lie about the truck.

Survivor has challenges that involve standing on a small shelf for hours or holding a ball on a plate or standing on your toes while balancing a block of wood on your head. Anyone might win these. Unlikely people go far in *Survivor* all the time. On season 35, Ryan, a bellhop and a classic pale 98-pound-weakling type, says he's "never had an advantage in my life." People keep pulling him aside and telling him what to do. "I don't *know* why everybody wants to work with me," he says. But he knows how to use his goat status. "I think I'm a freaking weasel, but the closer you are to somebody, they can't really see you go behind their back and backstab them." Ryan comes in third. He doesn't win a million dollars, but $85,000 isn't bad for a bellhop who's never had an advantage.

In *San Juan del Sur*, Keith, a cranky, wiry firefighter from "Loozianna" with a grizzled beard and perpetually backward baseball cap, doesn't understand alliances and seems wholly out of place among the hardworking young schemers. But he finds an idol, makes friends, wins immunity, and comes in fourth. In *Island of the Idols*, Elaine, a gay factory worker from Kentucky, almost cruised into a position of power. She describes herself as "five foot two, a little busted can of biscuit." In private, she says she came on the show because she wants "that soul-searching, that lifetime journey everybody talks about." Elaine made a few strategic errors, but she was sincere, funny, and likable, and she had a great hard-luck story. When Missy is voted out, she hugs Elizabeth and whispers, "You realize now you have to kill Elaine? Slowly and methodically?" But Elaine lasted until day 35. She is one of the only people who walk out for their first night on the jury still looking like they did on the beach. A little cleaner, but not cleaned up.

A few seasons have been divided into three teams called Brawn, Brains, and Beauty. This was done on season 28, *Cagayan*, and all through the season, the Brains made stupid errors, the Brawn team couldn't win challenges, and Beauty was only beautiful on the outside. In a swimming-diving-underwater-knots-and-puzzle challenge, Brawn solved the puzzle first. Beauty couldn't swim but still came in second. Said Kass, "We're not the Brain tribe. We're the crap-for-brain tribe. Just a rolling logjam mess with a couple of nerds on top." When J'Tia dumps all their rice into the fire in a fit of pique, Kass asks, "How did we come up with the criteria for brains? I'd like to see that data."

The 32nd season, *Kaôh Rōng*, had the same divisions, but this time, the tribes had ringers. Alecia, a skinny blond real estate agent with massive breasts, is on the Brawn tribe. Tai, a skinny, bald former boat refugee from Vietnam who works as a gardener and cries at the drop of a hat, is on the Beauty tribe. Tai says to the camera, "*Why am I* here?" And his teammate Caleb adds, "Why in the world is Tai on this tribe? 50, 60-year-old Asian guy, eyebrows like three or four inches long, dude's got Mr. Miyagi glasses, like, I don't understand. Like, maybe there's a lot more that people don't really see." Later in the season, Jeff explains that Alecia qualifies as "Brawn" because she has a strong *character*, because she doesn't "take any lip." Tai is the one with a beautiful character. He cries when they consider killing the chicken, which he has named Mark. He gives people massages and actually seems to enjoy it. That he ties himself in knots in a sabotaging, deceptive alliance is, well, just *Survivor*. But he is a talented underdog, charming his way along while finding idols and winning advantages. Tai comes in third. And he saves the chicken. He brings Mark to the final Tribal Council and holds him on his lap during the interrogation. I would have voted for him to win for that alone.

One of the tropes of *Survivor*, now a common plaint in many reality shows, is the declaration, "I'm not here to make friends." But really, if you want to actually win, you *are* here to make friends. You need to make friends. In *Panama*, "I didn't come here to make friends with 24-year-olds," Terry says after they all snipe at each other after Council. Terry is arrogant with reason; he's played a nearly perfect physical game. But he hasn't made friends. "What I need from you is an apology," he says to Aras about a stray comment Aras made, "or we don't have a relationship for the next three days." Aras graciously apologizes, and it is at that moment the viewer knows, probably everyone knows, there is no way Terry can win the game. (Aras does. Aras wins a million dollars.)

There are players who ride for a while, derided as passengers by the more proactive or frenetic. Passengers let other people decide; they follow the crowd or an obvious leader. These are the utility players, the bench. This is Amber in *All-Stars*, hanging with Boston Rob and laughing at everyone's jokes and not making a move until the end. No one needs to push the quiet players out. No one minds keeping them around because quiet players are seen as easily manipulated, when in fact they may be plotting a coup for weeks. Such players often make it to the finals, and sometimes, like Amber, they win. Sandra won her first game doing this, saying over and over, *Whatever you guys want, as long as it isn't me.* Eventually, there was no one left.

In *China*, Denise talked about how she was never popular as a child, was always picked last for games "or not picked at all." This is true even in *China*; no one would have bet on her to make it to the final four. But she got that far because people saw her as disposable. Meat. A lot of power players, the ones who are flashy, alternately charming and alarming, think such uncharismatic people are the best ones to take to the end. Sometimes the meat turns into a sympathetic person who will shine in front of a jury resentful of her tribemates' deal-mongering. At some point, in every season, the game suddenly shifts; intensely bound alliances begin to collapse, and everyone turns as though on a signal to look at the quiet lunch lady from Revere, Massachusetts. The one who is never picked first.

One thing about winning *Survivor*: you don't have to have any survival skills. You really don't. You'll be more comfortable, but that's about it. "Did anyone tell her what show she was on?" Tina says of Cirie on the first day in Panama. Cirie, a round African-American nurse from New Jersey, has never gone camping. She is scared of bugs and animals and even piles of leaves. But Cirie is one of the stealth missiles of the game. She laughs a lot and never argues. She just hangs in there, fun and completely unthreatening. Cirie can't *possibly* win. The other players, who think she has no business being on *Survivor*, matter-of-factly inform her she will be voted out "first or second, nothing personal." Alone, she is pragmatic and clear. She seems amused by the bickering and favor-mongering around her, and subtly targets other, more visibly strong people in a series of eliminations that no one else even seems to notice.

She lasts and lasts. When there are only six players left, the city girl scared of bugs decides to try fishing, and almost immediately catches a big one. "I kind of underestimated myself for thirty-five years," she says, and decides to learn how to make a fire. Which she does, with sheer delight, hopping and giggling around the flames. She comes in fourth and is voted fan favorite, winning a GMC Yukon. She played again in Micronesia, came in third, and was again voted fan favorite and won another car. She was dispatched early in *Heroes vs. Villains* because people had figured her out. In *Game Changers*, with its plethora of twists and advantages, Tai plays both his idols at one Tribal Council, then Sarah plays her legacy advantage for immunity, then Troyzan plays his idol. That leaves Cirie as the only player who can be voted out, the first person in 34 seasons to be voted out because there is no other choice. "I'm going out in grand style," she says, and the jury gives her a standing ovation. Many people think of her as the best player who hasn't won. Cirie's doing okay.

JURY MANAGEMENT

When the jury finally has a chance to speak at the end of the game, they are supposed to ask questions of the finalists that will help them decide who should win. But often as not, it's just a chance to unload. The original jury takedown was by Sue Hawk, at the end of the first season. She told Kelly she wouldn't give her a sip of water if she were dying of thirst, that the island was filled with "snakes and rats," and they should let nature take its course. Let the snake—Richard—eat the rat—Kelly. He did.

I don't know when the term "jury management" first appeared, but it reflects the growing strategy people brought to the game. The people you are lying to, blindsiding, and voting out will become the jury that may award you the prize. Jury management means lying to, blindsiding, and voting out people in such a way that they aren't too mad. Jury management means not being too much of a jerk. As Jeff reminds a tribe early in season 24 when they are contemplating (and then rejecting) an act of mercy, "The single biggest mistake made in this game is doing decisions early that nobody will forgive you for in the end." The tribe does not learn this lesson and every single one of them is eliminated.

Good jury management: On *Vanuatu*, Chris apologized to the jury, saying that the only reason he was in the final instead of one of them was because they were nicer people. Remember: he won a million dollars.

Excellent jury management: On *Kaôh Rōng*, Michele won an advantage that allowed her to vote someone off the jury. She chose Neal because he didn't like her and he was articulate enough to sway others. As he walked off, he looked at her and took his only shot: "You came to this game like you were a badass bitch, but you're more like a cute little puppy still suckling at the teat. And I don't think you stand a chance." Good choice, Michele. She won a million dollars.

Bad jury management: In *Guatemala*, Cindy gets to the final five and then wins a new car in the reward challenge. She is offered the chance to give up her car and instead give a new car to each of the other four players. Jeff reminds her of the famous "Car Curse" of *Survivor.* No player who has won the car in a challenge has ever won the game. She keeps the car and they vote her out.

Really bad jury management: In *One World*, Kat, a naïve young woman who is half lost the entire season, wins the loved ones reward. It's obvious who she should pick, who needs it, who might then look kindly on her when they're on the jury. Instead she picks Alecia and Kim, her closest allies. She says, "I just really wanted to spend time with Kim and Alecia on a genuine friendship level. Maybe I shouldn't have picked those two people strategically," she says. "Am I going to dwell on it? No. I'll eat my cake, get drunk, and I'll go back to the tribe and deal with them later." Meanwhile, back at camp, they're resentful and making a deal to vote her out next. At Tribal Council she says picking people to go with her was the "hardest thing I've ever had to do in my life," and "it does hurt my feelings." Jeff: "It hurts *your* feelings?" She says yes, because she didn't want to see their mad faces. Then she cheers up, there's more talk, and she exclaims, "Blindsides are fun!" Then she is blindsided. (The video of her ride to Ponderosa is painful. She sits in the back of an SUV beside a psychologist, weeping uncontrollably and saying over and over, "No one wants me.")

Terrible jury management: On season 37, the tribe is running out of rice. Angelina considers herself a suave negotiator, a "closer." Her schemes are clumsy and obvious. At the next challenge, she tells Jeff that the tribe will give up their fishing gear, most of the cooking gear, and the hammocks to get a bag of rice. (There's nothing else to give, and her tribemates are looking at her in astonishment.) Jeff is amused and points out the flaws in her "lowball offer." Instead, he says he'll give them enough "rationed rice" to get them to the end if someone sits out on the immunity challenge. Angelina volunteers. She says to the camera, "It's a big moment for my *Survivor* story, and my resumé . . . It shows I'm a risky player who's willing to make big moves and big sacrifices to make things happen." But later, when she's not picked for a reward, she clearly feels cheated. "I do not want any reciprocity or favor because of the rice but I stepped out of a puzzle challenge in order for us all to have rice, so it's like, c'mon, Davie." Then she makes "revenge rice" for herself, using up most of the supply they just received.

Nick picks her to go to the final three, and she says, "Super proud of myself." But he picks her because she's least likely to win. She doesn't get a single vote and Nick wins a million dollars.

"Final four, baby!" Players shake hands, promising to go all the way together. *Almost* all the way. "Final four" means *We stick together until the moment when we have no choice but to turn on each other.* "Final three!" means *Everyone will get serious money.* And "Final two, just us, just you and me, pal," means *I think I can beat you.*

But to get to the end, you mustn't be too deserving. Having a disability is, well, a disability. On *Vanuatu*, Brady, a handsome FBI agent, is depressed to learn that his teammate Chad has a prosthetic leg. "Great! The guy with the mechanical leg's gonna win for sure! He's nice, he's smart, he's quiet"—Brady ticks the sins off on his fingers—"and he's got the underdog thing going on. So *we're* screwed." During the season in Nicaragua, Kelly Bruno, a medical student, quickly admitted that she has a prosthetic leg. "I could almost cry, I felt so bad for her," said Shannon Elkins, but his compassion was focused. "Like if I went to the final three with her, or two, I'd be like, 'Just give her the money, you know. Just cut her the check.' Because no money in the world could replace what she's probably gone through in her life." Better she be voted out with nothing.

Probst sometimes asks the players who deserves to go to the end. It's a wildly misleading question in a game where the point is to survive challenges, destroy threats, and then charm the jury you've eliminated into giving you a lot of money. The only *point* of the game is to be the last one there. Every sporting contest comes to this: regular season play leads to quarterfinals, semifinals, last heat, last lap. You knock down your rivals one by one until you are the last one left standing. In the first season, before anyone knew how to play, this question made more sense. Kelly says to the jury that she was sincere, the better person; she wasn't just *playing a game.* She *deserves* to win. Richard replies, in so many words, Sorry, girlfriend. It *is* a game. I played best. Richard won a million dollars.

ak to the other jury members. "Half of you are the most
le I've ever met in my life," she says. "Angry at people who
er than you. You are all *so* mad at Mike for *playing*! Like,
eaks out that he went and tried this strategy and it didn't
 this strategy, didn't work—what else was he supposed
guys were so on your whole *group* thing bull crap, you
out of his own house, set up a barb wire fence and said,
e in, I dare you.' Mike is the only person that outwitted,
nd outlasted." She's not done yet. "You guys say that
-fans. Well, if you're a fan, then you're actually going to
deserves it. Get over it, prove that you're a fan. The end!
ons!" Mike won a million dollars.

In the second season, *Australia,*
this equation and finally decided t(
able and stalwart player, to the en
of course (Of course! Go figure!) 7
guy, a good guy, and a sucker; Jeff
the more deserving player as doin
sense of humor. He appeared as
where he gets into a bread-thro
survivor about which of them su

Players often don't behave i
even seem to understand self-in
who risk their chance to win ir
million-dollar prize becomes
down in order to preserve on
defeated but triumphant sur
then his or her tested person
a donaldson.

On *Palau,* Gregg said, "{
to stay around, but in the
game is hardly about deser
be here or not. If you have
be here so you can help m

Sometimes, even now
who love the game as much
the game right, by *beatir*
planning to betray each
least objectionable way
someone will say, *This i*
the game. In *Worlds Apa*
a proper social game—

turn to sp
bitter peop
played bett
everyone fi
work, tried
to do? You
kicked him
'Try to com
outplayed a
you're super
vote for who
Congratulati

THE BIGGEST VILLAIN, THE WORST PERSON, AND THE BEST PLAYER EVER

Now that the show is on hiatus for the first time, fan action has shifted and lists are proliferating: funniest player, most attractive, wackiest. Best location? Worst location? Who was the worst villain? The worst *person*? Best player? Best player not to win? Granted that all we are doing is responding to edited character arcs, that we are seeing a fraction of what happens and maybe none of the private interactions of players and often none of the happy or helpful acts of a certain player: lists are fun. Let's make lists.

Let's start with most annoying player. Annoying players can go a long way in the game, since they make good goats, but lack the razor-sharp instincts of a true villain. A villain has the ability to be charming if required, always playing the long game. Annoying players are just annoying. This is probably the most controversial list because it's such an individual experience. One person's favorite player (Boston Rob) is another person's most annoying player (Boston Rob). One viewer will be annoyed by a player's hat (Jonathan's fedora) or hair (Joe's curls) or voice (Noura's) or laugh (Noura's). Annoyingness is not just editing, either. At the reunion show for *Worlds Apart*, Dan complained that his ugly behavior was a creation of the producers. So Jeff played back unedited raw footage to prove that things were actually worse than we'd seen. Lists of annoying players often include NaOnka, who buried the tribe's food and tripped a tribemate with an artificial leg. (One critic called Brian Heidik, who played in *Thailand*, "an oil slick incarnate." My favorite Brian moment: He literally pats himself on the back and says, "You've come a long way, baby." Then he treats himself to a long monologue. "What skills come into play at this part of the game? Skating skills. Who's the best skater, ice skater? Who's got the longest skates on? Who's the best at cutting corners, going around in circles? Usually in skating, you gotta be ice cold. You can't lose your cool. You gotta be like ice. You gotta have friendships, you gotta cut off those friendships. You gotta keep stringing people along, and bam! Throw 'em a nice slider. Mr. Freeze is in the house. I've got my skates on." I'm sorry to say that Brian won a million dollars.) Russell Hantz is on lots of annoying player lists as well as villain lists, but I put him over to the side, in the small but significant subset of players with what seems to be pathology. For anyone to behave in public view as he has done consistently, day in and day out, over four seasons, takes more than bad manners or lack of insight.

The difference for me between a good season and a bad one is often whether or not there is a player for whom I can root. Is there a character I care about, the way I care about characters in novels, wanting to see how their story ends? Linda Holmes, writing for NPR in 2011, observed that "competitive reality shows operate upon audiences almost exactly the way competitive sports do. It's no different from following a baseball season, with the exception of the fact that when the season starts, you have a game you know, and you have a familiar host like Jeff Probst (whom you may think of as the San Diego Chicken, for a whole variety of reasons)." Holmes compared Boston Rob to the Red Sox; it doesn't matter if you love the team or hate it, you watch to find out how the game ends. I need to care about the team in order to care about the outcome. If *every* player is annoying, I just don't care.

I have a special award for most annoying pair, which relates to the most annoying twist, which is *Blood vs. Water*, in which people play with a so-called loved one. It's been used twice, in the original *Blood vs. Water* season in which returning players brought a relative or partner, and later in *San Juan del Sur* featuring all new players. People behave abominably in this twist, tangled up in weird knots and playing out endless family scripts; Jeff helps to milk it, planting fears about how one's *loved one* is doing on the other tribe, or ranting about self-sacrifice during a challenge. *San Juan del Sur* was an unpleasant mess of a season. It was redeemed only by its excellent winner, Natalie, the first Asian-American woman to win. A lot of time was given to the tedious relationship between Missy and her daughter, Baylor. We learn about Missy's multiple divorces and Baylor's daddy issues. Missy spends half the season in a sky-blue fringed bikini and cowboy boots, calls herself "Mama Bear," and loses her temper at anyone who would dare vote for her kid while they're on a show that involves voting people out. She just wants to *protect her kid*, so she votes someone else's kid out. Baylor says being sent to Exile Island was like getting lost in a store looking for her mommy and Missy says it's terrible that she couldn't go search for her daughter when she's lost in a store looking for her mommy. Missy votes for Reed because he calls Baylor a brat. Baylor tries to vote out Jon because he reminds her of one of Missy's several ex-husbands. Almost the entire cast is in arrested development. Parental dysfunction, marital bickering, and leftover resentments don't make for entertainment. (I can just hear people shouting that these are central themes in reality television. Maybe, but I don't watch those shows.) If it weren't for Natalie, I probably would have bailed.

Abi-Maria won Best Villain at the 2015 Reality Television Awards, but she wasn't evil. She didn't seem smart enough to be evil. In her first season, *Philippines*, Abi is an obvious goat: deeply unlikable and lacking almost all self-awareness. She is lazy around camp and doesn't even attempt most challenges. She is canny but not bright, riding on the petite prettiness that has obviously been enough until now. She's called out at Tribal Council for her behavior. The next day she announces that she is "done cooking, but of course, I want to eat"—said while lying in the sand in a bikini with her eyes closed.

"Since the beginning of this game, *everyone* has wanted Abi gone. Abi is *so* detrimental to morale," says Malcolm. "She's like a soul sucker around camp. She's like the dementors in *Harry Potter*."

Denise, a therapist, says "Very challenging to diagnose, that's for sure." Abi is Brazilian and claims people don't understand her culture. "It is *not* a cultural thing. It's her personality. It's this histrionic, dramatic, passive-aggressive martyr. It's not culture. It's the culture of Abi."

Malcolm: "I'm considering making a really bad strategic decision just for my, like, morale. That's how terrible of a human being Abi is."

Skupin wins a reward and leaves Denise alone at camp with Abi. Denise says, "It's going to be a painful afternoon. It's like the first date with the kid who, like, pulled your hair all the time in kindergarten or spit in your lunch, and then suddenly you're on a date. I'm just going to make nice. I just want to get to the end of the day." Denise spends the day practicing therapeutic communication and talking to the producers in confessionals as long as they will let her. "I want to hang myself, gouge my eyes out. If I could have needles that go right into my eardrums, I would be good for the afternoon."

At a Tribal Council, Jeff sums up: "With respect—which probably means without any—you've been detested, laughed at, and then told you're not likable, not a good person, has nothing to do with her culture, you're just not nice, no one here wants you around. That's what you've been told." Which obviously makes her the best person to take to the end. "If that's the way you want to play the game of *Survivor*," says Denise, "Abi's the *perfect* person to take because you want to bring someone who truly hasn't outwitted, outplayed, and outlasted." But they can't stand it anymore.

Denise says to the camera when she writes down Abi's name, "If this vote doesn't go as planned, there's something *seriously* wrong in the universe." Abi is voted out and as the remaining players leave, they start dancing.

Can you be the biggest villain if that's actually your intention? In season 7, *Pearl Islands*, the eejit who calls himself Jonny Fairplay speaks of himself in the third person. His real name is Jon Dalton, and he can't be on camera (and he is often on camera) without striking a self-conscious pose and flashing crossed hand signs. The pose somehow means *Jonny Fairplay*, he smugly informs Jeff. Easily one of the most obnoxious people I've seen on reality television, Dalton says, "I'm a freaking puppet master." He's goatish, but not entirely a goat, because he says he's doing all this on purpose. He's in about four conflicting alliances, disliked and not trusted. To the camera he says—not once, but twice—"A promise to me can be broken about as easily as a fat woman on wicker furniture." Jeff asks him, "Jon, self-proclaimed 'good strategist,' what are you basing your vote on tonight?" He says, "Whatever the astrological signs tell me." In the countless lists of villains and irritating people on *Survivor*, you don't see a lot of consistent descriptions of people, but Dalton is frequently described with one word: *douche*.

When his friend visits during the loved ones reunion, Dalton asks him why his grandmother hadn't come. His friend whispers loudly that his grandmother had died. The others feel sorry for him and let him win the challenge. Back at camp, he and his friend chortle over it. "The fake dead grandma could easily go down as the dirtiest thing ever to be done in this game," Dalton laughs. He milks this all the way through the rest of the season. At one point, he swears on his "grandmother's grave." After the show he said in interviews that he consciously chose to play as a villain, because being outrageous gets you more screen time. But if you choose to behave in an obnoxious and deceitful way, you *are* obnoxious and deceitful. And yes, I know that the fact that he is the most obnoxious person I've seen on reality television means that I haven't watched that much reality television. But still. During the reunion show, Dalton still flashes his stupid hand sign, grinning while the audience boos. "I wanted to be the most hated *Survivor* of all time," he says. The healthy grandmother is watching from her seat. Jeff explains that they had called Jon's home to see if there was anything they could do "and you answered the damned phone."

The postgame dish about Dalton holds that Jeff disliked him greatly and asked that he not be invited back. This was overruled by producers, and Dalton returned for the season in Micronesia. He lasted three days and then quit. His behavior at an after-party was so loathsome that he is now banned from official *Survivor* events.

Maybe Dalton can take credit for spawning the odious pig edit, and maybe he is even proud of this. But it's hard to imagine why anyone would be. At a Fox Reality Show awards event in 2007, Dalton was booed. When Danny Bonaduce (I know, I know!) took the mike and said, "They're booing because they hate you," Dalton jumped on Bonaduce, who promptly flipped him over his head, supposedly knocking out a few teeth.

Cheating is a subset of villainy. Jeff Probst accused Hatch of smuggling matches between his butt cheeks for *All-Stars*. Players are now strip-searched. (Hatch denies the charge.) Jenna wore a wired hat for *The Amazon* and used the wire for fish hooks; supposedly Peih-Gee wore earrings made of flint and fish hooks on *Cambodia*. Supposedly, Boston Rob and Tyson stole kerosene from crew boats to make fires. Russell Hantz has said that it's easy to smuggle drugs in. These obvious violations of the rules don't seem to have brought on any consequences, but most of this is just rumor. The NDAs don't just mean you can't talk about your own progress on the show—you can't talk about anyone's and you can't talk about what happened during production unless it is aired. Even then, be careful. Bloggers endlessly try to track down the rumors and endlessly fail to prove most of them.

Then there's Colton. You watch him and wonder, *What is this guy's deal? Does he understand this is all on film?* On *One World*, Colton can't stand anyone; he's either whining or crying or making shockingly nasty remarks. He does nothing around camp and continually wanders over to hang out with the women, who don't want him there and kick him out. He makes a point of saying he's a Republican because he doesn't "believe in handouts"; when he is then given an immunity idol, he becomes a megalomaniac. He drags the men to Tribal Council when they don't have to go—that is *not* how you play the game—just so he can kick someone off his own tribe. He calls Leif, a person with dwarfism, a Munchkin and an Oompa Loompa, and complains that the sole Black player on his tribe should get "a real job." When Jeff asks Colton if he knows any Black people in his regular life, he names "our housekeeper." Colton may be the worst person to ever be on the show. When he is evacuated for possible appendicitis, everyone on the island and everyone watching at home breathes a big sigh of relief.

Then he returns in *Blood vs. Water* to play with his boyfriend, Caleb. Colton claims to be a changed man but acts exactly the same, dissing the "YMCA camping trip" atmosphere, spreading rumors, and lying. Then he quits in just a week, leaving Caleb behind.

Best player ever? What does best mean? Is it how far you go in the game? Total amount of money won? Days played? What about come-from-behind persistence or sheer entertainment value? Is the best player the one who makes the most surprising moves, or the biggest moves, or the most last-ditch escapes? In *Caramoan*, Cochran won without ever receiving a vote against him. Earl was the first unanimous winner. Kim won four of the last five immunity challenges in her season, made it to the end without ever playing her idol, and won fan favorite as well. Denise had to go to every single Tribal Council in *Philippines* before winning.

Lots of really good players have never won. On *Edge of Extinction*, Devens played hard and well; he was the obvious winner. But the whole season becomes about not letting him win because he's playing too well. The jury applauds him as he leaves, in fourth place. Malcolm has played three times and won fan favorite in *Caramoan*.

He hasn't won the game, but he can get away with murder. Lisa said of him, "Malcolm is the kind of guy who will put his arm around you, stab you, then visit you at the hospital the next day. And you get out of the hospital saying, 'Was that the sweetest thing for him to come visit? He's such a nice guy!'"

Ozzy is lean and handsome and can be charming if he's in the mood. He's probably the best physical competitor in the history of the show and has played four times. He's on a few most-annoying-player lists. Ozzy has come in second place, fourth place, and twice in ninth place. When he was ejected from *Game Changers,* he said, "It's the greatest game. Who wouldn't want to play again?" He was voted fan favorite twice, but geez, won't someone just give this guy a million dollars?

On *Tocantins,* J.T., a young cattle rancher from Alabama, was used to heat and roughing it. He said, "The biggest challenge for me is going to be fitting in with the people." He's likable and competent, and a natural leader—a very rare combination on *Survivor.* Early in the game, he forms a strong bond with Stephen. "He might just be seducing me with his pretty country ways," says Stephen, a corporate consultant from New York City, "but I'm smitten." People like J.T. so much that they campaign on his behalf. J.T. wins a million dollars.

J.T. is the first person to play what is known among fans as a "perfect game," meaning he never received a single vote against him, won the fan favorite award, and won the million dollars in a unanimous vote. But J.T. also made one of the biggest mistakes in the history of the show when he came back in *Heroes vs. Villains.* He found an idol, but then gave it to a player on the other tribe—and of all players, gave it to Russell Hantz, apparently because J.T. believes in fairies. Russell blindsided him with that same idol a short while later.

Tyson has played four times and won once, in *Blood vs. Water*. To be fair, Tyson made a boneheaded mistake in *Heroes vs. Villains*, trying to split a vote without accounting for an idol, essentially voting himself out by accident; of such wonky confusion is Tribal Council made. But generally he has played a cool and thoughtful game, and he's unencumbered by sentimentality. He never forgets that he's playing. On *Blood vs. Water*, he and Gervase ran "Operation Coconut," sneaking off to drill the coconuts and drink the water, then leaving the empty coconuts behind, a mysterious plague eventually blamed on crabs. He's a veteran, so he's able to convince the new players they should eat as much rice as they can. "You do have to do a certain amount of work, or *appear* to be working," he says. While he's gathering coconuts for the others, he takes an extra for himself and grabs a banana while he's out of sight. When he wants to undermine Aras, he pretends to be his pal, and starts apologizing for him to the others: Sorry that Aras is bossing you around. Sorry that Aras is being so dominating. Sorry, Aras doesn't know better. Sorry he's *rocking the boat*. Tyson is friendly, a good listener, quick to laugh at jokes and listen to people's concerns. To the camera, he says: "Give me a rusty spoon so I can dig both my eyeballs out, and then try and jam it through my eye sockets into my brain. It's taking all of my patience. *All* of it." When he wins individual immunity, he tells Jeff he wants to receive it like a knight, and goes down on one knee. He tells the jury he did it all for his girlfriend, and then wins a million dollars.

Fabio is never on any of these lists, but he's one of my favorite winners. He's the youngest winner, barely 21 at the time, and most people seem to think he more or less stumbled into victory. But I think he played a long and interesting game.

His real name is Jud, but he gets nicknamed within a few hours. (He actually was a model at the time.) On the first day, Shannon says, "The guy with the long blond hair? He's a dumb blonde." Brenda says, "You never know what Fabio's going to do. He's clueless." Fabio gets splinters and stabs himself with thorns and cuts himself and burns himself and giggles and swings his blond mop. He grins all day no matter what happens, acting the stoned surfer. He wears the dive mask to start a fire because he doesn't like smoke in his eyes. He joins the first alliance that asks him and never suggests strategy.

Fabio isn't half as dumb as he's chosen to act (or as the editors made him look). Midway through the season, he says, "I gotta be cool. I can't let on that I'm playing the game." Facing a transparent attempt to vote him off, Fabio wins immunity.

A few days later, after Dan is voted off, Fabio wins immunity again. This time, it really is a million-dollar challenge. "It was awesome, man," he says to the camera. "I always knew that I would wait till the last minute to be aggressive." Barely strangling a laugh, grinning madly, he adds, "I'm *loving* this, man! I won the final immunity challenge and I'm going to come back to camp and watch the three of them plead their case for why *I* should take *them* to the final three! It's going to be fun watching them sweat about this one."

Every time one of the other players begs him to take them to the "final three," he outs that person to the others until everyone is mad. "It's like I walked into the kitchen and turned the light on and all these little cockroaches are scrambling to get out of the way."

At Tribal Council, he entertains the jury by calling out each of the other players in turn, always with a smile, for their lies and betrayals. Then they vote out Holly, the most sympathetic person left. Back at camp, Sash says, "To end up with you two guys, awesome. My two wing men." As if.

Fabio just laughs. To the camera, he says, "Dude, you can take a backseat. I'll let you take notes on how this is going to go. It's going to be fun."

Fabio wins a million dollars. (He was arrested for illegal skate-boarding while intoxicated afterward. I don't know if he was convicted, but he seems to be doing fine. For a while, he was the drummer for a band called Space Funk Odyssey. Because, why not?)

Parvati Shallow is on a lot of lists of best players. She has played 148 days, second only to Boston Rob. When she started out in season 16, her game was all about the bling. But she grew into strategy. She performed one of the game's great heists in *Micronesia*, her second time playing, when four women and Erik remained. He is a self-professed super-fan and is a little starstruck throughout the season. When he wins the immunity necklace and seems guaranteed to go to the final four, the women start working on him until he's a horny pretzel. During Tribal Council, Parvati keeps at him; you can see him wavering; viewers across the nation are shouting, "Don't do it, Erik! You putz!" and then he gives the necklace to Natalie. At which point he is immediately voted out. Jeff says, "That was a life lesson: Breasts can get you into a lot of trouble. Erik was surrounded by breasts, and it cost him quite likely a million dollars." (Jeff sounds like he knows what he's talking about.) Parvati won *Micronesia* with the vote of every woman on the jury.

Richard Hatch? "Hatch is different than anyone else, because he was the first one," says Paul Grassi. Grassi was a contestant on *The Mole* and then made a documentary about reality show contestants; he was both exploring this weird fame and taking advantage of it. "He's the Godfather of Reality TV. He started it all. At the end of the day, his experience differs from people because he was the first." Peter Lance came to see Richard Hatch as "vicious," "cutthroat," and "a red devil"; *TV Guide* named him one of the "60 Nastiest Villains of All Time"; he's #1 and #2 on a couple of "most annoying players" lists. He was also a very good player.

Hatch stood out from the start. He was chubby and jovial, a confident player. He predicted he would win before he was even selected as a finalist—but only to the camera. He was durable and relaxed, built fires, killed rats, caught a lot of fish. He didn't seem to get tired or cold and rarely showed any temper. I've read criticism that he won only because he was playing against people who didn't know how to play *Survivor*—but neither did he. No one had ever played it before.

Hatch saw the game as corporate politics, just like Burnett. He pointed out that he had also been a gay man in a homophobic culture all his life, and he knew how to be two-faced. He managed the tricky feat of turning the good sportsmanship of the other players, their earnest fairness, into their undoing. He was disdainful to the camera, attentive and cheerful in the group. In a late immunity challenge where the players had to answer questions about other contestants, he lost, because in fact he knew almost nothing about the other people on the island. It was a dangerous reveal of how shallow his intimacy really was.

In his statement to the jury, Hatch said, "I want the million. I really want the million. Oh, my god, it would change my life." And of course, he did win. He returned for *All-Stars* and was caught cheating, and accused of sexually harassing Sue Hawk—she of the "rats and snakes" speech—by banging into her. (Hatch denied any deliberate contact. Hawk appeared on television with Hatch after the show aired and said that they had had a chance to "hash it out" and she was moving on.) Some years later, Hatch went to prison for failing to report his *Survivor* prize money to the IRS. His was kind of a storybook marooning. It changed his life.

Then there's Rob Mariano, "Boston Rob," the first person to play *Survivor* four times. At this point he has played more than anyone else—151 days, almost half a year on the island. He's a controversial player; many viewers find his rocket to the stars unearned. I enjoy his relaxed, confident manner, in on the joke but not mean about it. He's a pleasure to watch in the cramped den of feral cats that the island sometimes resembles. Who else would call Jeff "Pretty Boy Probst"? In his first season, *Marquesas*, he was a real galoot—loud, lazy, homophobic. He disses another guy's penis size and doesn't seem to know how to handle people at all. He was out before the merge. But he came in second on *All-Stars*, where he met his wife, Amber. Then he was voted off in the middle of *Heroes vs. Villains*, but came back and won *Redemption Island*, where he was also voted fan favorite. He was an idol in *Island of the Idols*, where he spent his days building a gigantic two-story mansion of bamboo with a fireplace, kitchen, and furniture, and then went spearfishing. "I love *Survivor*," he says. "I love being out here. It feels like home to me. I've been here so many times over the past two decades. It's like riding a bike." He played again with Amber, in *Winners at War*. Rob and Amber also competed on *The Amazing Race*, where their very existence seemed to destroy the confidence of other players. They came in second. Rob has won more individual immunity challenges than any other contestant. But in all these months of play, he has found an idol only once. He doesn't even bother to look.

Has Rob become more likable because his edits got better? Or did he grow up a little? He actually got a degree in psychology from Boston University, not something you'd expect if you'd watched only his first season. I'm sure editing helps, but you can only be edited as a lunkhead if you say a few lunkhead things. The fact that he lied his way through the season isn't news—though he was setting a standard for manipulation right out of the gate. A story on NPR said of Rob: "Because the fact that he is obnoxious *and* infuriating *and* endearing *and* funny *and* smart *and* arrogant *and* so eminently quotable that he would make a great addition to any team of highly paid speechwriters is the best explanation you're ever going to get of how *Survivor* actually works."

On *All-Stars*, he starts falling for Amber early on. He says to the camera, "Make no mistake, I'm here to play *Survivor*. At the end of this, hopefully Amber and I can be having some fun together, and we'll be spending my million. Worse case scenario, we'll be spending hers." When he wins a video from home, he gives it up so everyone can have letters from home instead. In a confessional, he gets a bit weepy as he reads his letter. "It wasn't about strategy," he says. Pause. "It *was* about strategy, to a degree. It's a good move, yeah. It is. I'm not going to sit here and tell you it's not." Then he points at the camera and says, grinning, "But I'm still getting the million." When I watched this season again, I was struck by how badly people played against Rob. They made terrible decisions, got twisted into distrust and conflict. It happened again in *Redemption Island*, which Rob won. Perhaps it's hypnosis. At the end, when Rob and Amber are the final two, he says, "I'm sure there's people who took this game very, very personal, and that's their own frickin' problem." He wins a GMC Colorado pickup and picks Amber to go see a drive-in movie with him (*Lord of the Flies*, of course), and then Amber is given a pickup as well, just for being there. Things just seem to work out for this guy.

Jeff takes the votes, gets on a helicopter in Panama, and lands casually on the sidewalk in New York City, then walks across the street and into Madison Square Garden. Just before the votes are read, Rob kneels and proposes to Amber and she says yes and they clinch. Some people in the audience boo, others clap, and then Amber wins a million dollars.

They live in Pensacola now with their four children.

Sandra Diaz-Twine, the first person to win twice, is actually likable in her first season, *Pearl Islands*. She's not very strong; she can barely swim and doesn't feel like a threat. But she can turn people against each other with a single phrase, watching from a distance until everyone forgets she is there. She doesn't lead, votes with the group—a classic way to win. And she does, a million dollars. This goes to her head when she comes back to play on *Heroes vs. Villains*. She announces, many times, that she is "queen" of the game and it all gets pretty obnoxious. But she wins a million dollars again. One study of *Survivor* says, "Perceptions of having power are just as important as actual power." Sandra has both. She's adaptable, persuasive, willing to try anything, and she scares people.

Jeff Probst says, "She's a badass. Lots of people despise her. She doesn't care."

In *Game Changers*, she just leans back, complacently declaring her favorite phrase: *The queen stays queen.* "The reason Sandra has won twice is because she doesn't come off as the most dangerous person in this game," says Sarah. "I almost feel, the way Sandra talks to people, is she's grooming us. She doesn't pressure you, her voice never raises, it's calm, and she just starts to suck you in." "Sandra's so good, *I* was even considering what she was saying," says Ozzy, who knows better. Zeke: "We have to get Sandra out of this game before the merge. Otherwise she's going to beat you. People always say, you can get Sandra out of this game anytime, but you know what's happened to everyone who said that? They've lost a million dollars to Sandra Diaz-Twine." Enough people find their cojones and she is voted out sixth.

The most recent season was entirely made up of previous winners, and they played for $2 million. Tony is the king to Sandra's queen; he's a special case and I don't really understand him. He first played in season 28, *Cagayan*. This is the season that broke Edgic, because Tony did not have a winner's arc. It's considered one of the best seasons by many for that reason—unpredictable, with many layers of deceit and manipulation. From the start, Tony twists people up, playing like a toddler on espresso. He convinces Sarah that two cops can always trust each other. She likes his "sincere handshake." To the camera, Tony says, "I don't trust nobody here, none of them." This sets the tone for his entire season.

Tony lies, deceives, and blindsides people, including his allies, and throws a fit when anyone else does this. At the merge, Tony tells everyone he's really a police officer and not in construction like he'd said. LJ: "So, to solidify that he's trustworthy, Tony exposed that he lied. Different." He talks and talks and talks and somehow, it works. Jeremiah says, "Right now, I got to believe him a *little* bit. Still, I have my doubts. He might be playing us." You think?

Tony builds a hidey-hole in a bush near the well so he can eavesdrop on private conversations, knowledge he uses to hornswoggle everyone else. Someone calls him a "cult leader," and it's weirdly true that this chubby, bald, coarse, ill-mannered Jersey cop has somehow charmed everyone into submission. Kass calls him "the Don, aka Tony, our Mafia King. Anyone who crosses Tony gets their cement shoes and thrown in the pond."

Woo, a classic goat going all the way to the end, says, "I'd be the *stupidest Survivor* player, taking Tony to the end." Too little, too late, Woo. When the time comes, he can't make up his mind. Kass or Tony? In front of the jury, Tony becomes the Woo-Whisperer, saying that Woo's game has been all about loyalty and now it's his time to show it. "Do me this favor. I won't forget it." Woo seems to be in a trance. He chooses not to be a "hypocrite," and stays loyal to the guy who is the biggest hypocrite. And Woo is the *stupidest* player, because Tony wins a million dollars. (At the reunion, Jeff asks the jury if Woo would have won against Kass. Yes.)

Tony played on *Game Changers,* but was out early. Then he came back on *Winners at War* and won $2 million. To many fans, there is no question about the best player ever. Tony is the King.

TRANSFORMATION, CELEBRITY, AND A VERY SPECIAL MOMENT

At each Tribal Council, the jury members walk back onto the set: clean, coiffed, made up, and sparkling, with a *you can't hit this* stride. At the live finale, the transformation goes nuclear; many players are almost unrecognizable. Shaved heads, big hair, makeup, neat goatees, sitting carefully in sheath dresses and skinny jeans, suddenly very conscious of the endless gaze. They are, finally, *real* and a new game is about to begin.

Jeff sometimes makes a little speech toward the end of a season about how the players are *changed people*, they've gone through a *real journey*. Mainly the game changes people by making them into minor celebrities for a time, which creates a minor revenue stream. That's one kind of transformation—or *metamorphosis*, as Jeff likes to say these days.

Many players say their lives have been transformed, enriched, by the game; they "owe it all" to *Survivor*. Ethan Zohn started a charity with his prize; so did Yul, Earl, Bob, and Adam. Sophie finished medical school. J.T. created college funds for his nieces and nephews. A blog, a where-are-they-now interview in *People*, and an appearance on the Australian version of *Family Feud*, and that's about it for most of them. A few bit parts and a convention appearance—Amanda did an ad campaign for Scope mouthwash with Ryan Seacrest—and a few end up on another reality show. Former players have not proven themselves to be a particularly evolved group of people, and most disappear after a few months. (Many seem to want to disappear.) Plenty of people have been deformed by the game. Whether they made an unfortunate comment on camera or had a loser edit, people can be hurt by playing. This is another way the game changes people; they have to survive being on *Survivor*. Many get both hate mail and love letters, are heckled in public, or face a sex-tape scandal. Boston Rob is doing okay, but a lot of former players are not. *Survivor* may be a show about transformation, but it is also about attention, about wanting attention, needing attention, demanding attention, and finally, trying to dodge it.

Returning to ordinary life takes time. There's the obvious: "See a dentist the second you get back to civilization," said David Wright, who played twice. Many have needed medical care for parasites, malaria, malnutrition, kidney infections, fevers, and reactions to insect bites. Ian, who stepped off the platform after more than 12 hours and lost to Tom in *Palau*, was left with nerve damage in his feet from the challenge. Former players talk about hoarding food for months, having nightmares, or freaking out at work when they see people talking in a corner. The show offers counseling, but a few need real therapy.

Jenna, the winner of *The Amazon*, dated Ethan from *Africa*— and let me just say, from here that looks an unlikely match, but they lasted ten years and did *The Amazing Race* together. A few years after the breakup, Jenna was arrested for allegedly driving while intoxicated in a sports car with an AMAZON vanity plate. She was never charged and denies the event happened. The lunch lady from China, Denise, said during the reunion show that she lost her job because of being on the show. Mark Burnett offered her $50,000 as compensation, until Martin's school district stepped in to say it wasn't true. She had taken a promotion before filming began and her old job was filled. She donated the money Burnett gave her and apologized. Paschal English, who came in fourth on *Marquesas*, resigned as a judge after he was caught in an affair with a public defender, and then accused of turning a blind eye on another judge's harassment.

Katie Gallagher, who came in second on *Palau*, was arrested for alleged drunk driving. Brian Heidik, the winner of *Thailand*, bought several sports cars and was charged with cruelty to animals for shooting a puppy with a bow and arrow; he said he thought it was a coyote. So many former players have posed nude or gotten half-naked in straight-to-video films that I can't keep track. Michael Skupin played in *Australia*, was evacuated with burns, returned to play in *Philippines* and was a runner-up. Then he was convicted of larceny and possession of child pornography and served a year in prison. He won't be playing again.

Todd Herzog, who won the season in *China*, is an alcoholic who has had several ugly and very public relapses. He was so drunk when he went on *Dr. Phil* with his parents that he had to be carried to a chair. In what may be the purest (and most hateful) moment of modern reality television, Dr. Phil filmed himself collecting Herzog after another relapse and flying with him to rehab. Herzog appears to be sober now, and recently proposed to his boyfriend during a charity event with several other reality show veterans.

Mark Burnett was also changed. Inspired by the book *The Art of the Deal*, he held the finale for *Survivor: Marquesas* at the Trump skating rink in Central Park. Trump basked in the front row. Burnett's place in Hollywood royalty now rests on the odd twin successes *Survivor* and *The Apprentice*. Burnett made oodles of money off the latter and is still raking it in as an executive producer for *Survivor*. He is going to make hundreds of millions more on Amazon's acquisition of MGM, where he is currently head of TV programming. But will he still have a job? His other ventures (*My Dad Is Better Than Your Dad*, *The Contender*, *Pirate Masters*) haven't gone very far and he will forever be linked with Trump, and what Trump did with the celebrity Burnett gave him. His is a kind of fantasy marooning.

John Jeremiah Sullivan wrote an article for *GQ* in 2005 about hanging around with The Miz, a contestant from *The Real World*. He describes the postgame life of signing young women's breasts and tossing back free shots. The Miz was one of several newly minted reality stars of the show, "all of them just going around *being somebody who'd been on The Real World*, which is, of course, a show where you just *be yourself*," writes Sullivan in only faintly ironic prose. "I mean, my God, bros. The purity of that . . ." Sullivan is fascinated by *The Real World* for the very reason I'm averse to it: its absolute meaninglessness, the way the people on the show are living a life in which the show and life become one. *The Real World* created its own community of viewers the way *Survivor* did. "Came a point at which the people being *cast* on the shows were for the most part people who thrilled back home to *watch* the shows, people (especially among the younger generation) whose very consciousnesses had been *formed* by the shows," he writes. "You're watching people who are *being on a reality show*." Sullivan writes in a breathless fan voice, deliberately not explaining anything, because if you have to ask—but he does explain a little, and then adds, "Oh, fuck it! You know how it works." Sullivan, like a lot of critical viewers (like me), is insider-chic but self-conscious about it, almost above it all—*almost*, because he really wants to be inside. He might enjoy being on *The Real World*. He wants to watch and be watched and watch himself watching being watched.

Sullivan's point 16 years ago was an obvious one: we are all on television now. There isn't much difference between real life and reality life anymore, no entirely clear demarcation between people who make reality shows, people who watch reality shows, people who go on reality shows, people who talk about reality shows, and all the rest of us, who are just being filmed all the time whether we know it or not. The producers already know everything I am saying. Well, they may *know* it, somehow, as a felt experience—I don't know if there's been a lot of deep thinking here. I suspect success in producing television shows involves luck, privilege, and good base instincts, not critical thinking skills. But it ends up in the same place.

The smartest thing I've seen about reality television in all this surfeit is a tiny bit of metaphysics from BRIC-TV, a local station in Brooklyn. It's called *The Show About the Show*. In episode 1, we watch Caveh Zahedi, a small-time filmmaker, try to convince a producer at local studio BRIC-TV to green-light a show. "The show is about making the show," he says, and he can't pitch the whole season because "I don't know what's going to happen." The entire episode is just various actors and crew acting out on camera the conversations they've already had in which they talk about whether to make a show about making a show. Episode 2 is largely devoted to how episode 1 was made—how they rehearsed the conversations they'd already had about whether to make the show before actually filming the conversations. Zahedi shows us his wife's resentment at having their private conversations revealed, the cameraman rehearsing how he criticized Zahedi's direction before being filmed saying this, the producer's discomfort with watching himself on film talking about not wanting to be on film, and Zahedi's own stoned revelation that the title should be *Self-Reflective TV Show About Its Own Making*. Each episode is about how the previous one was made. And so it goes, as Zahedi becomes increasingly confused about who is an actor and who is not, what happened and what he thinks might happen next. The show is about the show; there is no line where the show ends and life begins.

We hold the camera in our hands now; we are each other's camera. Television never dies; ours is the unfading capture of our lived performances. We look; we are looked upon; we perform; we watch the performance. Jacques Derrida wrote of codes and messages. He wanted to take apart literature—speech, expression—to expose hidden bias and subconscious agendas. Derrida believed that we could never truly decide, that there are no fundamentals in our speech, no unbreakable blocks of truth. We can't come to a conclusion; everything shifts like sand or fog, hiding something in itself. In deconstructing story, he added, "one does not know where to begin." I am not qualified to deconstruct *Survivor*, but when has lack of qualifications had anything to do with reality television? Reality television transparently subverts language; the genre steals definitions and invents vocabulary and twists the meaning of words. Logic is not its intent; overt plagiarism often is. Does it have a hidden agenda? I've already talked about *Survivor*'s brutal colonialism, the layers of oppressive bias, the endless pretense to some deeper personal growth. *Survivor* is deeply uninterested in studying its own point of view. Perhaps meaning is barely and only accidentally the result of our conscious intent—but reality television *begins* this way; it has already deconstructed itself.

Each season of *Survivor* depends on, refers to, and is constructed out of previous seasons. Out of the repetitions and rituals, the veteran players, the absorption of fans, the lessons of strategy, and the (often erroneous) belief people have that they "know how to play the game." Jeff Probst is a parody of Jeff Probst, and the show becomes ever more not real. As time goes on, *Survivor* is less and less about its apparent constructed purpose and ever more about how people respond to that construct—how they think about it, enter into it, behave within it. *Survivor* has become a show about what a show about pretend survival might be like. (*The purity of that, bro . . .*) Maybe no one can write about reality television without an internally self-referential wink. Which came first—reality or television? Derrida also said, "I love very much everything that I deconstruct in my own manner."

The show blooms, swelling into all-stars, game-changers, favorites, and finally, *winners.* When *Survivor* first used a cast of veterans for the eighth season, ratings were declining a bit. The producers wondered if anyone would want to watch players with whom they were already familiar. Why would we pursue these revelations of private life when we think we've already seen them? But *All-Stars* was a big hit. It featured two winners (Ethan and Jenna), old scores to be settled (Jerri and Colby), old relationships turning sour (Ethan and Lex), old relationships that were still sour (Sue and Hatch), and the start of new relationships (Rob and Amber). Everyone had the common goal of staying longer than So-and-So. The challenges were bigger, the rewards were bigger, and two people quit.

Veteran seasons have done well on many reality shows. Misha Kavka says that rather than boring the viewer, returning players are people "with whom viewers are *already intimate*," and thus we form an immediate connection. We know what we're going to get from this relationship. The thrill is different: Rather than the private person being revealed to us, we are meeting people we know as friends. (Or frenemies.) And once someone has a public persona with no need for a last name, we return to the thrill of getting to know the actual private life of a public person—the public person being the one they play on the show about real people.

In seasons filled with cunning veterans, the producers can add special advantages and harder challenges. There's more of what we could call production value. A few have played with each other on the show, a few have played on other shows or done celebrity poker games together or been to the same *Survivor* fan events. All have studied the show carefully; they think they know each other's game. There are old alliances and new alliances and lots of humming brain activity spent on whether to keep someone like Ozzy because he can win team challenges versus getting rid of someone like Ozzy because he can win individual challenges. They may know only what they've seen on television, and veterans are as subject to the loser edit as any other player. But they *think* they know each other's game. They've all been here before—they've been *edited this way* before—and they are playing people who are playing *Survivor*. Just as knowing how to play the game changes the game and playing with other people who know how to play the game changes it yet again, playing with people *you have watched playing the game* changes it again. And while you may have played the game before and played it well, you've never played this particular game with these people. You're always starting over.

In the most recent season, *Winners at War*—the 40th season and the last before the pandemic shut down production—all the players are former winners and they are playing for $2 million, supposedly the biggest cash prize in reality television history. Some are friends; Amber and Rob are married. Several of the women have had kids since they played; Ethan survived Hodgkin's lymphoma and Rob's got a bit of a potbelly. Most of all, they know each other in the way that matters; they've watched each other play. All openly fear the ignominy of being the first *winner* voted off. Jeff starts with the expected voice-over: these are people whose lives have been changed by the game. It's actually true this time; a million dollars will do that. At first they call each other "legends" and seem to be following a script about how *epic* and *awesome* the season is. They clap and hoo-rah at all of Jeff's jokes. Jeff calls *Survivor* "an all-encompassing challenge of the human spirit," and even though I know this was filmed before the pandemic, it still seems like a weird thing to say in 2020.

From the beginning you can see there are two games here. The older players from earlier seasons played a game without idols and twists. They are facing players who know the game as ceaseless skittering paranoia. At Tribal Council, people are cautious and reserved until Jeff complains about all they are not saying. "I just want to be a part!" he whines. The maneuvering is constant. The challenges are hard. The secrets are many. There's a lot of jockeying for position and quite a bit of overthinking. Sandra spreads rumors about everyone, including her allies, and they believe her. Don't they all know better? They know the game.

One by one, the old-school players are voted out and sent to the Edge of Extinction to scrape through their days. Then all the players who have been starving and suffering on a barren spit come back for a challenge, which they have to do while Jeff talks nonstop about all those days of starvation and suffering on a barren spit. Tyson beats Rob by one second and joins the tribe. The others all go back to starving.

"I'm honestly the only O.G. left on this beach," Tyson says. "I played three times before most of these people even put their *Survivor* diapers on. Are the kids that are coming up now changing the game so much that I can't adapt?" He doesn't think so. "If I was these people, I would get rid of me day one every single time I ever played." There are double agents and blindsides. Nick starts rumors and Tyson starts different rumors and Tony spies on people. When Tony tries to tell someone the truth, tries to explain the *real* plan, they don't believe him—why should they? I can't follow it all. Then I tell myself, see? That's why you wouldn't be a good player.

Once again, Natalie saved the season for me. Embarrassingly fit, alert to every detail but not frantic, quiet when she needs to be. She is voted out first, then spends 32 days in exile, earning advantages and collecting intel. She finds an idol and plays it perfectly. She wins her way back into the game at the last possible minute and then wins the last immunity challenge. She has a heck of a résumé.

Then the pandemic and *boom*. Instead of a crowded live finale, it's just Jeff alone in his garage. We see bicycles, a telescope, the carefully designed mess of the prosperous American family. He says he's using his home internet and personal ear pod and Jeff Probst is a *survivor*, man, he can do it from scratch. "This is as real as it gets!" he says, sitting in a fake Tribal Council set made from a kit. At the end, with only Natalie and Tony left, Rob leads the jury in a standing ovation. But Natalie comes in second, and Tony wins two million dollars.

*   *   *

In every season of *Survivor*, there is that one very special moment. In a climbing-swimming-balancing-throwing challenge in *Game Changers*, Cirie cannot finish. In the challenge, she can't even get out of the water onto the platform to do the balance beam; she's too weak. Sarah swims over to help her, but the other team wins before she gets across. Jeff announces that everyone will stay there and cheer Cirie on if she wants to try and finish, *just for the sake of finishing*. She tries again and again, and finally crosses the balance beam and everyone cheers.

"That is what happens when you believe in yourself!" exclaims Jeff. "*Anything* is possible!" All she did was walk across a beam that everyone else had already walked across, but over the course of the day and well into Tribal Council, this moment takes on mythic proportions. Cirie is applauded by all. At first, I thought, *C'mon*. It was *just a balance beam*. But now I'm beginning to wonder. She's set herself up nicely. Good move, Cirie.

RESOURCES

Battista, Paul, and Hughes, Hayley. *Reality Television Contracts: How to Negotiate the Best Deal.* New York: Allworth, 2016.

Burnett, Mark. *Dare to Succeed: How to Survive and Thrive in the Game of Life.* New York: Hyperion, 2001.

Burnett, Mark. *Jump In! Even if You Don't Know How to Swim.* New York: Random House, 2005.

Burnett, Mark, and Dugard, Martin. *Survivor: The Ultimate Game.* New York: TV Books, 2000.

Carter, Julia. "Push Me to the Edge: My *Survivor* Experience," https://thejuliacarter.com/2019/06/06/push-me-to-the-edge -my-survivor-experience/.

Chu, Andrea Long. *Females: A Concern.* New York: Verso, 2019.

Delisle, Jennifer Bowering. "Surviving American Cultural Imperial- ism: *Survivor* and Traditions of Nineteenth-Century Colonial Fiction." *The Journal of American Culture*, vol. 26, no. 1 (March 2003): 42–55.

Goffman, Erving. *The Presentation of Self in Everyday Life*. New York: Doubleday, 1959.

Gonzales, Laurence. *Deep Survival: Who Lives, Who Dies, and Why*. New York: W.W. Norton, 2003.

Hayes, Erich M., and Dunbar, Norah E. "Do You Know Who Your Friends Are? An Analysis of Voting Patterns and Alliances of the Reality Television Show *Survivor*" in Hetsroni, Amir, ed. *Reality Television: Merging the Global and the Local*, 7–24. New York: Nova Science Publishers Inc., 2010.

Holmes, Su, and Jermyn, Deborah, eds. *Understanding Reality Television*. New York: Routledge, 2004.

Jenkins, Henry. *Convergence Culture: Where Old and New Media Collide*. New York: New York University Press, 2006.

Kavka, Misha. *Reality Television, Affect and Intimacy*. London: Palgrave Macmillan, 2008.

Kraidy, Marwan M. *Reality Television and Arab Politics: Contention in Public Life*. Cambridge, UK: Cambridge University Press, 2010.

MacCannell, Dean. *Empty Meeting Grounds: The Tourist Papers*. London: Routledge, 1992.

Riley, Kathleen C. "Surviving *Survivor* in the Marquesas." *Anthropology News*, May 2002.

Sender, Katherine. *The Makeover: Reality Television and Reflexive Audiences*. New York: New York University Press, 2012.

Smith, Matthew J., and Wood, Andrew F., eds. *Survivor Lessons: Essays on Communication and Reality Television*. North Carolina: McFarlan and Col., 2006.

Wright, Christopher J. *Tribal Warfare: Survivor and the Political Unconscious of Reality Television*. New York: Lexington Books, 2006.

ACKNOWLEDGMENTS

My mother and I watched *Queen for a Day*, and I would so like to be able to do that again, side by side with the curtains closed. Lisa So'on Mann is responsible for sending me down the *Project Runway* rabbit hole in the first place. My many thanks to Jennifer Stoots, who was enthusiastic about an early version of this story without ever having watched the show. When I needed one most, Ryan O'Connell became an able assistant in every way. Thanks always to my agent, Kim Witherspoon, and apologies to my editor, Lauren Spiegel, who now finds herself obsessed with Rob and Amber.

ABOUT THE AUTHOR

Sallie Tisdale is the author of several books, including *Advice for Future Corpses (and Those Who Love Them)* and *Talk Dirty to Me*. Her essays have appeared in *Harper's Magazine*, *The New Yorker*, *Conjunctions*, and many other publications. Visit her online at www.sallietisdale.com.